BERLITZ®

D0059012

DISCOVER
NORMANDY

Edited and Designed by
D & N Publishing,
Lambourn, Berkshire.

Cartography by
Hardlines, Charlbury, Oxfordshire.

Printed by Butler and Tanner, Frome,
Somerset.

*Although we have made every effort to
ensure the accuracy of all the information in this book, changes occur in-
cessantly. We cannot therefore take
responsibility for facts, addresses and
circumstances in general that are constantly subject to alteration.*

Photographic Acknowledgements

All photographs by the author except
for those on the following pages:
© Berlitz Publishing Co. Ltd: 27,
64/65, 68, 134, 147, 152/153, 166, 173,
175, 178 (lower), 185, 187, 190, 228,
238, 244, 245, 271, 277, 282, 306, 307,
309; The Bridgeman Art Library, 183.

Cover photographs by the author.
Front cover: Etretet.
Back cover: Norman poppy fields.

The Berlitz tick is used to
indicate places or events of
particular interest.

BERLITZ®

DISCOVER
NORMANDY

Kim Naylor

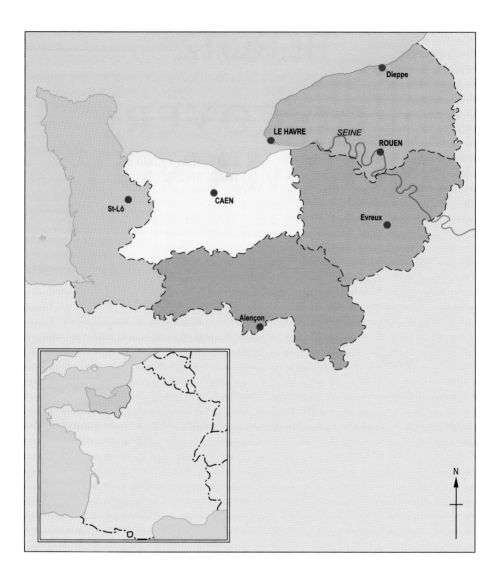

St-Lô

CAEN

LE HAVRE

Dieppe

SEINE

ROUEN

Evreux

Alençon

N

Contents

"Normandy Offers"

Lodge in a château or a farm house; travel along autoroute or country lane; transport by car, horseback, bike or foot; come in the rain or shine; visit on market day or holiday. There are always choices. Herewith are the "hows", "whens", "whys" and "wheres" of travelling in Normandy.

Getting There

By Plane
Travellers from outside France can arrange to fly direct to Paris from most major cities and pick up a connecting flight to Normandy from there. In some cases it may be possible to book a through ticket, but flights to various destinations in Normandy can be easily arranged in Paris.

Despite their highly pragmatic view of their land and all that grows upon it, the Normans have a great appreciation of flowers.

By Train
The French SNCF (*Société Nationale des Chemins de Fer Français*) is acknowledged as amongst the best railways in the world. SNCF offices provide full information about local and other travel, and where there are no trains there are well-organized rail–road links with coach or bus companies. Bookings can be made at most travel centres to various towns in Normandy via Paris. Students and senior citizens are entitled to appreciable reductions on rail travel.

By Coach
This is probably the most cost-effective mode of travel, and the level of service on inter-European coaches ensures a safe and comfortable journey. There

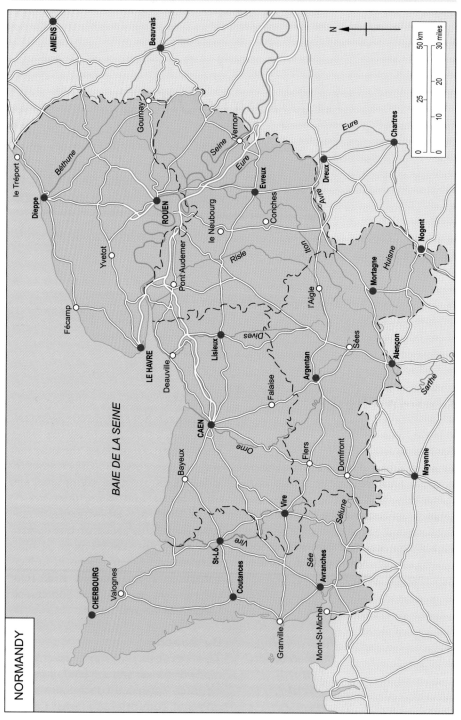

NORMANDY

are services to a number of destinations in Normandy—enquiries should be made at the travel office where the tickets are booked. As with rail travel, there are financial discounts available for students and senior citizens.

Cross-Channel Ferries

Dieppe, Le Havre, Cherbourg and Caen are the Normandy ports receiving cross-channel ferries from England and Ireland.

The Newhaven–Dieppe crossing takes 4 hours; the service is operated three or four times a day throughout the year by Sealink.

The Le Havre–Portsmouth crossing takes 5 hours 45 minutes for the daytime sailing and 7 hours for the nighttime sailing; the service is operated two or three times a day throughout the year by P & O European Ferries.

The Portsmouth–Caen (Ouistreham) sailing lasts 6 hours. There is one service a day during the winter months and up to three a day in summer. This route is run by Brittany Ferries

The Portsmouth–Cherbourg crossing takes 4 hours 45 minutes for the day-time sailing and 6 hours (Sealink) or 8 hours (P & O) for the night-time sailing. Sealink provide at least one service on all except one or two days in June, July and August, and one service on most days during the other months of the year. P & O's ferries operate this crossing between one and three times a day from mid-March until the fourth week of December.

The Weymouth–Cherbourg crossing takes 3 hours 55 minutes; the service is operated once or twice a day from the second week of April until October by Sealink.

The Poole–Cherbourg sailing takes about 4½ hours. This service commences on 15 April and there are between one and two crossings a day-operated by Brittany Ferries.

Tariffs vary considerably depending on the time of day you sail, the season, the size of your car, and the duration of stay abroad (special short break fare savers are usually on offer); cabins and Pullman chairs are available as extras on night crossings. Full information on rates and the sailing timetables are published in ferry companies' individual brochures; these are readily available from travel agencies or from the companies themselves (*see* USEFUL ADDRESSES). Bookings, which should be made well in advance during the summer months, school holidays and British bank holidays, can be made at travel agents or direct with the ferry company.

Most ferry companies operate a frequent travellers' club with free membership, which entitles members to discounts on future crossings.

Those with destinations in upper Normandy should bear in mind that the short crossing from Dover or Folkestone to Calais or Boulogne, followed by the drive south to Normandy, may prove a quicker door-to-door route than the long sailing direct to a Normandy port. A list of useful addresses and phone numbers for cross-channel ferries is provided below:

M ap of Normandy's main roads, rivers and towns.

Useful Addresses

Sealink UK Ltd
Charter House
Park Street
Ashford
Kent TN24 8EX
Tel: 0233 647047

P & O European Ferries
The Continental Ferry Port
Mile End
Portsmouth PO2 8QW
Tei: 0705 827677
P & O's telephone number in London
 is: 081-575 8555

Brittany Ferries
Wharf Road
Portsmouth PO2 8RV
Tel: 0705 751708

The following numbers are local numbers to call for latest information on
sailings:

Sealink
Newhaven: 0273 512266
Portsmouth: 0705 755111
Weymouth: 0305 760600
Dieppe: 35-82-24-87
Cherbourg: 33-20-43-38

Up-to-date recorded information is
provided on the following English
phone numbers:

0233 610340 (Dieppe sailings)
0233 610342 (Cherbourg sailings).

P & O
Portsmouth: 0705 772244
Le Havre: 35-21-36-50
Cherbourg: 33-44-20-13

Brittany Ferries
Portsmouth: 0705 827701
Caen (Ouistreham): 31-96-86-00
Cherbourg: 33-22-38-98

Irish Ferries
Le Havre: 35-21-36-50
Cherbourg: 33-44-28-96

Motoring in France

Aspects of Driving in France

Most obviously, as glaring roadsigns
alongside routes leading from France's
Channel ports remind forgetful British
motorists, the driving is on the right
and not on the left. A left-side wing
mirror is useful.

A thin strip of sticker should be
placed on each headlight to prevent
them dipping to the left; a set can be
bought at motorists' shops or can easily be cut out from household tape.

Traditionally, French motorists
have yellow-tinted headlights fitted to
their vehicles. British drivers need not
follow suit when travelling in France;
they are required, though, always to
carry a spare set of bulbs for their
main lights.

A warning triangle must also be
brought if the vehicle has no hazard
lights, and should be placed 50 m (55
yd) behind the vehicle during a break-
down.

A sticker indicating the country
where the vehicle is registered ("GB"
or otherwise) should be placed in a
conspicuous area on the back of the
vehicle.

Motorists should have with them
their full national driver's licence, the
vehicle's certificate of registration, valid

road tax and certificate of insurance. A Green Card is not obligatory, but is recommended, and is available on request from the vehicle's insurers. Separate short-term insurance, providing relay service and cover for garage fees, car hire and other costs in the event of an accident, is offered by the AA, RAC and Europ Assistance.

Police, stationed at their checkpoints, are all too ready to apprehend speeding drivers. They have the power to fine offenders in cash, a minimum of 1,300 F, on the spot. Allegations can be disputed but the culprit will then have to pay a "deposit" and attend a tribunal where the case will be decided.

The speed limits on dry roads are: 130 kph (81 mph) on the autoroute; 110 kph (68 mph) on dual carriageways; 90 kph (56 mph) on ordinary roads, and 60 kph (37 mph) in towns. On wet roads, the speed limit is reduced by 20 kph (12 mph) on autoroutes and by 10 kph (6 mph) on other roads. Other speed-limit signs, often emphasized by *rappel* (remember), are posted on the roadside. The end of a restricted speed zone is indicated by a similar sign with a black diagonal line through the speed limit. On flat, straight stretches of the autoroutes, and when the visibility is clear, there is a minimum speed limit of 80 kph (50 mph) in the fast lane.

A *"Vous n'avez pas la priorité"* (You do not have priority) sign commonly stands at the approach to roundabouts. Traffic already on the roundabout, travelling anticlockwise and appearing from the left, has the priority.

A *"Priorité à droite"* sign warns you to give way to traffic approaching from the right and *"Passage protège"* means that you have priority.

Seat belts must be worn by drivers and by front-seat passengers; children under ten cannot travel in the front, unless there is no back seat. Those caught by the police disobeying the rules are fined on the spot.

The drink-driving limit is similar to that in Britain, though in France the police can stop vehicles at random and take breath tests. Those discovered to be over the limit are given a hefty on-the-spot fine.

The French Road Network

Autoroute à péage (A), the toll motorways (at present the Autoroute de Normandie from Paris to Rouen and Caen is the only autoroute in Normandy); *National* (N), France's national roads which are both dual and multi-carriageways; *Départemental* (D), the departments' roads which are either single or dual carriageways; *Communale* (C), the local communities' minor roads, often barely the breadth of a car, linking hamlets and outlying farms. When actually talking about roads, the full category of the road and not just the letter abbreviation is used. Thus, for example, D123, as marked on the map or road sign, becomes "Departemental 123" in conversation.

Petrol in France is currently 20 per cent more expensive than in Britain. Prices can vary by about 60 or 70 centimes per litre for *"super essence"*: pumps at the large supermarkets tend to be the least expensive, similar to those in Britain, while those run by café or store owners in the small villages tend to be the most expensive; the well-known chains of service

*A*venues of tall trees *lining straight roads is so typical in France.*

stations, where unleaded petrol is also most readily available, charge somewhere in-between the two.

Road Maps
The *Michelin Carte Routière et Touristique* yellow series (1 cm: 2 km) is commonly used. Numbers 52, 54, 55, 59, 60 cover Normandy.

Accommodation

Accommodation in Normandy is varied, plentiful and, generally, good value for money.

For most of the year, there is no problem finding a place to stay. However, in the summer months, and in August in particular, vacancies are suddenly scarce.

Weekends and national holidays, the British ones included, are also peak periods in Normandy, so it is advisable to make reservations if you wish to be certain of securing a room in the hotel of your choice.

Hotels
According to the *Comité Régional de Tourisme de Normandie*, "The grading of hotels by stars (official classification) is decided by the standard of amenities and type of hotel:

****L	Luxury hotel (Palace)
****	Top-class hotel
***	Very comfortable hotel
**	Good average hotel
*	Plain but fairly comfortable hotel"

The vast majority of hotels fall into the 3-, 2- and 1-star categories; there are some 4-star, but no 4-star Ls in Normandy. All accommodation listed

12

by the Tourist Board in their "Hotels" booklet (readily available from tourist offices throughout Normandy) has to meet certain standards and 1 star hotels are generally clean, and usually have at least some rooms with private bathrooms.

The types of hotels vary from the *gîte* "bed and breakfasts", and the ordinary town and country houses which have been converted into small and midsize hotels, to the purpose-built hotels in larger towns and the unique châteaux hotels, which typically accommodate only a few guests.

The tariff quoted at hotels usually relates to the rate of the room rather than to the per head price and thus

*M*any of the old cob and pise cottages have been abandoned and have fallen into an irreparable state. Some, though, have been maintained with pride, love and care.

provides good value for couples. A "*lit supplement*", however, is normally paid for three or more people in a room.

The charge for a room in a 1-star hotel ranges from under 100 F to about 250 F a night; expect to pay 100 F–350 F for a room in a 2-star, 200–to 600 F in a 3-star and 300 F to in excess of 1000 F in a 4-star hotel.

Some of the Hotel Groups Operating in Normandy

Logis et Auberges de France

The well-known *"Logis et Auberges de France"*, a group founded in 1949 and now with some 5,000 establishments spread all over France, tend to be family-run hotels from the 2-star bracket,

though the chain does have some 1- and 3-stars amongst its fold. Normandy's 230 or so *"Logis et Auberges"* are recognizable by their symbol of a yellow fireplace on a green shield; they can be found in the countryside and in villages and towns and, to a lesser extent, in cities. They are reliable and provide adequately good, inexpensive accommodation, and their restaurants offer very reasonably priced set menus in addition to the à la carte.

A booklet listing all the *Logis et Auberges de France* is available from:

Fédération Nationale des Logis et
  Auberges de France
83, avenue d'Italie
75013 Paris
Tel: (1) 45-84-70-00

A list of their hoteliers in Normandy and, more specifically, in the various departments, can also be obtained from the above address or from the local tourist offices in Normandy.

Reservations are made directly with the hotels and may require a deposit, especially during the high season.

A small selection of Normandy's Logis are featured in the *"Logis Stop"* brochure and are affiliated with the Gîtes de France (*see* below).

Special car ferry–accommodation package prices are offered. Brochures and booking forms are available from:

Gîtes de France
Logis Department
178 Piccadilly
London
WIV 9DB
Tel: 071 493 3480 or
  071 408 1343

Reservations can be made at the above address; alternatively, present the booking form to an ABTA travel agent.

France Accueil

The smaller France Accueil group of hoteliers tend to be more up-market than the *Logis et Auberges de France*. Their dozen member hotels in Normandy are drawn from the 3- and 2-star categories and their excellent restaurants offer good value set-price meals as well as à la carte menus.

A directory of France Accueil hotels and booking facilities are available from:

Minotels France Accueil
85, rue de Dessous-des-Berges
F-75013 Paris
Tel: (1) 45-83-04-22

or

France Accueil Hotels
10 Salisbury Hollow
Edington
Westbury
Wilts BA13 4PF
Tel: (0380) 830125

Best Western

The large international Best Western chain of hotels have a small collection of members in Normandy whose 3- and 4-star hotels are amongst the best town accommodation. They also have a few country hotels, including a converted 18th-château and an old mill near Bayeux and Mont-Saint-Michel respectively.

A Best Western hotel directory and booking facilities are available from:

Best Western (France)
74, avenue du Docteur
Arnold-Netter
F-75012 Paris
Tel: (1) 43-41-22-44

or

Best Western (Britain)
Vine House
143 London Road
Kingston-upon-Thames
Surrey KT2 6NA
Tel: 081 541 0033

Châteaux Hotels

A growing number of private châteaux are being converted into hotels. At present there are about 50 "Châteaux Hotels" in Normandy and they range from local manor houses to the grander more classic châteaux.

There are several "Châteaux Hotel" organizations operating in Normandy. The largest is the *Châteaux Hôtels Independants et Hostelleries d'Atmosphere* with over 30 members in Normandy; their directory is available from:

Châteaux Hôtels Independants et
Hostelleries d'Atmosphere France
BP12
41700 Cour Cheverny

The directory is also widely circulated to French Tourist Offices abroad as well as to local Tourist Offices in Normandy. Reservations are made directly with the proprietor.

Members of the relatively small Château Accueil chain tend to have only a few rooms in their homes available. Their directory is available from:

Mme la Vicomtesse de Bonneval
Château de Thaumiers
18210 Charenton-du-Cher
Tel: 48-61-81-62

Rather like the Château Accueil, the B & D de Vogue is a group of château owners who prefer not to call themselves hoteliers. They view their customers as house guests in their homes whom they treat as part of the family during their stay. B & D de Vogue currently have nine members in Normandy; their directory is available from:

B & D de Vogue Tours
15, rue Mesnil
75116 Paris
Tel: (1) 45-53-56-00

or from their British representatives, who can also organize reservations:

Destination Marketing Limited
2 Cinnamon Row
Plantation Wharf
York Place
London SW11 3TW
Tel: 071 978 5222

The Relais & Châteaux is an international group with only a few members in Normandy; their handbook is available from:

Relais & Châteaux
9, avenue Marceau
75116 Paris
Tel: (1) 47-23-41-42

In addition to the above groups there are two English-based companies, Allez France and Unicorn Holidays, specializing in a variety of package holidays which include accommodation in châteaux (some of the châteaux are members of the organizations mentioned above).

For further information contact the following:

Allez France
27 West Street
Storrington
Pulborough
West Sussex RH20 4DZ
Tel: 0903 745793

Unicorn Holidays
Intech House
34–35 Cam Centre
Wilbury Way
Hitchin
Herts SG4 ORL
Tel: 0462 422223

The local tourist offices in Normandy can provide you will full details of châteaux and manor hotels and accommodation with character in their district.

Gîtes de France

The *Federation Nationale des Gîtes de France*, more commonly referred to as the *Gîtes de France*, offers self-catering (*Gîtes Rural*) and bed and breakfast (*Chambres d'hôtes*) accommodation in typical rural French homes. An organization linked to the French Ministries of Agriculture and Tourism, the *Gîtes de France* are privately owned houses, individual in character, usually traditional cottages or farmhouses, and are often off the beaten track and in the heart of the countryside.

17

Gîtes Rural and the "Gîtes Elite" Club

The idea of a *Gîte Rural* is that guests can live the French rural life, independent and catering for themselves, in a suitably modernized country home. There are over 150 *Gîtes Rural* in Normandy, some are only available during certain months, and they are easily identified by their green circle symbol.

Rates are reasonable and are gauged according to the standard of accommodation, ears of corn serve as grades, and the number of occupants; children often stay for free. There are also different seasonal rates: winter: from 4 November to 28 April; low: from 28 April to 2 June and 30 September to 3 November; mid: from 3 June to 30 June and 2 September to 29 September; and high: from 1 July to 1 September.

Gîtes are normally booked from a Saturday to a Saturday with one week being the minimum period of stay (two weeks is the minimum period during most of the high season). The owner of the property usually welcomes the guests and helps them settle in. He can be called upon if there are problems, though, in the unlikely event of intractable disputes over the standards provided, you can turn for assistance to the local *Relais Departement* whose address is provided on booking.

There is a scheme whereby British residents can join the *"Gîtes Elite"* club. The membership fee is nominal and entitles you to the current *Gîtes de France Handbook*, which lists well over 2,000 *gîtes* in France, each entry featuring a photograph and details of the accommodation. This hefty directory provides other useful information and includes a typical inventory of what you can expect to find in a *gîte* and advice on what you should take: sheets (standard French beds have different dimensions to those in Britain and bolsters rather than pillows are the norm), towels, a teapot and so forth.

For membership, bookings and further details about the *Gîtes Rural* contact:

Gîtes de France Ltd,
178 Piccadilly
London W1V 9DB
Tel: 071 493 3480 or 071 408 1343

Members of *"Gîtes Elite"* are given a detailed IGN map of their region when they book, and can take advantage of special all-inclusive *gîte* and ferry rates.

Chambres d'Hôtes

These are French equivalent of the English bed and breakfast. Guests stay with families who provide a room, with basin and sometimes a private bathroom, and a continental breakfast. Evening meals, normally home-made traditional fare, are extra and should be requested in advance. By living with the locals, guests are dipped into their culture. There are around 600 *Chambres d'Hôtes* in Normandy and they are recognizable by the *Gîtes de France* green circle symbol.

Tariffs, per person rates rather than room rates so as to account for the breakfasts, range from about 100 F for one person to 300 F for four people. An evening meal is usually available. Gîtes de France Ltd in London can make reservations at the small selection of *Chambres d'Hôtes* which are

featured in their "Chambres d'Hôtes Book" and they offer all inclusive accommodation–ferry packages. The complete list of the Normandy *Chambres d'Hôtes* is available from tourist offices in Normandy or from the *Gîtes de France* headquarters in Paris:

Maison des Gîtes de France
35, rue Godot-de-Amuroy
75009 Paris
Tel: (1) 47-42-25-43

Other organizations also provide self-catering accommodation in a similar way to the *Gîtes de France*. These include Allez France and Unicorn Holidays, see above for addresses.

Three Other Categories of "Gîtes"
Le Gîte d'Enfants: a chance for city kids to spend time in the countryside during their school holidays. *Gîtes de France* approved families, often

A genial welcome into the front room.

farmers, take in children, up to a maximum of 11 per household. A supervisor-cum-co-ordinator is provided for groups of more than six children. *Le Gîte d'Enfants* is not used that much by foreigners, and it therefore offers an excellent chance for English children to learn French.

Le Gîte de Groupe: lodgings for groups of between 10 and 18 people.

Le Camping à la Ferme: small campsites, with washrooms, in a farmer's field. Caravanners are welcome.

Camping and Caravanning
The French with their 11,000 officially graded campsites are well geared to campers and caravanners. In Normandy, there are some 500 sites, their

greatest concentration being along the coast and near the popular beach resorts.

Campsites are graded from 1- to 4- stars. Their ratings correspond to the amenities, standard and the camper-to-land ratio. In a 1- and 2-star site, for example, a minimum of 10 per cent of the area is devoted to washrooms and other basic facilities, with each camping lot being at least 90 m^2 (108 ft^2); 4-star sites provide double the space for communal facilities and 100 m^2 (120 ft^2) per tent. The more modest sites may offer no more than the mere basics, toilets, showers (though not always hot water), and electricity in the public areas. At the fancier sites, you can expect more and better washrooms, hot water, shops, children's playground, baby-sitting, possibly a swimming pool, a higher standard of paths and lighting around the site, day and night guards and, especially at the 4-star *grand confort* sites, direct electrical and water hook-ups to each camp allotment.

Besides these, the conventional campsites, there are the small rural sites. Typically, these are fields owned by farmers, "non-professionals" in the world of camping, who provide on-site running water, toilet and washing facilities, but little else. There are over 100 such sites in Normandy which are affiliated to one of two groups, the *Aires Naturelles de Camping* and the *Gîtes Camping-Caravanning à la Ferme*; camper density is restricted to a maximum of 25 lots and 100 campers, and 6 lots and 25 campers respectively. These sites are not star graded, though they are officially recognized.

Tariffs are posted outside the site and are either per lot or per person rates (children are sometimes given discounts). The range of prices varies from approximately 75 F for a car, tent and family of four in a 1-star site to two or three times this rate in a 4-star site. Tariffs at the "farm sites" are lower than those of a 1-star.

Several publications can help campers with the planning of their trip:

Camping Caravanning, and annual listing of all campsites in Normandy, including the "farmsites", giving relevant details about each site, is published by the Normandy Tourist Office.

The Camping Traveller in France, a magazine providing hints, useful information and addresses for campers and caravanners travelling to France, is produced by the French Tourist Office in London.

The annual *Official French Federation Camping and Caravanning Guide*, which lists sites throughout France, is available from Springdene, Shepherd's Way, Fairlight, Hastings, East Sussex TN35 4BB.

The annual *Michelin Camping Caravanning* is available from travel bookshops as are other publications on camping and caravanning in France.

Various caravan clubs, their advertisements and listings appear in *The Camping Traveller in France* (see above), offer their members specific advice and special ferry–campsite packages.

Normandy on Foot

France's *Grandes Randonnées* (GR), public footpaths, cover some 40,000 km (25,000 miles) nationwide of which over 3,000 km (1,900 miles) are in the meadows and forests, and along the rivers and coast of beautiful rural Normandy.

The Fédération Française de la Randonnée Pedestre (FFRP), France's national ramblers' association, was founded in 1948. It created the splendid and ever-expanding network of *Grandes Randonnées*. The FFRP works in close conjunction with its associates at departmental and at a more local level, whose responsibility it is to maintain existing routes and to provide suggestions for new ones.

The *Grandes Randonnées* can be many hundreds of kilometres in length and one of Normandy's famous footpaths, the 300 km (186 mile) long GR2 commences on the right bank of the Seine north-west of Paris, follows much of the remainder of the river's course, entering Normandy just before Giverny and terminates at Le Havre. Other marathon treks to conclude on the coast of Normandy are the GR 22 and the GR 26, both start in Paris and reach their finale in Mont-Saint-Michel and Deauville respectively; another is the GR 36 which runs from the Pyrennes to the mouth of the Orne.

Most *Grandes Randonnées*, though, are contained within Normandy and are sometimes signed as "Tours"

T *he Chemin de Randonnée, a quiet path through the heart of the Normandy countryside.*

implying they are circular routes, returning the rambler to his point of departure. Furthermore, the footpaths often cross each other, allowing the walker to devise his own itinerary incorporating more than one *Grande Randonnée*.

There are also the *Grandes Randonnées de Pays*, GR de Pays, and the *Moyennes Randonnées* which are routes concentrating on a particular region. The more modest *Petites Randonnées*, PR, are walks devised by locals which originate and end in a small town or village and pass through the countryside in the vicinity; the walk may take anything from an hour to a day and a sketch map of the course is usually only available from the local tourist office (*syndicat d'initiative*) or *association de randonneurs*.

Grandes Randonnées are identified easily at various stages by a red sign marked GR followed by the number of the footpath. Elsewhere along the way, two small horizontal lines, the top one white, the lower one red, are painted conspicuously on trees, walls, gates to indicate to ramblers that they are on the right path. An arrow, as well as these lines, points the change of direction at the relevant places, and the two lines crossed is notice that the wrong direction has been taken.

*T*he poppy blossoms briefly in June-July, forming patches of blood red across the landscape; the flower of the Wars is a reminder of those who lost their lives on these fields.

Similar signs mark the routes of the GR de Pays and the PR, though the colour codes are different: yellow and red lines and a single yellow line respectively (yellow is not always standard in the case of the latter, so check before embarking on the walk).

Listed below are the current *Grandes Randonnées* in Normandy. The Topo-guides are published in association with the FFRP and give detailed information on certain routes:

GR 2   The Seine Valley (Eure, Seine-Maritime); Topo-guide No. 203.

GR 21–211–212   The coastal cliffs and countryside of the Pays de Caux (Seine-Maritime); Topo-guide No. 205.

GR 22   Paris–Mont-Saint-Michel, from Verneuil-sur-Arne east–west along the lower regions of Normandy (Eure, Orne, Manche); Topo-guide No. 207.

GR 23–25   Region around Rouen, including the Forêt de Brotonne (Eure, Seine-Maritime); Topo-guide No. 209.

GR 26   Paris–Deauville, from the Seine near Vernon through the Bocage to the sea (Calvados).

GR 36 Pyrennes–The Channel, entering Normandy at the Parc de Normandie-Maine, passing through Suisse Normande and then along the River Orne to the coast (Orne, Calvados).

GR 221 Coutances–Suisse Normande, via St Lô (Manche, Calvados); Topo-guide No. 208.

GR 222 Valley and forests of the Eure (Eure).

GR 223 The west and north coasts of the Contentin peninsula and the Saire Valley (Manche); Topo-guide No. 200.

GR 224 Risle Valley and Pays d'Ouche (Eure); Topo-guide No. 210.

GR 261 Caen–Port-en-Bessin–Grandcamp (Calvados).

Grandes Randonnées de Pays and Moyennes Randonnées

Pays de Bray, the Andelle Valley (Seine-Maritime, Eure); Topo-guide No. 002.

Walks in the Parc Normandie-Maine (Orne); Topo-guide No. 039.

The Bresle Valley, Le Tréport to Aumale (Seine-Maritime).

Walk through southern Manche, former GR 226 (Manche).

Circuit around Suisse Normande (Calvados, Orne).

Walks around the Odon, Caen to Aunay-sur-Odan (Calvados).

Tourist paths of Bessin: Ouistreham, Caen, Bayeux and the beaches of the Normandy landings to Grandcamp (Calvados).

Walks in the Bocage, Vire to the Souleuvre (Calvados).

The Ornais area of the Parc Normandie-Maine: 5 circuits (Orne); Topo-guide No. 1.

Perche–Pays d'Ouche: 18 circuits (Orne); Topo-guide No. 2.

The Auge–Argentan countryside: 10 circuits (Orne); Topo-guide No. 3.

The Ornais Bocage–Suisse Normande: 10 circuits (Orne); Topo-guide No. 4.

Accommodation for Ramblers

Lodgings thought appropriate for dedicated ramblers and cyclists, *Hebergements du Randonneur*, are found along the courses of the *Grandes Randonnées* and cyclists' circuits.

A *gîte d'étape* is a generic term for a resting place, but for those in the accommodation business the *gîte d'étape* is a specific type of simple, inexpensive lodging and, typically, has a communal room, kitchen with cooking facilities and utensils, toilet and showers and individual rooms or dormitories. Many have received the Gîtes de France (*see* page 17) stamp of approval "G.F." which means they are of a guaranteed high standard.

"*Baladhôtels*", literally the "Wanderer Hotels", are a small group of country inns and modest hotels with a particular aim to cater for the rambler; often they have boxes for horses. Further information about the balad-hôtels is available from: Hôtel de France, 14350 Le Beny-Bocage; tel: 31-68-63-10.

There are also Youth Hostels, *Auberges de Jeunesse*, though they tend to be in towns (membership is required and is obtainable at hostels) and the *Centres d'Accueil* which usually accommodate parties of schoolchildren, but can provide lodgings for others if there is room.

A list of *Hebergements du Randonneur* is included in the *Randonnées en Normandie* pamphlet published by the Normandy Tourist Board. It also indicates lodgings which provide boxes for horses.

And for the dedicated, or even the casual walker, there is a Normandy ramblers' get-together held each year on the first weekend of October. People at the addresses below will know the time and venue.

Useful Addresses for Ramblers

Fédération Française de Randonnée Pédestre
8, avenue Marceau
75008 Paris
Tel: (1) 47-23-62-32

In addition to the national organization of the FFRP, there are the individual departmental ramblers' associations:

Departmental Ramblers' Associations
Calvados: Association Départementals de Tourisme Pédestre, 6, promenade Mme de Sevigne, 14039 Caen.

Manche: Association de Tourisme Pédestre de la Manche (ATP), 2, rue du Roc, 50400 Granville.

Orne: Fédération Ornaise pour le Tourisme de Randonnée, 88, rue St Blaise, BP 50, 61002 Alençon Cedex.

Ramblers' associations in Eure and Seine-Maritime can be contacted through the respective departmental tourist offices (*see* page 29).

Normandy on Bike

"Cyclotourisme" has been given a high profile within the tourist industry. The *Fédération Française de Cyclotourisme* has its headquarters in Paris and has two branches in Normandy; the *Comités Départementaux de Cyclotourisme* are departmental bodies dealing with cycling (*see* below).

Bikes, including mountain bikes, can be hired from scores of places, including about 30 railway stations which makes a "one-way cycling–return by train" excursion all the easier.

Lists of the cycling routes, bike hiring depots (*"liste des locations de bicyclettes"*), inclusive bike hire-accommodation holidays and other information for cyclists are available from the *Fédération Française de Cyclotourisme* and the departmental and local tourist offices.

Useful Addresses for Cyclists
Fédération Française de Cyclotourisme
8, rue Jean-Marie Jego
750013 Paris
Tel: (1) 45-80-30-21

Strong bikes offer the option of rough tracks across empty countryside.

The addresses of local cycling associations can be obtained from national organizations.

Normandy on Horse

Some of France's great national stud farms and equestrian centres, notably Le Haras du Pin and Le Haras de Saint-Lô, are in Normandy.

The *Randonnée Equestre*, Normandy on horseback, is an increasingly popular way of seeing Normandy. There

are some 150 stables in Normandy which offer riding holidays to all levels of rider from the novice to the accomplished, providing them with a horse and tuition and full board if required.

Some of the *Grandes Randonnées*, referred to as the *Itineraire Equestres*, are suitable for riders. Alternatively, the stables have their own routes, called *Randonnées Attelées*, through the best of the surrounding countryside.

A list of stables and what they offer and a calendar of equestrian events is included in the brochure *A Cheval en Normandie* available from the tourist offices. There are hotels, such as the *baladhôtels* and some *gîtes d'étapes* (*see* above) which provide boxes for horses. For full information about these and other aspects relating to riding in Normandy contact the relevant addresses below.

Useful Addresses for Riders

Association Nationale de Tourisme
  Equestre
15, rue de Bruxelles
75009 Paris
Tel: (1) 42-81-42-82

Association de Tourisme Equestre
  Haute Normandie
381, rue P. et M. Curie
76480 Duclair

Association Régionale de Tourisme
  Equestre Basse Normandie
Chambre d'Agriculture
6, promenade Mme de Sevigne
14009 Caen Cedex

Ligue de Normandie des Sports
  Equestres
BP 6092
14063 Caen Cedex
  (They produce the bi-monthly *Normandie Equestre* with full details of equestrian events.)

Departmental Committees for Horse Riding

Calvados: Same as the Association Régionale de Tourisme Equestre Basse Normandie (*see* above).

*H*orse riding is not restricted to the countryside: low tide exposes long wide stretches of firm sand.

Eure: Centre Equestre de Bec-Hellouin, 27800 Brionne.

Manche: Le Poirier de Milieu, 50000 Saint Lô.

Orne: Coterrel, 25, rue des Iris, 61250 Damigni.

Seine-Maritime: Centre Equestre des Pommerolles, 76570 Limesy.

Useful Publications

Randonnées en Normandie: a pamphlet produced by the Normandy tourist board includes practical information, a sketch map of *randonnées* and a list of suitable accommodation. It is available from the Comité Regional de Tourisme de Normandie (*see* TOURIST OFFICES) and some departmental and local tourist offices.

Topo-guides: guides to individual *Grande Randonnée* footpaths—published in association with the FFRP (*see* above for address).

Institut Geographique National (IGN) maps: the French equivalent of the Ordnance Survey publish 1/50,000 (1cm: $\frac{1}{2}$ km, $1\frac{1}{4}$ in: 1 mile) maps of Normandy in their orange series (*see* below) and 1/25,000 (1 cm: $\frac{1}{4}$ km, $2\frac{1}{2}$ in: 1 mile) in their blue series. These are available from the Institut Geographique National, 107, rue de la Boetie, 75008 Paris; tel: (1) 42-25-87 90.

McCarta Map and Guide Shop, 122 King's Cross Road, London WC1X 9DS; tel: 071-278 8276 also stock IGN maps and produce their own guides on some of Normandy's *Grandes Randonnées* in conjunction with the *Topo-guides*.

The Office National de Forêts: Direction Regionale de Normandie, 58, rue Bouquet, 76042 Rouen; tel: 35-71-00-15, produce 1/25,000 (1 cm: $\frac{1}{4}$ km, $2\frac{1}{2}$ in: 1 mile) maps of many of the forests in Normandy.

Tourist Offices

Normandy's tourism is administered by its five separate departmental bodies. The headquarters are in the respective departmental capitals and there are hundreds of local tourist offices and *syndicat d'initiatives* in the towns, resorts and other places of interest.

A mass of material, pamphlets about the sights, listings of hotels and events, maps and so forth, is readily available at all levels: the headquarters can provide general information about the whole department, whereas the local offices can supply detailed information about its catchment area.

Comité Regional de Tourisme de
    Normandie (the overall
    headquarters)
46, avenue Foch
27000 Evreux
Tel: 32-33-79-00
Telex: 172739
Fax: 32-31-19-04

Calvados

Comité Départemental de Tourisme
    du Calvados
Place du Canada
14000 Caen
Tel: 31-86-53-30
Telex: 171343
Fax: 31-79-39-41

Eure

Comité Départemental de Tourisme
  de l'Eure
35, rue du Dr Oursel
BP 187
27001 Evreux Cedex
Tel: 32-38-21-61
Telex: 770581
Fax: 32-38-73-39

Manche

Office Départemental de Tourisme
  de la Manche
Maison du Departement
Route de Villedieu
50008 St Lô Cedex
Tel: 33-05-98-70
Telex: 772138
Fax: 33-05-96-90

Orne

Comité Départemental de Tourisme
  de l'Orne
88, rue Saint Blaise
BP 50
61002 Alençon Cedex
Tel: 33-28-88-71
Telex: 171556
Fax: 33-29-81-60

Seine-Maritime

Comité Départemental de Tourisme
  de Seine-Maritime
2 bis, rue de Petit Salut
BP 680
76008 Rouen Cedex
Tel: 35-88-61-32
Telex: 770940
Fax: 35-71-00-37

Opening Times

The opening times of the local offices
vary according to the importance and
popularity of the place.

The French Tourist Office in London
produces its own series of publications
aimed at the huge British market and
their *Travellers in France* series includes
useful general information and addresses for visitors to France. These,
and brochures on ferries and accommodation, as well as a limited stock of
publications specifically on Normandy,
are available from:

The French Government Tourist
  Office
178 Piccadilly
London W1V 0AL

Markets, Festivals and Public Holidays

Most towns and many villages in
Normandy have their regular market
days, and all, it seems, have a festival
at least once a year (usually during the
summer). In addition, there are a host
of religious celebrations when locals
pay homage to their saint or remember some folkloric tradition. Such
events add a dash of colour to daily
lives as well as to a visit. Local tourist
offices can provide full information.
Some market days and festivals are
listed below:

Calvados

Beuvron-en-Auge: late November,
  Cider Festival
Cabourg: July, Regatta; end August,
  William the Conqueror Festival
Caen: Wednesday (place Saint
  Sauveur) and Sunday (place
  Courtonne); September, Caen fair
Courseulles-sur-Mer: Tuesday and
  Friday

White gloves, smart shades, black hat, red plume are de rigeur *at the country fair.*

La Déliverande: 15 August and 8 September, Pilgrimage to the Black Madonna

Deauville: Tuesday; August, Horse Racing Grand Prix

Honfleur: Saturday; Whit Sunday, Seamen's Festival

Isigny-sur-Mer: Every other Saturday

Lisieux: Sunday in mid-July, mid-August and last Sunday in September: festivals relating to Saint Theresa

Orbec: Wednesday

Saint Pierre-sur-Dives: Monday

Saint Sever: Saturday

Trouville: Wednesday and Sunday

Villers-Brocage: Wednesday

Vire: Friday

Eure

Les Andelys: Monday

Bernay: Saturday; end March–early April, Spring Flower Festival

Brionne: Thursday

Conches-en-Ouche: Thursday

Gisors: Monday, Friday and Sunday

La Haye-de-Routot: 16–17 July, Le Feu de Saint Clair bonfire night

Ivry-la-Bataille: Wednesday and Saturday

Louviers: Saturday; September, Saint Michel Festival

Lyons-la-Forêt: Thursday after 9 October, Saint Octave de la Fête Dieu

Le Neubourg: Wednesday

Pont-Audemer: Monday

Verneuil-sur-Avre: Saturday

Manche

Avranches: Saturday

Barneville: Saturday

Bricquebec: Monday

Carentan: Monday

Cherbourg: Tuesday, Thursday, Saturday (place Général de Gaulle); also daily fish market, except Sunday

Coutainville: Tuesday, Thursday and Saturday

Coutainville: Thursday

Coutances: Monday

Granville: February, Mardi Gras celebrations

Lessay: Mid-September, Saint Cross Fair (farm animal market-fair)

Mont-Saint-Michel: May, Saint Michel's Spring Festival; July, Pilgrimage across the sand; September, Saint Michel's autumn festival

Mortain: Saturday

Saint Lô: Saturday

Saint Vaast-la-Hougue: Saturday

Valognes: Tuesday and Friday

Villedieu-les-Poêles: Tuesday

Orne

L'Aigle: Tuesday

Alençon: Thursday and Saturday

Argentan: Tuesday and Friday

Bagnoles-de-l'Orne: Wednesday

Bellême: Thursday

Ferté-Macé: Thursday; March, Tripe Festival

Flers: Wednesday and Saturday

Gacé: Saturday

Longny-au-Perche: Wednesday

Mount Cerisi: last Sunday in May, Rhododendron Fair

Mortagne-au-Perche: Saturday

Saint Christophe-le-Jajolet: last Sunday in July and first Sunday in October: the blessing of cars

Sées: Saturday; 15 December, Foire aux Dindes

Soligny-la-Trappe: Tuesday

Vimoutiers: Monday; mid-October, Apple Festival

Seine-Maritime

Auffay: Friday

Aumule: Saturday

Blangy: Sunday

Caudebec-en-Caux: Saturday; last Sunday in September, Cider Festival

Dieppe: Saturday; November, Herring Feast

Duclair: Tuesday

Elbeuf: Tuesday, Thursday, Saturday

Eu: Friday

Fécamp: Saturday

Forges-les-Eaux: Thursday; July, Horse Market

Goderville: Tuesday

Gournay-en-Bray: Tuesday, Friday and Sunday

Le Havre: Tuesday, Thursday and Saturday; July, the Regatta; Sunday after mid-August, Flower Festival

Yvetot: Wednesday

Jumièges: July, the Cherry Market; August, Plum Market; October, Apple Market

Neufchâtel-en-Bray: Saturday

Rouen: Tuesday, Wednesday, Friday and Saturday in place Vieux Marché; Sunday nearest 30 May, Fêtes de Jeanne d'Arc

Smartly dressed for market day, farmers pass the time chatting. The flat cap, rather than the beret, is à la mode.

Dieppe's large Saturday morning market spreads over much of the old town. Baskets are made and sold on the western side of the church of Saint Jacques (previous page).

Saint Valery-en-Caux: Friday and
    Sundays in summer; Herring and
    Cider Festival in December

Public Holidays
1 January (New Year's Day)
Easter Monday
1 May (May Day)
8 May (VE Day)
Ascension Day
Whit Monday
14 July (Bastille Day)
15 August (Assumption Day)
1 November (All Saints' Day)
11 November (Remembrance Day)
25 December (Christmas Day)

Money

The French Franc (FF or F) is divided
into 100 centimes (ct).
    Coins: 5, 10, 20, 50 ct; 1, 2, 5, 10 F
    Bank notes: 20, 50, 100, 200, 500 F

An endless landscape of meadows, chequered by forests and dotted with villages.

Bank Opening Times

Generally 9.00 a.m. to 4.00 p.m., often with a lunch-break from 12.00 p.m.–2.00 p.m., from Mondays to Fridays. In some towns, the banks will remain open on Saturdays, especially if this is market day, and close on Mondays.

Credit cards and Eurocheques are all widely accepted; a passport will be required as means of identification when paying.

Opening Times

Opening times vary according to the town, the type of shop, the local market day, the season and so on. Very typical is the universal French practice of taking a 2-hour lunch-break. And so 9.00 a.m. to 12.00 p.m. and 2.00–6.00 p.m. are fairly usual opening times. Banks, shops and museums may well be open on Saturdays, but closed on Mondays.

Climate

It is commonly said that Normandy's climate is much the same as that of southern England, though temperatures are a degree or two warmer. Indeed, England's weather often blows onwards to northern France and Normans will look at England's forecasts to see what is in store for them the following day.

Winters are relatively mild for northern Europe; rain is plentiful and gives rise to the famous lush green pastures. In recent years, the summers have been particularly dry and hot.

Average Temperatures in Normandy				
	Min		**Max**	
	°F	°C	°F	°C
January	40	4	47	8
February	39	4	47	8
March	41	5	51	10
April	45	7	54	12
May	49	9	59	15
June	54	12	64	18
July	57	14	67	19
August	54	14	67	19
September	56	13	65	18
October	51	10	60	15
November	46	8	53	12
December	42	5	49	9

Children

The Briton, in search of an accessible and inexpensive place to take the family on holiday, has discovered Normandy. In terms of modern travel and convenience, what could be easier than piling into the car and hopping on a ferry to Normandy?

The Norman, aware of the demand, has prepared the land, for the most part tastefully, as a "family destination". The "gîtes" (*see* ACCOMMODATION) are ideal self-catering family lodgings; the larger campsites, in particular, are usually geared for kids and often provide a variety of amusements and facilities for youngsters; in hotels, the "extra bed" in the room, for example, is easily arranged at little further cost to the normal tariff. Family restaurants cater for kids by offering "children's menus", familiar food, smaller portions, lower prices. And, even in this land of fine customs and food snobbery, there are the universal, not to say ubiquitous MacDonalds or their equivalents.

Nature, too, seems to favour children. Normandy's long coastline consists largely of beaches, many sandy and with shallow waters, and at the seaside resorts there is typically a variety of children's amusements, ranging from watersports and playgrounds to aquariums and fairgrounds.

Family walks around the countryside are devised by local tourist offices and, increasingly, local museums aim exhibitions, particularly about local flora, fauna and environmental concerns, at the youngsters. Overall, there is a positive attitude towards the family, children are to be seen *and* heard, and it is a smart attitude: happy families mean healthy tourist revenues.

The Region, its History and its People

Two major events, almost 1,000 years apart and which were to change the course of world history, took place in Normandy. First was the rise and success of the Norman dynasty, creators of a medieval empire which included England after William the Conqueror's victory at Hastings in 1066. Second, the Allies' D-Day landings and their subsequent success in the battle for Normandy, which was to lead to Germany's eventual defeat in World War II.

A land of extraordinary richness is the strong, lasting impression one has of Normandy: a long coastline of giant white cliffs, craggy windswept headlands and wide, sandy beaches. An interior with its lush rolling pastures grazed by the plumpest dairy cows, its open plains, its beautiful river valleys and majestic beech forests. A land which bore the Dukes of Normandy, who were to shape the destiny of the Western world, and where early Christian monasticism took seed and flourished. The castles, châteaux, city cathedrals, country churches, and ruined monasteries are legacies of a great history and reflect the pioneering styles, and the highest standards of architecture and design of the medieval ages.

Normandy's dramatic skies and seas were the inspiration of Impressionism whose "father", Eugène Boudin, and most celebrated artist, Claude Monet, were both Normans; so, too, were Gustave Flaubert and Guy de Maupassant who used Normandy and its people as the scene and subjects in their novels. The Normandy portrayed by these 19th-century artists and writers is there behind the veneer of the 20th century.

T emptation in Normandy's Garden of Eden: a country girl offers a smile and an apple to a passer-by.

The cuisine—a people's most enduring tradition—is rich, plentiful and wholesome in Normandy. A land as fertile as this provides an abundance. The idyllic image of meadows and orchards—of full fat cheeses and earthy cider—has changed little with time.

But Normans have always been at the cutting edge of progress, and energy, pragmatism and a sense of innovation are factors behind their remarkable success over the centuries. It was a credit to their character that, after the fighting and bombings of the Second World War—which ravaged their lands and destroyed many of their cities—they picked themselves up from the ruins, rebuilt and prospered.

In this book, Normandy's five administrative departments: Seine-Maritime, Calvados, Manche, Orne and Eure, are covered separately. The object is to provide a comprehensive touring guide—itineraries along the well-worn paths as well as circuits off the beaten track—through the rich and varied lands which make up Normandy.

Geography

Normandy—a varied country of rolling pastures, plains, woodlands and with a dramatic coast of white cliffs, rugged headlands and long, sandy beaches—is not dissimilar to southern England, a land it once joined.

The province can be divided into Upper (*Haute*) and Lower (*Basse*) Normandy. The higher chalk and limestone region to the east, comprising the departments of Seine-Maritime and Eure, tends to be more populated and industrialized, and with an affinity towards Paris. The lower sandstone and granite region of the west, comprising Calvados, Orne and Manche is more akin to Brittany. Within these two regions there is a great diversity of local geography.

Coast

Normandy's white chalk cliffs—the evocatively named Alabaster Coast—stretch from le Tréport to le Havre at the estuary of the Seine. Rivers have, over eons, breached this wall and, at their mouths, have evolved fishing villages and small resorts, fronted by pebble beaches and flanked by the towering cliffs. The settings are often stunning and no more so than at the resort of Etretat.

The coast from Honfleur—on the opposite side of the Seine estuary from le Havre—to Cabourg is known as the Côte Fleurie and is characterized by long, wide stretches of sandy beach. Thriving ports from the past—Dives-sur-Mer and Honfleur, for example—have silted and it is the resorts, such as Deauville and Cabourg, which now command attention.

Beyond Cabourg stretches the Calvados coast and the Côte de Nacre—the Coast of Mother of Pearl. Flat, sandy and broken by headlands, this is where the Allies made their D-Day landings on 6 June 1944. The beaches still retain their wartime code names: Sword, Juno, Gold and Omaha. The resorts along this stretch of coast are more modest than those of Côte Fleurie.

The Cotentin Peninsula—with its 300 km (180 miles) of beach and craggy cliff washed by the Channel

and the Atlantic—sticks up like a stubby thumb at the western end of Normandy. Utah—the westernmost Allied landing beach—is at the eastern base of the peninsula and at the top are the bleak, flat, exposed extremities of Normandy. The short northern coast becomes increasingly dramatic after Cherbourg and reaches its most rugged at Cap de la Hague and Nez Jobourg. Some of Normandy's finest and emptiest sandy beaches are along the western side of Cotentin. On a clear day you can see the Channel Islands. At the lower end of the peninsula the shore swings west for Mont-Saint-Michel—France's most spectacular monument—a powerful climax to the coast of Normandy.

Countryside

Wet winters, mild temperatures and warm summers provide Normandy with pastures as lush as any in Europe. And this translates into the huge quantities of rich dairy produce for which Normandy is so rightly famous.

U tah and Omaha, the latter pictured here, were the two American D-Day landing beaches under the command of General Bradley of the 1st US Army; to the east lay Gold, Juno and Sword, the British beaches.

Pays de Bray, the inland northernmost quarter of Normandy, is cider country and is one of the major suppliers of dairy goods to Paris—hence the nickname "Dairy of Paris". Neufchâtel-en-Bray and Gournay-en-Bray are the region's two famous cheese centres, producing the "Neufchâtel" and "Petit Suisse".

Pays de Caux, the hinterland of the Alabaster Coast between the Seine and Dieppe, is the flat to undulating chalkland more characterized by crop cultivation—the growing of wheat and sugar beet—than dairy farming. The region provides an interesting—and

43

N orman and the dog out walking the cows.

welcome—contrast to the richer fields of Normandy; the monotony of the countryside is broken by pretty river valleys. These open plains extend across Upper Normandy, beyond Rouen to Norman Vexin and to the flat Neubourg Plain which stretches from the far side of the Seine towards Evreux.

Beyond the Neubourg Plain are the woodlands of Pays d'Ouche which give way—to the south—to the forests and meadows of the undulating Pays de Perche, where horse breeding is the preoccupation. And to the west of Pays d'Ouche—in the lands between the Touques and the Orne—are the rich meadows of Pays d'Auge. This, too, is a prime orchard and dairy region—the home of cheeses such as Pont l'Eveque, Livarot and Camembert. Flatter lands and forests predominate south towards Alençon. West—up by the coast—are the grazing marshlands of Bessin, famous for their Isigny-sur-Mer blend of butter and *présalé* lamb; further south are the granite quarries near Vire and the extraordinary Suisse Normande—Normandy's Little Switzerland. Beyond is the heart of the Bocage, the open land of hedge-bordered fields and woods which characterize much of the Cotentin Peninsula.

The bomb damage of the War—which destroyed so many of Normandy's towns—has now been repaired. Today, Normandy smacks of

M ap of the Val de Seine.

44

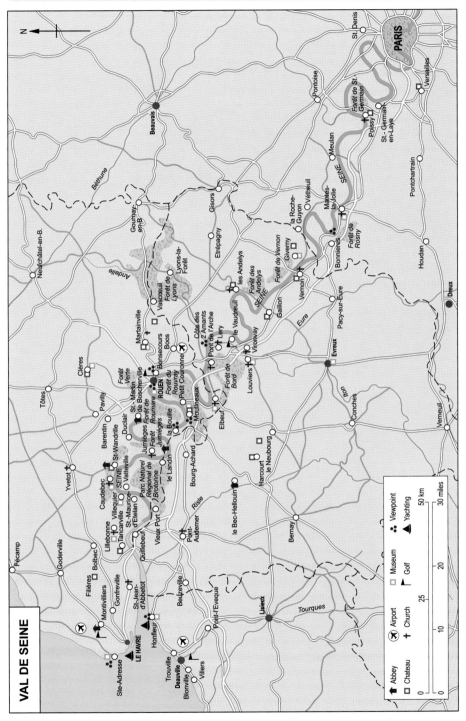

VAL DE SEINE

Scale key:

- Abbey
- Chateau
- Airport
- Church
- Museum
- Golf
- Viewpoint
- Yachting

0 25 10 20 50 km
0 30 miles

well-being and this is reflected in the prosperous street life. Rouen—capital of Seine-Maritime and Normandy—is one of France's great cities; the other departmental capitals—Caen, Evreux, Alençon, Saint Lô—flourish but are more provincial in character. In contrast, houses tumble in the villages as people move from the country to the city; but now new life is coming into the rural areas as outsiders are buying up the old properties.

*T*he quiet corners of Normandy, such as stretches of the Durdant where houses, half hidden by orchards and weeping willow, overlook the narrow stream.

Rivers

Journeys along rivers are frequently the most rewarding travels through a country. The great and beautiful Seine has always been the avenue into the heart of France: it was the Vikings' passage of discovery and conquest and for 4,000–5,000 years it has been an all-important trade route deep into France. As Napoleon remarked, "Le Havre, Rouen and Paris are but one single town of which the Seine is the main street".

The Seine may be Normandy's most celebrated river, but there are scores of others, many cutting through attractive countryside and each with its own history. Some rivers remain important but there are those, little more than trickles today, which lie forgotten with their old settlements ignored by progress.

Forests

Dense forests once covered much of Normandy. What is left now—a fairly impressive hectarage for modern-day Europe—is well protected. For example, the Brotonne Forest along the banks of the lower Seine was created a Regional Nature Park in 1974 and covers 40,000 hectares (98,840 acres). This, and many of the other smaller forests—they are predominantly beech—are accessible to the public. Maps of forest trails are often issued by local tourist offices.

History

The Norman Evolution and the Birth of Normandy

The perennial plundering of the North-men—the Vikings of Scandinavia—along the eastern shores of England and Scotland and of north-west France during the 9th century AD was to develop into a more lasting conquest during the following centuries.

In AD 911, the Northmen sailed up the Seine in their longboats. They were familiar with the river because they had ransacked settlements along its banks on previous invasions, including Paris which they had besieged in AD 885. By now, too, some had chosen to live in this lusher, more tolerable country instead of returning to their bleaker, native lands. The result of this particular venture was a contract for more legitimate and permanent foothold in France. At Saint Clair-sur-Epte—50 km (30 miles) south-east of Rouen—Rollo, the chief of the Northmen, struck a deal

A marble Catherine de Cleve at ease on her tomb in the College Chapel in Eu. Such images of famous figures colour our history of Normandy.

with Charles, king of the western Franks and the man they called "The Simple" because of his integrity rather than because of any suggestion of idiocy. The treaty, endorsed merely by a handshake between the two leaders, gave Rollo the lands contained within the river Bresle, Epte, Avre and Dives—which included the city of Rouen—and ensured for Charles the reassurance that the Northmen would not maraud his territories to the east.

Thus *Terra Northmanorum* (the land of the Northmen) was born. The regions of Bessin (Bayeux district) and Hiemois (Falaise district) were granted to Rollo in AD 924 , and the Cotentin peninsula and the Avranchin (Avranch district) were added in AD 933; it was more than another century before the Alençon district was annexed, to give, more or less, the present Normandy outline.

The First Dukes of Normandy

The Northmen took root surprisingly quickly in their new colony. They displaced the existing nobility, created a solid army, became merchants and fishermen, while, at the same time, allowing the Frankish majority to continue working the land as they had done for generations.

They also assimilated much of the culture. Rollo, now the Duke of Normandy, adopted Christianity, the religion the Vikings had traditionally brutalized; he may have converted merely for political reasons, but at least he had given the faith his blessing. He was succeeded in 933 by Guillaume Longue-Epée (William Longsword), his second son, who set about restoring the churches and monasteries which had suffered the sword from earlier Viking raids. They adopted and streamlined the local feudalism and Frankish became their *lingua franca,* with their Nordic language fading into virtual extinction.

Duke William passed the duchy on to his son, Richard I the Fearless, in AD 942, who left it to his own eldest son, Richard II the Good, in AD 996.

The 11th Century—The Golden Age of Norman Expansion

By the end of the 10th century, the descendants of Rollo and their Norman aristocracy had consolidated their position in their new motherland. The Viking spirit still flowed through their veins and their military prowess was to win them further territories. The catalyst which gave the Normans lasting success in their conquered lands was their ability to adapt in their colonies, mixing aspects of the indigenous culture with those of their own to provide a winning, dynamic result to the formula. The 11th century was to be the golden era of Norman expansion and Normandy was the birthplace for some of the greatest knights and adventurers of the medieval age.

In AD 999–1000 a band of Norman knights—many were probably the younger sons of nobles with little opportunities for large estates at home—took it upon themselves to defend from the Saracens the old Christian Pilgrim routes. Quickly proving themselves as proficient warriors, they were employed by the Italian counts to fight local wars and, *in lieu* of services, they were granted domains. One family in particular, that of Tancred of Hauteville—possibly from the village of Hauteville-le-Guichard in Cotentin—excelled.

During the mid-11th century, most of Tancred's 12 sons went to Italy and won countships for themselves, with Robert Guiscard and Roger becoming Duke of Apulia and Calabria and the Great Count of Sicily respectively. Under the two of them, south Italy and Sicily effectively became Norman Kingdoms.

Meanwhile, back in Normandy, the dukeship had passed from Richard II to his son, Richard III, who died in 1028 having reigned for only two years. He was succeeded by his brother, Robert the Magnificent, sometime known as the Diabolical, whose affair with Arlette, a tanner's daughter from Falaise, resulted in the birth of William the Bastard, later to become William the Conqueror.

The Norman seed had, by now, already been sown in England. Ethelred the Unready, king of England in the early 11th century, married Emma, the sister of Duke Richard II of Normandy, who bore him Alfred and Edward. These two boys were sent to Normandy after their father had died and after their mother had married Canute, the new king of England.

Twenty-five years later, in 1042, the English throne was vacant and Edward, the younger son of Ethelred and Emma, returned from Normandy to claim it. As Edward the Confessor, so-called because of his piety, he invited his old Norman colleagues over to England, giving them senior positions in the church and in his court.

The Rise of William the Conqueror

William the Bastard became Duke of Normandy in 1035, aged seven, and as a young man proved to be a formidable leader through his skills in local wars and politics. Calculated brutality, the ruthless elimination of opposition and pretenders, was the necessary policy for any man with ambition during these ages. William, ever

Château d'Eu, the town hall, was the home of Louis-Philippe, the Citizen King, who twice entertained the young Queen Victoria here before abdicating

ready to spill his quota of blood to secure his interests, is also known to have indulged in lascivious manslaughter on occasion. When he besieged Alençon, its inhabitants draped old skins over the walls, taunting the duke about his illegitimate birth by a tanner's daughter; on capturing the town he gave vent to his fury by allowing his men to run riot through the streets, massacring and looting at will.

William's claim for the English crown was based on two promises. First, from Edward the Confessor who had, apparently, bequeathed it to William, the son of his cousin Robert. Second, from Harold, Earl of Wessex and the most powerful man in England during Edward's last years, who, during an expedition to Normandy in 1064, had met with William; some sources maintain that Harold had been captured by a French adversary and William had secured his release on condition that England pass to him after Edward's death.

Edward died childless in 1066, and Harold was quick to succeed him on the throne. William acted sharply, securing papal approval for an attack on England, and enticing barons and knights from around Normandy and mercenaries from elsewhere in France with splendid offers of English estates and spoils. By the late summer of 1066, he had gathered his army of 4,000–5,000 infantry and 2,000–3,000 mounted knights and cavalry.

Lack of wind delayed his crossing the Channel until 27 September. Meanwhile, Harold was in the north of England, having just scored a remarkable victory over Harald Hardrada, the Norwegian king, at Stamford Bridge. Hearing of William's landing at Pevensey he rushed south, collecting fresh forces along the way.

1066: William Wins Hastings and England

Don't Look Up
A Battle author recounts the famous story of Harold's death by an arrow in the eye:
"William, so devious and sly Shouted, 'Hey Harold look at the sky',
  Our king, so easy to confuse,
  Fell for the cheeky French ruse
  And "whack" came that flying iron in the eye."

The Battle of Hastings was fought between Harold and William on 14 October on Senlac Hill in the present town of Battle. Harold was killed by an arrow piercing through his eye, or so we are led to believe from the Bayeux tapestry, Matilda's remarkable account of her husband William's conquest of England, and hence England was lost to the Normans.

The victorious William marched his army through southern England, mopping up pockets of resistance and finally winning London. He ascended the throne on Christmas Day 1066, receiving the crown of England in Westminster Abbey: the Norman-styled abbey completed by Edward the Confessor shortly before his death. The Norman seed, planted when Ethelred married Emma 60 years earlier, had started to blossom on English soil.

There were revolts against Norman rule over the next few years, but they were unco-ordinated and ultimately unsuccessful. By 1072, William had all England under his control, and he

The Northman's Great Legacy

By the late 1000s, in less than 200 years since Rollo's treaty of Saint Clair-sur-Epte, the Northmen had created a solid homeland. They had gradually acquired all southern Italy and Sicily, though unity of the whole region under their rule would come in the 12th century. In about 15 years they had won England's crown and conquered all its major dissidents; and now, at the close of the century, they were on the brink of gaining another kingdom.

In November 1095, Pope Urban II proclaimed the Holy War against the Moslem occupants of Jerusalem. Joining this, the First Crusade, were groups of Norman aristocrats, including Duke Robert Curthose himself and, what proved even more significant, a contingent of the illustrious Hautevilles led by Bohemund, son of Robert Guiscard.

These crusaders, on a divine mission endorsed by the papacy, went on to win against huge odds in the harsh lands of the Levant. They extended the frontiers of Christendom, regaining from the Moslems the birthplace of their religion. They covered themselves in glory, eulogized then and ever since, and Bohemund, the most magnificent of their number, created a principality of his own in 1099 on the eastern shores of the Mediterranean, with its centre at Antioch.

A smooth-featured gentle boy is how Rollo is depicted on his tomb in Rouen cathedral. Hardly the image one has of the ex-Viking and founder of the Norman dynasty.

The impact the Normans had in Europe in the 11th century was tremendous. Even after their ruling lineages had petered out in their colonies, their influences: the administrations, laws, aspects of religion and learning, politics, continued. And they left their great heritage of architecture: the castles, cathedrals, churches, monasteries which still stand impressive throughout the old Norman world. Having settled amongst the mellow pastures of north-west France, the once rampaging Vikings had, in a short time, refined their reckless aggression into effective conquest and colonization; simultaneously their invigorating culture evolved, to leave an indelible mark on civilization then, and ever since.

Strong and blond—Viking ancestry revealed in the features of a Norman farmer.

Line of descent of the dukes of Normandy.

Rollo 911–933

William Longsword 933–942

Richard I The Fearless 942–996

Richard II The Good 996–1026

Richard III 1026–1028   Robert The Magnificent 1028–1035

William The Conqueror c. 1028–1087
King of England 1066–1087
Duke of Normandy 1035–1087
m. Matilda of Flanders

Robert Curthose 1054–1134   William Rufus c. 1056–1100   Henry I Beauclerk 1069–1135
Duke of Normandy 1087–1106   King of England 1087–1100   King of England 1100–1135
                                                                      Duke of Normandy 1106–1135

Empress Matilda
m. Geoffrey Plantagenet 1113–1151
Duke of Normandy 1135–1150

Henry II 1133–1189
King of England 1154–1189
Duke of Normandy 1150–1189
m. Eleanor of Aquitaine

Richard Lionheart 1157–1199   John Lackland 1167–1216
King of England 1189–1199   King of England 1199–1216

continued to invest estates and high positions around the land to his faithful Norman relations and friends. His conquest was irrevocably to link England with Normandy (and consequently France), more often as enemies than friends, over the following centuries.

Normandy remained William's home, England being the duchy's colony, and here he spent most of his last years. The branches of the Norman family tree were by now well intertwined with the noble households of the neighbouring domains and with the more distant lands in France, England and south Italy. Marital bonds sometimes secured allegiance between families, as in the case of the marriage of William's daughter to the Count of Brittany, though often they did not and the relationship between William and his in-laws (the House of Flanders) degenerated to the extent that the Counts of Flanders became one of the greatest threats to the stability of Normandy.

During his final years, William was kept busy maintaining the security of Normandy through pact and suppression. He died in Rouen in 1087—later to be buried in the church of St Etienne at Abbaye-aux-Hommes in Caen—leaving Normandy to his eldest son, Robert Curthose. The English crown was inherited by William Rufus, his second son.

Reversing the Verdict of Hastings

Of all the Normans' foreign territories, England was to have the closest ties with Normandy itself. William's successful conquest in 1066, an invasion of England yet to be repeated, locked together the two lands on either side of the narrow Channel and was to determine not only their subsequent histories but also the course of events elsewhere in Britain, France and beyond.

King William Rufus' death by arrow, whether an accidental act or a murderous one, it was never proved, while hunting in the New Forest in the south of England in early August 1100 gave Henry, his younger brother, the chance to take the English crown. In doing so, he pipped his eldest brother Duke Robert Curthose, who was away on a crusade at the time, to the throne. And, indeed, Robert felt that the kingdom of England, his right by primogeniture, had been denied him for the second time. He landed in England and marched towards London with a large army, threatening to wage war and grab the English crown. However, his aggression was cooled and he returned to his duchy sufficiently content after Henry offered to relinquish to him his own possessions in Normandy, on condition Robert dropped his claims to England.

Many of the senior Norman nobles had estates on both sides of the Channel, their families having been awarded lands in England after the Conquest. Now they began to polarize becoming "English" or "Norman" in their allegiance. People in Normandy regarded Henry as an Englishman, nicknaming him Godric, and his wife, a princess of English heritage, Godiva, both solid Saxon names.

The prominent Normans in England who fell out with Henry, of whom there were a fair number, had lands confiscated, and a fair number took refuge back in Normandy. This exodus led to the reduction of Norman aristocratic stock in England; at the same time, Robert suppressed the Normandy estates of the pro-Henry faction of nobles. This state of events led to the clash of the brothers: Henry I, King of England, crossed the Channel and invaded the land of his forefathers and on 28 September 1106, exactly 40 years after his father had landed on the shores of Sussex, he defeated Robert at Tinchebray in present Orne and thus, as commonly said, "reversed the verdict of Hastings".

Normandy: A Duchy within an Empire

Duke Robert Curthose, a fine crusader, though feeble leader and with a nickname probably originating from the short breeches (*courte heuse*) he wore, spent the remainder of his life detained in Cardiff Castle, dying there in 1134. Meanwhile, Henry, whose own nickname "Beauclerk" probably stemmed from his ability to read and write, reunited Normandy and England under his rule.

Normandy, which had degenerated into anarchy under Robert, regained some of its former stability, but total peace was never lasting in an age when war was a way of life. Henry became embroiled in an almost incessant string of conflicts against his own Norman subjects: some of them supported Robert's son's claim to the duchy, while others allied themselves with the neighbouring counts or King Louis VI of France.

Henry died on 1 December 1135 after over-indulging in lampreys at a

*B*arfleur, the medieval Channel port for Norman dukes and English kings and watery graveyard for those who sank with the White Ship, is now little more than a picturesque fishing village.

dinner in Mortemar Abbey in the Forest of Lyons. His son and heir had drowned 15 years earlier when his ship, the White Ship, had smashed against rocks soon after leaving Barfleur bound for England. With him sank Henry's hopes for a legitimate filial heir through male issue. He had, therefore, initially named Matilda, his daughter, as his successor. However, he subsequently married her off to the young Geoffrey Plantagenet, the future Count of Anjou, whose family were traditional enemies of the neighbouring Normans, and after she had given birth to a son in 1133 he hoped his crown would pass directly from him to his grandson.

But the lad, Henry, was only two when his grandfather died. The legacy of Normandy and England fell to Henry Beauclerk's favourite nephew, Stephen, who spent his unhappy 19 year reign bogged down in civil wars against contenders to his throne, most notably his cousin Matilda.

Stephen's battlefields were mostly in England. He paid little attention to Normandy, which fell into anarchy as he lost the support of its nobles who eventually recognized the now teenage Henry Plantagenet as Duke of Normandy. Henry crossed to England in 1153 where Stephen, saddened by the recent death of his first son, accepted him as his successor.

Stephen, the last of the Norman kings of England, died a year later. Henry Plantagenet became King Henry II, adding England to his domains of Normandy, including the vassalage of Brittany, his Angevin territory of Anjou and Aquitaine, which had been gained through marriage to Eleanor of Aquitaine.

Normandy lay in the middle of an empire which stretched from Scotland to Spain. The plans Henry made to make Rouen capital of his vast domain did not materialize; indeed, while he managed to maintain his inheritance intact, he did not impose a standardization policy in the empire, and each region did retain its identity.

Richard the Lionheart

Henry was succeeded in 1189 by his son Richard, the Lionheart, famed for his courage, crusades and compassion, who spent the first half of his reign fighting for Christianity in the Levant and the other half embroiled in conflict against his former crusading companion, Philippe-Auguste, King Philip II of France. Encouraged by John, Richard's younger brother, Philip had invaded Normandy during Richard's absence intending to extend the western frontier of his French kingdom.

On his return in 1194, Richard drove Philip out of Normandy and showed characteristic mercy by allowing him his freedom, though in doing so he failed to snuff out the French king's ambitions. To protect Normandy's eastern limits, in 1197 Richard built the formidable Château Gaillard high above a meander of the Seine at the present town of Les Andelys. The broken ruins of the castle remain Richard's greatest legacy to the duchy.

John Lackland

John succeeded Richard in 1199 and proved to be as unable as his two predessors had been able. He lost the support of his old ally Philippe-Auguste, who now saw his best opportunity of winning Normandy. In March 1204, the French king captured Château Gaillard, the frontier's solid bastion, and went on to conquer the entire duchy apart from the Channel Islands. Normandy was once again a French domain, nine generations after Rollo had been granted the territory by Charles the Simple at Saint Clair-sur-Epte in AD 911.

John also lost almost all the rest of his French possessions, managing to hold on to only Guienne and Gascony from the once immense Angevin inheritance. Henry II's great empire had now been reduced to little more than England; the "landless" John earned himself the name John Lackland. As John's powerbase was reduced, that of the King of France was increased.

The loss of Normandy meant that the nobles who had held estates in both England and in the duchy forfeited their Normandy interests. As a consequence, and ultimate blessing for England, they became even more "English" now that their opportunities were exclusively on that side of the Channel. Meanwhile, Normandy, now annexed to France, became increasingly susceptible to French influences.

Normandy and England had become separated 138 years after William's Conquest of 1066 had brought them together. The union of the two lands during that period had led to the cross-fertilization of people and ideas resulting in the irrevocable mixing of cultures. And today, over 900 years later, the Anglo-Norman inheritance lives on, on both sides of the Channel.

1204 to D-Day 1944

1204—King Philippe-Auguste confiscates Normandy.

1259—The Treaty of Paris and the official recognition of the French conquest of Normandy.

1315—The granting of the Norman Charter: Normandy the Province.

1329—The Duchy of Normandy is revived in favour of John, son of King Philip VI of France.

1338–1453—The Hundred Years War rages intermittently between the English and French: in 1346 Edward III, answering the call from Godfrey d'Harcourt of Saint Sauveur, invades Normandy. On 12 July Edward lands at Saint Vaast-la-Hougue. Two weeks later he besieges Caen and goes on to ravage the lands as far as Poissy. Normandy remains in French hands

After a lull, hostilities intensify in 1415 with the invasion of France by England's Henry V. Leading an army of 60,000, Henry lands at the mouth of the Seine on 14 August and captures Harfleur a month later. He pushes

---

Hi-Tech Weaponry Wins the Day

The Duke of Somerset, under threat in Caen from Charles of France, sought relief from England. Sir Thomas Kyriel was despatched with a force of 4,500 to provide assistance. At Formigny on 15 April 1450 Kyriel encountered Comte de Clermont with his 3,000 lances and infantry and two small cannons. The English went on the defence, confident that their bowmen would repel the enemy's attack. The French wheeled on their cannons and blazed into Kyriel's men, who, totally disrupted, ran forward to capture the artillery. Unable to use their bows in close quarters, the English became easy prey under a fresh assault from the French knights. It was a resounding defeat for Kyriel who lost 3,750 men compared to 1,200 deaths suffered by the French. Formigny was one of the last decisive battles in the Hundred Years War, furthermore it heralded the arrival of the all important cannon.

---

north, achieving his famous victory at Agincourt before winning the whole of Normandy by 1420; Rouen bravely withstands a tough English siege from 29 July 1418 to 13 January 1419.

With the rise of Jeanne d'Arc, the peasant girl from Domremy, the English position of power looks less stable. Joan is captured by the Burgundians in 1430 and handed over to the English; she is burnt at the stake in Rouen the following year.

The people of Caux and Val de Vire rise up against the English in 1435 and 1436 respectively. It is not until 1450 and the Battle of Formigny, however, that the French fully recover Normandy. Famous amongst the French–English contests was the resistance of

Salut! A fireman drinks to the memory of the Revolution at the village's 14 July celebrations.

Mont-Saint-Michel. The Mont never fell to the English, despite the latter having an active military base across the bay at Granville.

1469—Normandy the Dukedom is abolished with the breaking of the ducal seal after the dispossession of King Charles. Normandy becomes, once again, a province of France.

1499—Exchequer of Normandy becomes a permanent court of justice, which in effect is the parliament of Normandy.

16th C—The Protestant Reformation movement gathers strength. It is countered by the Catholics and, amongst the clashes, is the Saint Bartholomew's Day massacre of 1572 when over 500 Protestants are killed.

1789—The French Revolution.

1944—D-Day.

D-Day and the Battle for Normandy

D-Day 6 June 1944: Operation Overlord, the long-awaited Allied invasion of German-occupied north-west France, was finally launched. The Germans, alert to the probability of an attack from across the Channel, were not, however, aware of when or where such an offensive would occur, or the extent of its force.

The Build-up to Operation Overlord

After their evacuation from the continent at Dunkirk in May 1940, the British had sought the opportunity to return to liberate France from German occupation. Initial attempts made by the Allies to secure a foothold on French soil, like the cataclysmic Operation Jubilee assault on the Dieppe coast in August 1942, had failed. Back at the drawing board, new tactics were debated and, at the Quebec Conference in August 1943, the draft of the major Operation Overlord was given the go-ahead.

For the Allies, General Eisenhower was Commander-in-Chief of the operation. Under him were Marshall Leigh-Mallory and Admiral Ramsay, in charge of the Air Force and Navy respectively, and General Montgomery, who held overall control of the land forces. General Bradley, of the 1st US Army, and General Demsey, of the 2nd British Army, were Montgomery's senior officers. In command for the Germans was Field Marshal von Runstedt, one of Hitler's most experienced soldiers, who had been given control of the Western Wall, as these western German defenses were known, and as his deputy he had Field Marshal Rommel.

Logistically, Operation Overlord was a massive task, and its success lay in the surprise and supplies factors. Landing, taking the beaches and winning a foothold was the prime and vital objective, but an extremely ambitious and hazardous one.

Von Runstedt believed that the Allies would launch the inevitable offensive against the Pas de Calais region, where the Channel was at its narrowest. And so it was here that the defences, in the hands of the German 15th Army, were at their strongest, while the Western Wall in Normandy, under their 7th Army, was less protected.

The German supply routes, such as those crossing the Seine and Loire, were more vulnerable than those to the north in Pas de Calais. The destruction of these became the Allies' aim before the landing of troops.

In early March, the Allied bombers, co-ordinating with the French Resistance, acted, blowing up strategic points. Correctly interpreting this to be the breeze before the storm, Rommel initiated a programme to strengthen the Normandy defences, laying mines off the coast, booby traps along the shore and building pillbox gun turrets above the beaches. Despite seeing where the Allies targeted their initial attack, von Runstedt still maintained that the landings would be in Pas de Calais.

D-Day

Operation Overlord, postponed from 5 June due to bad weather, finally got under way in the early hours of 6 June.

The Allied armada cautiously picked a path through the mined waters of the Channel and, soon after first light, the initial wave of ships disgorged its load of soldiers on to French soil. At the same time, airborne divisions dropped parachutists within the enemy lines, on the eastern and western flanks of the invasion front, whose mission was to take key positions and then link up with their compatriots after they had secured the beaches.

That day, 6 June 1944, 135,000 men scrambled on to the beaches of Normandy. The Germans were unprepared for such an onslaught and they were never able to recover from this initial blow. They were unable to cope with the wave after wave after wave of Allied forces which were to pour in during the following days and weeks. The element of surprise had been achieved. Over the next few months, tens of thousands of ships and planes participated in the ferrying of soldiers and cargo to northern France, and by the end of August over two million men had been put ashore along with three million tonnes of goods. The all-important supplies kept on coming through, constantly furnishing the Allied war effort. Logistically, these aspects of the Normandy invasion were an outstanding success.

The Beaches and Battlefields

On the battlefields, where they have to count the dead and assess the destruction, the picture is always grim. There were two main directions of attack: the British and Canadian forces pinpointed their assault on the stretch of coast between Ouistreham and Arromanche, on the beaches they had

code-named Sword, Juno and Gold. The Americans' approach was further to the west at Omaha beach, the shore at Colleville and Vierville-sur-Mer, and Utah beach by la Madeleine at the base of the Cotentin peninsula.

The initial phase of the invasion was deemed a success and the first day's death toll of around 2,000 Allied soldiers was regarded as low. However, the objective of linking the victorious forces of the different beaches and then capturing Caen, Bayeux and a 5 to 15 km (3 to 9 mile) wide stretch of the coast's hinterland by midnight on D-Day was not accomplished. In response to the attack the Germans, calling upon their limited reinforcements, quickly consolidated their positions, effectively employing their panzer divisions against the Allies. The battle for Normandy was fought by the tank corps, infantry and paras in the fields amongst the hedgerows of the *bocage*, in country lanes, in town streets; and by the bombers and fighter pilots from the air; and by the navy off the coast. It was to continue into the latter part of August and cause devastating destruction.

By midnight on the 6 June, Dempsey's divisions had taken Sword, the beaches of Lion-sur-Mer and Ouistreham-Riva Bella, and pushed inland capturing the villages of Hermanville, Colleville-Montgomery (Montgomery being added after the war), Periers, Beuville, Bieville and Blainville and had linked with the airborne division which had earlier secured Bénouville, and what is now called Pegasus Bridge across the Caen canal and River Orne. The German panzer tanks countered and formed a wedge between the Sword invaders and their Canadian colleagues at Juno and, furthermore, their troops held Caen, denying the Allies one of their prime D-Day goals.

The Canadian and British soldiers landing at Juno and Gold won their beach heads, capturing villages such as Saint Aubin and Courseulles before heading inland. Bayeux, the first major town to fall, was taken the following day.

Further west, Bradley's US contingent at Omaha, the beaches at Colleville, Saint Laurent and Vierville, were faced with difficult sea and landing conditions and, suffering heavy losses, they made little headway inland that first day. Compatriots at Utah were more successful along the beaches at Les Dunes-de-Varreville and were able to capture the coast and drive inland; they teamed up with their parachute squads which had landed earlier, just a few kilometres from the coast at Sainte-Mère-Eglise and around the villages to its south. But the American objectives of Isigny and Carentan were not reached.

Over the succeeding days, the Allies capitalized on their footings and the forces of the five beach heads managed to join to form a front 80 km (48 miles) long. Planes pressurized the enemy, raining massive bombardment from the air, while the navy maintained the coast, ensuring a clear passage for supplies crossing the Channel. Arromanche and Omaha beach were selected as sites for the Mulberries, the remarkable prefabricated harbours which the Allies assembled after the landings and which were to provide docking for their vessels.

The Winning of Cotentin

At the eastern end of the battle front, the Germans continued to hold Caen. Tilly-sur-Seulles, 16 km (10 miles) to the west, was captured on 18 June and from here the Allies secured a crossing over the Odon and then took Hill 112, south-west of Caen, to allow a further line of attack on the city. The Germans then had to draw reinforcements from around Normandy to maintain

Caen, thus weakening their defences elsewhere. Looking westwards once again, in the early stages, the inland penetration had reached its farthest at Caumont-l'Evente 30 km (18 miles) from the coast, on 13 June.

On the Cotentin peninsula, the US divisions dispersed, their purpose being to quickly capture the key points and isolate the peninsula from German reinforcements. They defeated

A generation ago their fathers were enemies. Today young French soldiers invite their German counterparts to Normandy as friends.

the Germans at Vagnoles on 20 June, and thrust northwards for the assault on Cherbourg, winning the vital port on 27 June. However, on the eve of

61

their victory, Admiral Hennecke ordered the demolition of the port facilities, rendering them useless to the Americans. This act of sabotage won Hitler's approval and earned Hennecke the Knight's Cross.

Having cleared the debris and mines, the Americans rebuilt Cherbourg port as a substantial replacement to the prefabricated Mulberries, which had always been "stop gap", temporary docks. As the Allies' major goods depot on the French coast, Cherbourg also became the terminus for PLUTO, an acronym for Pipe Line Under The Ocean, the oil-supply line laid on the bed of the Channel from the Isle of Wight.

Three days after Cherbourg fell the Americans had control of the Cotentin peninsula. Other towns succumbed in July, notably Caen on the 9th and St Lô, after an equally devastating battle, on the 19th. By the beginning of August, the Allies held a line between Caen and Avranches, having liberated all of Normandy to its north.

The invasion on the western front had by now gathered its momentum. General Patton struck eastwards from Avranches, cleared the way to Le Mans, and then headed northwards to take Alençon on 12 August. The progress of the British army at the eastern end was less spectacular. They took Villers-Bocage on 4 August, Vire on the 8th and Thury-Harcourt on the 12th as they slowly pushed towards Falaise.

The Final Clash and the Overall Cost

Meanwhile, Hitler, having replaced von Runstedt with Field Marshal von Kluge, and no longer with the services of Rommel, who had committed suicide, ordered the remnants of his tank divisions to counter the Allies' offensive at Mortain, to fight westwards to Avranches and to cut Patton's supply routes. The Germans' stoic efforts were thwarted and, having suffered severe casualties, they were forced to retreat eastwards on 12 August.

On 13 August, the American force, a French contingent under Leclerc, marched into Argentan. With Falaise under the control of the British–Canadian army by 16 August, the last pocket of German resistance in Normandy now lay surrounded on three sides. Only the land between Falaise and Argentan, known as the Falaise Gap, had yet to be breached. The Germans took advantage of the Gap and some 40,000 escaped through it heading eastwards to continue their struggle, before the Allies managed to close it down on 20 August. Having failed, von Kluge took his own life.

The Allies continued their drive eastwards, salvaging the rest of Normandy, liberating Paris on 25 August and pushing the Germans ever on towards the Rhine.

It had taken two and a half months to win Normandy. The cost of repairing the damage caused during this period was incalculable. In lives too it had been expensive, though the Germans' losses were significantly higher: their 240,000 dead dwarfs the toll of 37,000 Allied troops killed. In addition, there were the civilian deaths.

In Their Memory

The summer of 1944 is well remembered in Normandy. Every city, town

and village has its sons and daughters who died, either as soldiers, Resistance fighters or citizens caught in the crossfire, and a monument dedicated to them stands in the heart of even the smallest of villages. The Allied soldiers who fell in the bid to liberate Normandy have been buried in parish churchyards, a fact which is usually announced by a green plaque at the entrance of the village, or in the large immaculately manicured cemeteries, under the neat rows of mass-produced white stone crosses, each one bearing, if known, the name, the birthday, the deathday and the regiment of the deceased. The Germans, too, have their cemeteries.

The cemeteries are open to the public and are places of pilgrimage for the relations, colleagues-in-arms and countrymen who want to remember their family, comrades and nationals.

A village remembers family and friends who died fighting for liberty.

Monuments, plaques and street names to the regiments and individuals who served and died for liberty are found in the old war-zones all round Normandy. Further information about the memorials can be had from: Monsieur le Directeur du Service Departemental de l'Office National des Anciens Combattants et Victimes de Guerre, 16, avenue du 6-Juin, BP 268, 14008 Caen.

Many museums commemorate the Battle of Normandy. In the smaller towns they recount the local events during that summer of 1944 and exhibit collections of the military curios gathered in the neighbourhood. Several

museums at larger towns, notably the Memorial Museum at Caen, document the whole War.

Circuit Normandie 44

"Circuit Normandie 44" is an itinerary along the coastal region of Calvados and lower eastern Manche which incorporates the landing beaches, key points and towns and villages involved in the fighting that summer, and the cemeteries and the main war museums.

The Suggested Route

Day 1: Caen and "Memorial Museum for Peace"; Bénouville and "Museum of Airborne Forces"; Sword, Juno and Gold beaches (a short detour inland to Canadian Military Cemetery at Reviers-Beny-sur-Mer); Arromanche and the "Landing Museum".

*T*he roses of Britain *fell before they could blossom. Their hearts lie buried in the soil of France.*

La Cambe, the German Military Cemetery.

The "Carte Normandie 44" is a ticket allowing discounted entry into the six museums mentioned above and is available at any one of them.

*M*ort pour la France, *a gravestone at the Eu War cemetery remembers a 19-year-old soldier who died in the last days of World War I.*

Day 2: Bayeux and the "Memorial Museum of the Battle of Normandy 1944" and the neighbouring British cemetery; Colleville, Saint Laurent and Omaha beach and the American Military Cemetery; Pointe du Hoc and the monument to the Rangers.

Day 3: Saint Marie-du-Mont and the "Museum of the Landing Day of Utah Beach"; Utah beach; Sainte Mère-Eglise and the "Airborne Museum";

Just the Essentials

On a first-time visit to Normandy you may be overwhelmed by the wealth of choice you have wherever you start. The major landmarks and places to see are proposed here to help you establish priorities.

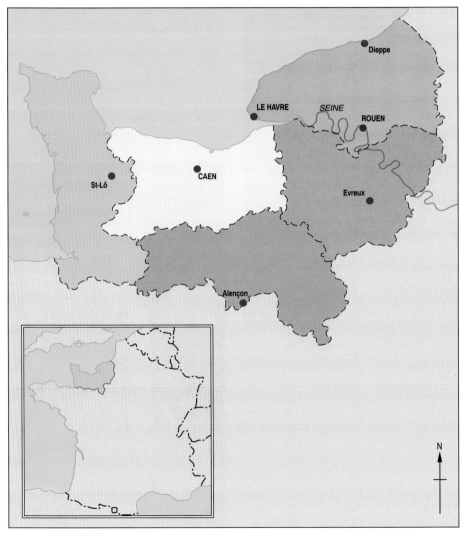

Seine-Maritime

Dieppe: the heart of Normandy
Eu: Gothic church, Norman château, ancient forest
Roads to Rouen: Andelle valley, châteaux at Vascoeuil and Martainville, Ry, Forêt d'Eawy: beech woodlands
Varengeville: Parc de Moustiers
Etretat: dramatic chalk cliffs
Rouen: historic, cultured city, cathedral
Saint Ouen: huge Gothic church
Jumièges: skeletal remains of great abbey
Saint Wandrille: monastery

Calvados

Caen: ancient roots, medieval castle
—Abbaye aux Hommes, built by William the Conqueror
—le Mémorial: a museum for peace
Deauville: Grand Prix (horse racing)
Honfleur: picturesque old harbour
Cider Country: la Route du Cidre
Lisieux: Ste Theresa Basilica
Suisse Normandie
Bayeux: 11th-century cathedral, Tapestry
Saint Laurent-sur-Mer: American Military Cemetery

Manche

North-eastern tip of Cotentin peninsula: pretty promontory
Carteret: la plage de la Vieille Eglise
Lessay: Benedictine Abbey church, 1056
Pirou: splendid 11–12th-century moated castle
Coutances: cathedral; one of the finest in Normandy
Haras of St Lô: important stud farm
Granville: fort, port, resort
Hambaye Abbey: great ruined abbey
Mont-Saint-Michel
Sélune Valley

Orne

Carrouges: château
Bagnoles-de-l'Orne: spa resort
—south: convenient base for Forêt des Andannes
West of Flers: attractive "bocage" countryside
Domfront: a "pear route"
Sées: ancient see and fine Gothic cathedral
Le Bourg Saint Leonard: 18th-century château
Haras du Pin: "Versailles of Stallions"
Médavy: château
Château d'O
l'Aigle to Mortagne-au-Perche: interesting route
Mortagne-au-Perche: home of black pudding
—south: circuit incorporating villages, manors, historical sites
—east: Forêt du Perche, lovely towns

Eure

Evreux: plundered throughout history
Conches-au-Ouche: medieval town
South-western Eure: Forêt de Conche and Pays d'Ouche
Vernon: 10th-century Norman town
Giverny: home to Claude Monet
Château Gaillard: magnificent view from ruined château
Les Andeleys
Thuit and la Roquette: splendid views
Fontaine-Guérard: 13th-century abbey
Vascoeuil: 14–16th-century red-brick château and cultural centre
Forêt de Lyons: lovely beech forest
Abbey de Mortemer: Cistercian abbey
Beaumensil: red-brick and stone château
Le Bec-Hellouin: abbey
Mandelles Nature Reserve

Going Places with Something Special in Mind

The following suggestions are for leisure routes and themes which cater for all kinds of interests. Some are given as itineraries which can be followed, while others are simply lists which will appeal to the visitor interested in certain aspects of Normandy life, architecture or history. The maps will help you locate the places mentioned, but a detailed road map will be needed in most cases to find the sites.

The Ivory and Spice Route

In 1364 two caravels departed from Dieppe bound for Africa. At "Little Dieppe", on the Guinea coast, they loaded up with a rich cargo of ivory and spices before returning home. Subsequently Dieppe became a centre for ivory and Fécamp a market for spices. A route around the Seine-Maritime coast and its Pays de Caux hinterland incorporates places relevant to these

Normandy offers something for everyone, from cider routes to glass works—and the architecture is worth seeing too.

trades as well as other points of interest along the way:

1 DIEPPE
Château Museum with its ivory collection.

2 VARENGEVILLE
Manoir d'Ango; Parc de Moustiers; church of St Valery.

3 VEULES-LES-ROSES
Seaside resort; les chaumières cottages.

4 SASSETOT-LE-MAUCONDUIT
18th-century château-hotel.

5 FECAMP
Arts Museum with its ivory collection; spices at the Benedictine museum.

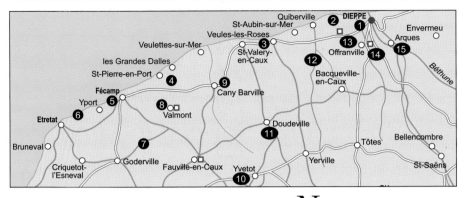

6 YPORT AND ETRETAT
Two seaside resorts with spectacular white cliffs.

7 BAILLEUL
16th-century château.

8 VALMONT
11th–16th-century château.

9 CANY-BARVILLE
17th-century château.

10 YVETOT
Ivory collection at Town Hall.

11 DOUDEVILLE
17th-century Château de Galleville.

12 BRACHY
15th-century Manoir de Gourel.

13 OFFRANVILLE
17th-century Manoir du Tot.

14 TOURVILLE-SUR-ARQUES
17th-century Château de Miromesnil.

15 ARQUES-LA-BATAILLE
Ruined medieval castle.

*N*ormandy's ivory and *spice route.*

Museums of Eure

15 museums, well spread around Eure and covering a diverse and curious array of subject matter, form a basis for an interesting tour of the department.

1 EVREUX
Museum at the Old Bishop's Palace.

2 VERNON
Alphonse George Poulain Museum.

3 GIVERNY
Claude Monet Museum and Gardens.

4 LES ANDELYS
Nicolas Poussin Museum.

5 BEZU-LA-FORET
The Roman Farm Museum; open May–November on weekends (tel: 32-49-66-22 for weekday viewings).

6 VASCOEUIL
Michelet's House and Museum.

7 LOUVIERS
Museum of Stage and Cinema Sets.

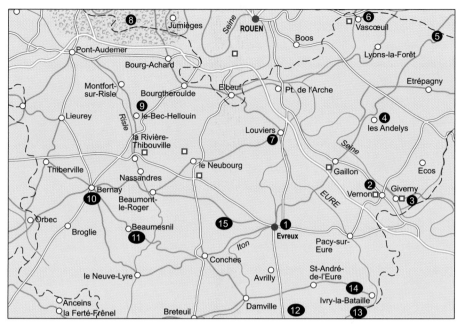

8 PARC NATUREL REGIONAL DE BROTONNE

The Brotonne Nature Reserve Museum.

9 LE BEC HELLOUIN

The Abbey Car Museum.

10 BERNAY

The Cart Museum.

11 BEAUMESNIL

The Château Bookbinding Museum.

12 FRANCHEVILLE

The Iron Works Museum; limited opening hours (tel: 32-32-64-00 or 32-32-67-66 to arrange viewing).

13 EZY-SUR-EURE

The Comb Museum.

14 LA COUTURE BOUSSEY

The Wind Instrument Museum.

*M*useums *of the Eure.*

15 CAUGE

Museum of Rural Normandy Tools.

Historic Studs and Châteaux of Orne

Stud farms and châteaux are Orne's principle fame. A cluster of the best of them is in the vicinity of Argentan. The route extends further to the west to include other sights of central Orne.

1 ARGENTAN

Church of St Germain.

2 BOURG SAINT LEONARD

18th-century Château de Bourg Saint Léonard.

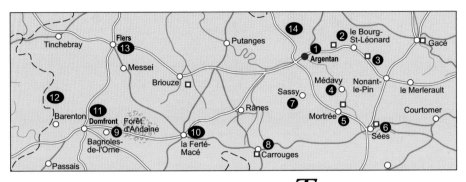

3 HARAS DU PIN
The Haras du Pin stud.

4 MEDAVY
15–18th-century Château de Médavy.

5 MORTREE
15–17th-century Château d'O.

6 SEES
The medieval Sées cathedral.

7 ST CHRISTOPHE-LE-JAJOLET
18th-century Château de Sassy.

8 CARROUGES
14–17th-century Château de Carrouges.

9 BAGNOLES-DE-L'ORNE
Famous spa town.

10 LA FERTE-MACE
11th-century Romanesque chapel.

11 DOMFRONT
Medieval church of Notre Dame-sur-l'Eau.

12 LONLAY L'ABBAYE
Medieval abbey church.

The Bresle glass route.

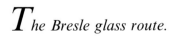

*T*he historic studs and châteaux of Orne.

13 FLERS
16–18th-century Château de Flers.

14 HABLOVILLE
13–15th century village church.

Bresle Glass Route

They say glass has been made in the Forest of Eu, on the Bresle's west bank, for 2,000 years. Certainly quality glassware has been made here since the 15th century. Today the local speciality is the *flacon d'odeur*, the scent bottle. This route is along the Bresle valley, from the coast up to Aumale.

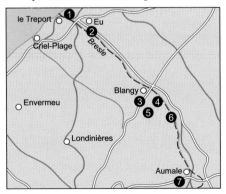

1 MERS-LES-BAINS
Verrerie Saint-Gobain.

2 EU
Glass museum in Château d'Eu.

3 BLANGY-SUR-BRESLE
Verrerie Waltersperger.

4 NESLE-NORMANDEUSE
Verreries-cristalleries de Nesle-Normandeuse.

5 ROMESNIL
Abandoned verrerie beside Château de Romesnil.

6 LE COURVAL
Verrerie le Courval.

7 AUMALE
The local verrerie now manufactures glass for the pharmaceutical industry.

Route of the Dovecotes

Colombiers, Dovecots, are common in various quarters of Normandy.

1 VALMONT
At la Hêtrée, near Thérouldeville, north of Valmont.

2 VERTOT
At Manoir de Vertot.

3 BAILLEUL
At Château de Bailleul.

Route of the Dovecotes of Normandy.

4 HATTENVILLE
South of Hattenville.

5 BENNETOT
West of Bennetot.

6 SAINT-PIERRE-LAVIS
At nearby la Chaussée.

7 HERICOURT-EN-CAUX
At nearby Petit-Veauville.

8 OHERVILLE
At nearby Château d'Auffay.

9 BOSVILLE
At nearby Bieurville.

10 LA HANOUARD
To the west, off the D150.

11 MONT MOREL
By the D131.

12 GRAINVILLE-LA-TEINTURIERE
At the "King of the Canaries" castle.

13 HOCQUEVILLE
Colombier off the D10.

14 GERPONVILLE
At Ferme des Grandes Portes.

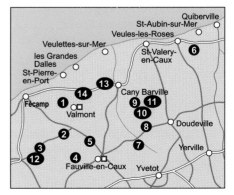

Parks and Gardens of Upper Normandy

1 GIVERNY
Monet's home and garden.

2 BIZY
Gardens of the Château de Bizy.

3 SAINT JUST
Picturesque informal park; open 12 June to 31 July.

4 EVREUX
Public gardens around the 17th-century Capucin cloister.

5 BEAUMESNIL
Formal French gardens around the Château de Beaumesnil.

6 HARCOURT
Created in 1802 the arboretum in the

Harcourt gardens is the second oldest in France.

7 ROUEN
A variety of plants in the Jardin des Plantes on the left bank of the Seine.

8 CLERES
Gardens and bird sanctuary by the Renaissance Château de Cleres.

9 GOMMERVILLE
Beech avenue and Le Notre park at Château de Filières.

10 GONFREVILLE L'ORCHER
Park high above the Seine by medieval château.

11 BAILLEUL
Park with oak, chestnut and herb garden by Château de Bailleul.

12 DOUDEVILLE
Birch rows and park at Château de Galleville.

13 CANY
Part formal, part informal gardens and park at Château de Cany.

14 LES MOUSTIERS
English gardens designed by Miss Gertrude Jekyll at Varengeville.

15 MIROMESNIL
Park and gardens around Château de Miromesnil.

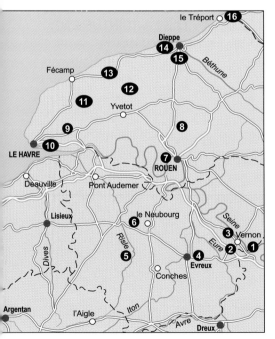

T he parks and gardens of Upper Normandy (left). La Route Normandie-Vexin (opposite).

16 EU

Formal gardens at Château d'Eu; includes famous 16th-century birch.

Route Normandie-Vexin

An attractive winding 200 km (120 mile) route between Rouen and Paris incorporating places of historical and architectural importance.

1 ROUEN

"Ville-musée"; the city itself is a museum.

2 CHATEAU DE MARTAINVILLE

15th-century château.

3 CHATEAU DE VASCOEUIL

14–16th-century château.

4 ABBAYE DE FONTAINE-GUERARD

Medieval Cistercian abbey.

5 LYONS-LA-FORET

"Site classe"; attractive town in heart of the forest.

6 ABBAYE DE MORTEMER

Medieval Cistercian abbey.

7 CHATEAU DE GISORS

12th-century frontier fort.

8 CHATEAU DE BOURY

17th-century château.

9 CHATEAU D'AMBLEVILLE

16–17th-century château.

10 MUSEE ARCHEOLOGIQUE DEPARTEMENTAL DE GUIRY-EN-VEXIN

Val-d'Oise archaeological museum; which is 20 km (12 miles) north of Pontoise.

11 CHATEAU GAILLARD

Richard the Lionheart's 12th-century fortress above the Seine.

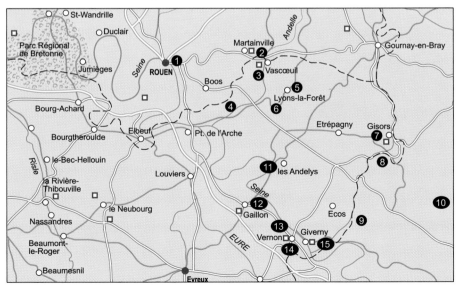

12 CHATEAU DE GAILLON
Re-styled Renaissance château.

13 VERNON
14th-century church and half-timbered houses.

14 CHATEAU DE BIZY
18th-century château.

15 GIVERNY
Monet's home, museum and garden.

The Writers' Houses

The route starts outside Paris and continues, for the most part, along the banks of the Seine to Villequier and links houses-museums associated with well-known writers.

1 CHATENAY MALABRY
Maison de Chateaubriand; house of François Réné de Chateaubriand (1768–1848).

2 BOUGIVAL
Datcha de Tourgueniev; cottage of Ivan Tourgueniev (1818–1883).

3 PORT MARLY
Château de Monte Cristo et Château d'If; residence of Alexandre Dumas (1802–1870).

4 MEDAN
Maison d'Emile Zola; house of Emile Zola (1840–1902).

5 PRESSAGNY L'ORGUEILLEUX
Château de la Madeleine; residence of Casimir Delavigne (1793–1843).

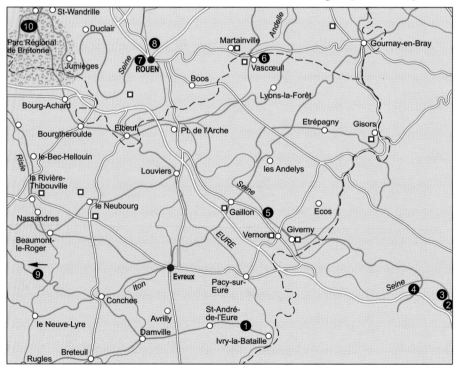

6 VASCOEUIL

Château de Vascoeuil; residence of Jules Michelet (1798–1874).

7 PETIT COURONNE

Maison des Champs; house of Pierre Corneille (1606–1684).

8 CROISSET

Pavillon Flaubert; house of Gustave Flaubert (1821–1880).

9 LE CHAMBLAC-PAR-BROGLIE

Maison de la Varende; residence of

The Route Mont-Saint-Michel (below). Route of the writers' houses (opposite, below).

Jean de la Varende (1887–1959). Private property, visits arranged through; Mme de la Varende, Château de Bonneville, 27270 le Chamblac-par-Broglie. (Off map.)

10 VILLEQUIER

Musée Victor Hugo; holiday home of Victor Hugo (1802–1885).

Route Mont-Saint-Michel

An inland route from Caen to Mont-Saint-Michel: châteaux and abbeys.

1 FONTAINE HENRY

15–16th-century château. (Off map.)

2 CREULLY

Medieval château. (Off map.)

3 BRECY

17th-century château and gardens.

4 VAULAVILLE

18th-century château with collection of "Porcelaines de Bayeux".

5 BALLEROY

17th-century château.

6 ABBAYE DE MONDAYE

18th-century abbey church.

6 ABBAYE DE CERISY LA FORET

Medieval abbey.

7 TORIGNI-SUR-VIRE

16th-century château and gardens.

8 ABBAYE DE HAMBYE

12th-century ruins of the abbey.

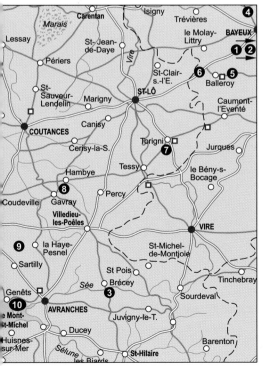

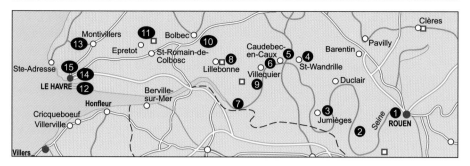

A bbeys along the banks of the lower Seine.

9 ABBAYE DE LA LUCERNE
Medieval abbey.

10 LE MONT-SAINT-MICHEL
Spectacular medieval church complex on its rocky mount.

Road of the Abbeys

Some of Europe's earliest monasteries were built along the banks of the lower Seine. The riverain route from Rouen to le Havre includes these abbeys and some other sights on the way.

1 ROUEN
Abbey of Saint Ouen.

2 SAINT MARTIN-DE-BOSCHERVILLE
Abbey Saint-Georges.

3 JUMIEGES
Abbey of Jumièges.

4 SAINT WANDRILLE
Abbey of Saint Wandrille.

5 CAUDEBEC-EN-CAUX
Church of Notre Dame; House of Knights; Seine Marine Museum.

6 VILLEQUIER
Victor Hugo Museum.

7 SAINT MAURICE-D'ETELAN
Château d'Etelan.

8 LILLEBONNE
Roman amphitheatre and museum.

9 MESNIL-SOUS-LILLEBONNE
Church with collection of minerals and fossils.

10 GRUCHET-LE-VALASSE
Abbey of Valasse.

11 GOMERVILLE
Château de Filières.

12 GONFREVILLE L'ORCHER
Château d'Orcher.

13 MONTVILLIERS
Abbey church of Saint Saveur.

14 HARFLEUR
Priory Museum.

15 LE HAVRE
Graville Priory.

Museums of Manche

1 AVRANCHES
Musée Municipal; manuscrips from Mont-Saint-Michel.

2 BARENTON
Maison de la Pomme et de la Poire.

3 BRICQUEBEC
Musée d'Archeologie et Ethnographie Regionale.

4 CERISY-LA-FORET
Musée Lapidaire de l'Abbaye with old furniture and statues.

5 CHERBOURG
Musée Thomas Hardy with a collection of JF Millet paintings; Musée du Parc Liais specializing in the natural sciences; Musée de la Liberation is here too.

6 COUTANCES
Musée Municipal with local pottery and art.

7 GRANVILLE
Musée de Vieux Granville displaying local history.

8 HAMBYE
Abbey museum.

9 MONT-SAINT-MICHEL
Musée Historique, about the Mont.

10 MORTAIN
Musée Africain de l'Abbaye Blanche with African ethnographica.

11 SAINT LO
Musée Municipal with art collections.

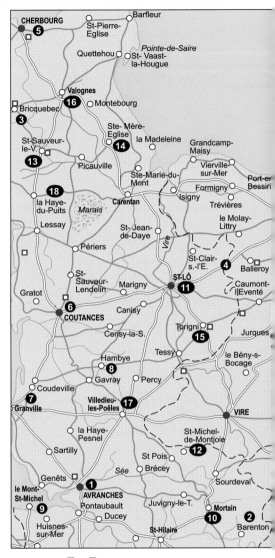

*M*useums *of Manche.*

12 SAINT MICHEL-DE-MONTJOIE
Musée du Granit.

13 SAINT SAUVEUR-LE-VICOMTE
Musée Barbey d'Aurevilly, a museum about the writer.

14 SAINTE MERE-EGLISE

Musée des Troupes Aeroportees; Musée de la Ferme du Cotentin.

15 TORIGNI-SUR-VIRE

The Château Museum with furnishings and art.

16 VALOGNES

Musée Regional du Cidre.

17 VILLEDIEU-LES-POELES

Musée du Cuivre (copper); Fonderie de Cloches (bell foundry); musée du Meuble Normand (Normandy furniture).

18 VINDEFONTAINE

Town Hall exhibition of old pottery.

Cider Route (Calvados)

There are several "Cider Routes" in Normandy. One is in Pays d'Auge to the west of Lisieux. Cider and other home-made produce can be bought at farms with the "Cru de Cambremer"

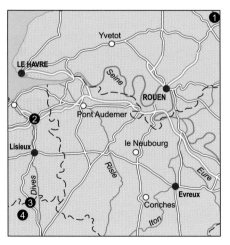

sign. The circuit also incorporates sights of local interest and is sign-posted "Route du Cidre" between the following towns: Beuvron-en-Auge, Cambremer, Bonnebosq and Beaufour.

Cheeses of Normandy

Route linking the homes of Normandy's four great cheeses. Factories and farms making and selling these cheeses, and museums displaying their history, are in and around the environs of the towns. The local tourist offices have lists of those involved in the cheeses.

1 NEUFCHATEL-EN-BRAY

Coninue west through St Saëns, Totes, Yerville, Yvetot, Caudebec-en-Caux and through Forêt de Bretonne to Pont Audemer; then west to:

2 PONT L'EVEQUE

Continue south to Lisieux and on to:

3 LIVAROT

(The cheese box centre of Saint Pierre-sur-Dives is to the west). Continue south to Vimoutiers, with its Camembert Museum, and on to:

4 CAMEMBERT

Sites of Normandy's four great cheeses.

80

Cheeses in the Pays d'Auge

An opportunity to branch off from the cheese route outlined above and follow the signposted "La Route du Fromage" along minor roads. The circuit is centred around Livarot and stretches to Saint Pierre-sur-Dives to the west and the D64 to the east.

La Route des Moulins

"La Route des Moulins", the route of the mills, is a signposted circuit in the countryside between Caen and Arromanches. A rectangular route, it follows minor roads between the towns/villages of Thaon, Reviers, Villiers-le-Sec and Rucqueville.

La Route des Marais

This is a signposted circuit around the fens to the east of Caen. The route incorporates the towns/villages of Troarn, Bavent, Varaville, Grangues, Dozule, Brocottes and Janville.

La Route des Traditions

"La Route des Traditions" is a signposted circuit around pre-bocage countryside between Bayeux and Thury Harcourt. The route incorporates places relevant to traditional Normandy and links the towns/villages of Vilers-Bocage, Epinay-sur-Odon, Aunay-sur-Odon, Saint Georges d'Aunay and Cahagnes.

La Route du Granit

In the heart of granite country, this signposted route follows a course west of Vire and incorporates places relevant to granite along a circuit between: Vire, Champs-du-Boult, Saint Michel-de-Montjoie, le Gast, Saint Sever and Saint Manvieu Bocage.

La Route des Douets

In the countryside around Pont l'Eveque, this signposted route follows a course along and across rivers between Saint Etienne la Thillaye, Beaumont-en-Auge, Clarbec, Saint Hymer, Pierrefitte-en-Auge, le Mesnil-sur-Blangy and Saint Julien-sur-Calonne.

La Route des Gorges de la Vire

This signposted route is to the west of le Beny-Bocage and follows the course of the River Vire through its gorges; places along the way include Saint Martin Don, Sainte Marie-Outre-l'Eau, Pont Bellanger, Pleines Oeuvres, Malloué, Montbertrand.

La Route de la Forêt des Bairds

The signposted "La Route de la Forêt des Bairds" is through a forested region lying between Bayeux and Saint Lô and incorporates Noron-la-Poterie, Balleroy, Cerisy-la-Forêt, Moulin de Marcy, le Molay-Littry.

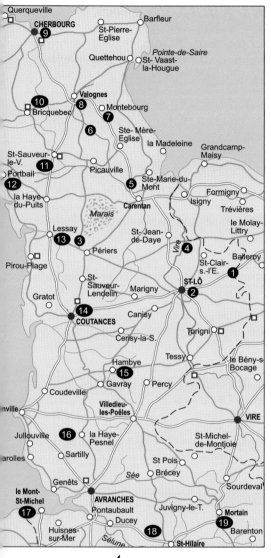

Abbeys and priories of La Manche.

Abbeys and Priories of La Manche

An itinerary linking the abbeys and priories of la Manche provides a predominantly inland itinerary through the department. The châteaux listed below (The Châteaux of la Manche) can be incorporated into the circuit.

1 CERISY LA FORET
Benedictine abbey of Saint Vigor.

2 SAINT LO
Ancient abbey of Sainte Croix.

3 MARCHESIEUX
Ancient priory.

4 SAINT FROMOND
Abbey church.

5 SAINTE COME-DU-MONT
Ancient priory.

6 LE HAM
Remains of medieval Benedictine abbey church.

7 MONTEBOURG
Abbaye Notre-Dame-de-l'Etoile.

8 VALOGNES
Abbaye Notre-Dame-de-Protection.

9 CHERBOURG
Abbaye du Voeu.

10 BRICQUEBEC
Abbaye Notre-Dame-de-Grace.

11 SAINTE SAUVEUR-LE-VICOMTE
Abbey dating from 11th century.

12 PORTBAIL
Site of ancient priory.

13 LESSAY
Restored medival abbey.

14 COUTANCES
Medieval cathedral.

15 HAMBYE
Abbey dating from 12th century.

16 LA LUCERNE-D'OUTREMER
12th-century abbey.

17 LE MONT-SAINT-MICHEL
The great abbey church and buildings dating from the Middle Ages.

18 ISIGNY-LE-BUAT
Chapelle de "Pain d'Avaine".

19 MORTAIN
12th-century Cistercian Abbaye Blanche.

Châteaux of La Manche

1 AVRANCHES
10th-century keep.

2 BRICQUEBEC
Medieval castle

3 CROSVILLE-SUR-DOUVE
15–17th-century château.

4 GONNEVILLE
16–17th-century château.

5 GRATOT
14–18th-century château.

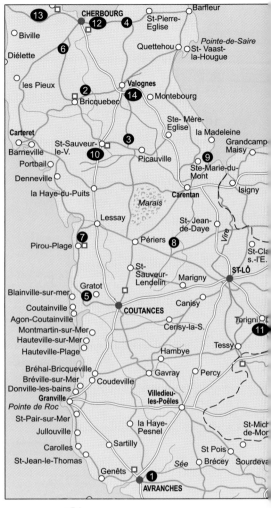

Chateaux of La Manche.

6 MARTINVAST
Site of medieval castle; also more recent château.

7 PIROU
12th-century château.

8 REMILLY-SUR-LOZON
15–16th-century Château de Montfort.

9 SAINTE MARIE-DU-MONT
15–16th-century construction.

10 SAINT SAUVEUR-LE-VICOMTE
Big fort in the Hundred Years' War.

11 TORIGNI-SUR-VIRE
16th-century château.

12 TOURLAVILLE
Renaissance construction.

13 URVILLE-NACQUEVILLE
16th-century château.

14 VALOGNES
The 18th-century Hôtel de Beaumont and Hôtel de Grandval Cligny.

Circuit 44

A route incorporating the D-Day Landing Beaches, some military cemeteries, memorials and War museums.

1 CAEN
Memorial Museum.

2 BENOUVILLE
Museum of Airborne Forces.

3 ARROMANCHES
Landing Museum.

4 BAYEUX
Memorial Museum of the Battle of Normandy 1944.

Circuit 44, a route about the D-day landings.

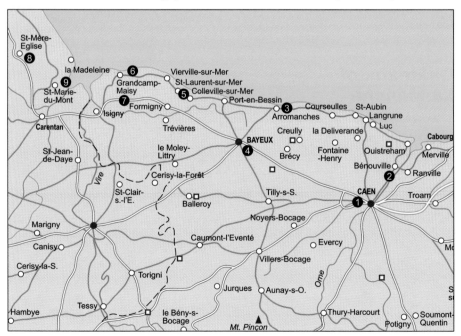

5 COLLEVILLE-SAINT-LAURENT
American Military Cemetery.

6 POINTE DU HOC
Monument in memory of the Rangers.

7 LA CAMBE
German Military Cemetery.

8 SAINTE MERE-EGLISE
The Airborne Museum.

9 SAINTE MARIE-DU-MONT
Museum of the Landing Day at Utah Beach.

Suisse Normande

An "anti-clockwise" itinerary around Normandy's "Little Switzerland" can be made by linking the following places: Thury Harcourt, Saint Martin de Sallen, Culey Patry, Saint Pierre la Vieille, Pontécoulant, Condé-sur-Noireau, Pont Erambourg, Cahan, Pont d'Ouilly, Cossesseville, Le Bo, Clécy, Saint Remy, Saint Omer, Esson.

Cider Route (Seine-Maritime)

The signposted "La Route de la Pomme et du Cidre" is an "apple and cider circuit" through countryside lying to the south of Dieppe. Along the way are Aubermesnil-Beaumais, Torcy-le-Petit, Torcy-le-Grand, le Catelier, Auffay, Longueville-sur-Scie.

Le Perche and its Forests

A route through the countryside and forests of Perche in the department of Orne. The circuit includes Soligny-la-Trappe, Mortagne-au-Perche, Courgeon, Monceaux, Logny-au-Perche, Autheuil, Tourouvre.

Le Perche and its Manors

A route through the countryside south of Mortagne-au-Perche, incorporating the manors in the southernmost corner of Perche. The circuit includes Mauves-sur-Huisne, Maison-Maugis, Moutiers-au-Perche, Conde-sur-Huisne, Saint Jean-de-la-Forêt, Preaux-du-Perche, Saint Germain-de-la-Coudre, Bellême, la Perrière.

Cheeses of Neufchâtel

A route through Pays de Bray, the heartlands of the Neufchâtel, cheese-making country. The circuit includes Neufchâtel-en-Bray, Nesle Hodeng, Mesnil-Mauger, Forges-les-Eaux, Sainte Genevieve-en-Bray, Massy, Esclavelles, Bully, Mesnières-en-Bray.

Towering White Cliffs, Rolling Countryside and the City of Rouen

Fish and cliffs are the speciality of the Seine-Maritime coast. The former are hauled onto wharves wedged between the latter. A clique of artists weaned in Le Havre developed an insatiable appetite for such scenes, reproducing them in innovative styles such as Impressionism. In the interior is a countryside of rolling pastures and wheatfields and well-to-do market towns and farming villages. Seine-Maritime also has Rouen, a city as rich in history and culture as any beyond Paris.

Dieppe

Take a boat to Dieppe and you enter the heart of Normandy. The ferry pushes deep into the harbour and moors alongside the famous quai Henry IV. Dieppe spreads out below you. This is a thoroughly Norman town, and especially on Saturday mornings when its huge weekly market centred in the shadows of the church of Saint Jacques draws local fishermen, farmers, traders and shoppers from

A ground eye view of the ceiling inside Caudebec's flamboyant Notre Dame, Henry IV's favourite church.

along the coast and from far in the countryside.

Dieppe, sheltered in a gap of the towering white cliffs of the Alabaster coast, has long been a port. Its very name is said to be derived from *Deope*, the Saxon word for "deep", and ancient reference to this, one of the deepest harbours on either side of the Channel.

Fishing continues as a foremost activity, with sole, turbot, bass, brill, and mackerel being the main catches; furthermore, it is estimated that two out of five shellfish consumed in France come from Dieppe. The port's excellent and celebrated, though often unassuming, fish restaurants line quai Henry IV and the adjoining quai Duquesne.

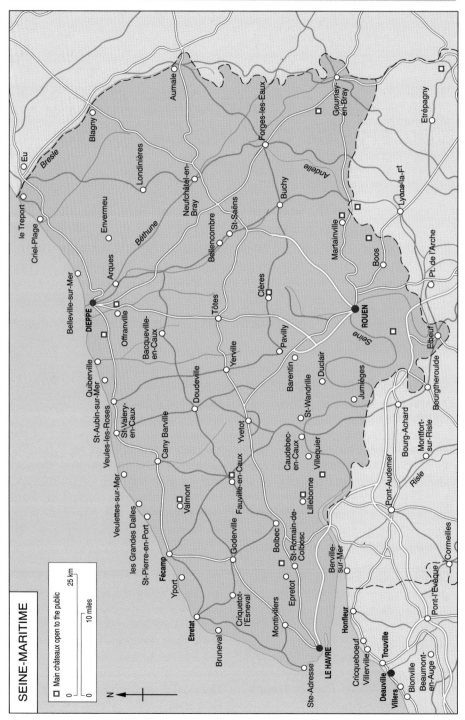

SEINE-MARITIME

☐ Main châteaux open to the public

25 km
10 miles

N

le Treport
Eu
Bresle
Criel-Plage
Blagny
Aumale
Londinières
Neufchâtel-en-Bray
Forges-les-Eaux
Gournay-en-Bray
Erépagny
Belleville-sur-Mer
Envermeu
Béthune
Bellencombre
St-Saëns
Buchy
Andelle
Lyons-la-Ft
Pt. de l'Arche
DIEPPE
Arques
Offranville
Bacqueville-en-Caux
Tôtes
Clères
Pavilly
Martainville
Boos
ROUEN
Quiberville
St-Aubin-sur-Mer
Veules-les-Roses
St-Valery-en-Caux
Doudeville
Yerville
Barentin
Duclair
Jumièges
St-Wandrille
Bourgtheroulde
Etbeuf
Seine
Cany Barville
Yvetot
Caudebec-en-Caux
Villequier
Bourg-Achard
Montfort-sur-Risle
Veulettes-sur-Mer
Valmont
Fauville-en-Caux
Lillebonne
Pont-Audemer
Risle
Cormeilles
les Grandes Dalles
St-Pierre-en-Port
Goderville
Bolbec
St-Rômain-de-Colbosc
Berville-sur-Mer
Fécamp
Yport
Epretot
Montivilliers
Criquetot-l'Esneval
Honfleur
Cricqueboeuf
Villerville
Deauville
Trouville
Blonville
Beaumont-en-Auge
Etretat
Bruneval
Ste-Adresse
LE HAVRE
Villers
Pont-l'Evêque

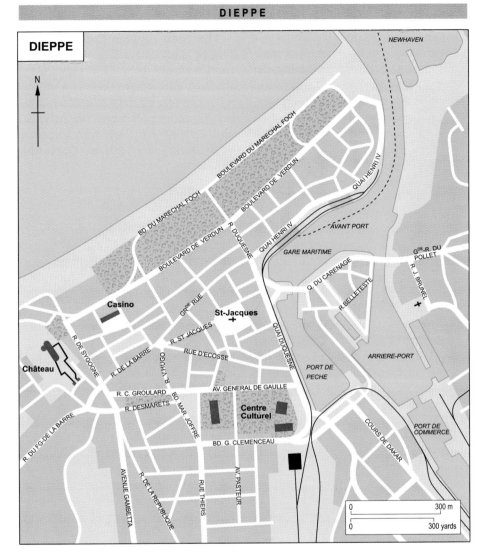

*T*own plan of Dieppe.

It was as a naval and merchant base between the 12th and 17th centuries, however, that Dieppe won recognition. The French and British regularly fought over the port, destroying much during battle.

*M*ap of
Seine-Maritime region.

The 16th-century Dieppois folklore is dominated by Jean Ango, an influential shipbuilder with the ear and the support of King François I. He constructed a fleet which successfully checked the seafaring ambitions and arrogance of the Portuguese, who, it seems, treated most sailors they encountered as pirates. The Ango privateers are said to have captured some 300 Portuguese ships and he himself became governor of Dieppe and resided in a splendid château on quai Henry IV. Ango died a forgotten man and his home was razed by the British in 1694. His legend is remembered and his unusual country house at nearby Varengeville is also a survivor of the time.

These were also great pioneering days and Dieppe, along with Honfleur down the coast, was one of the main gateways to America. And among Ango's employees was Verrazano, the man who, in 1524, discovered the land upon which New York was created. Many of Canada's earliest immigrant families left France from Dieppe. And their descendants were amongst the 5,000 Canadians who constituted the main force in Operation Jubilee, the Allied attack on Dieppe on 19 August 1942.

Eight German strongholds on the coast either side of Dieppe were targeted. The Allied sortie was repelled emphatically and the majority of their men were killed or captured by the Germans. Having suffered this disaster, the Allies were forced back to the drawing board. They learnt from their mistakes and, when they returned to Normandy two years later, under the banner of Operation Overlord, they went on to win France and the War.

The bond between Canadians and Dieppe is remembered in the **Square of the Canadians** below the château on the west cliff, where there is a monument commemorating Normandy's pioneers who set off across the Atlantic, and a plaque for those who lost their lives during the fateful Operation Jubilee.

*S*plendid gargoyles leap from the much weathered soot-covered walls of Dieppe's church of Saint Jacques.

Dieppe, the resort, still survives. Indeed, this is where French society inaugurated sea-bathing. The vogue gained popularity after the trend-setting Marie-Caroline de Bourbon, the Duchesse de Berry, took a dip in the Channel at Dieppe in 1824. The waterfront does not have the elegance of the past, though there are a few buildings evoking a hint of aged grandeur, nor the intimacy of corniches at resorts elsewhere on the coast. None the less, the sea-bathers still turn out on the long pebble beach during the warm summer days.

As for the town itself, gloomy lanes lead off quai Henry IV and constitute something of an old town; a recent

The 18th-century Café des Tribunaux, in place du Puits Sale at the junction of Grande Rue and rue de la Barre, is a popular rendezvous.

regeneration of interest in this quarter will doubtless brighten it up. Westwards, across rue Duquesne, named in memory of Dieppe's famous 17th-century naval captain Abraham Duquesne, the quai Henry IV gives way to Grande Rue, the long, busy pedestrian shopping street. About half-way up is place du Puits Sale with its famous 18th-century Café des Tribunaux: an acknowledged rendezvous in the heart of the Dieppe. Just to the left

of this, the lower end of Grande Rue, is the fine grime-covered church of Saint Jacques.

The original Saint Jacques was still under construction when Philippe-Auguste destroyed it, and much of Dieppe, in 1195. Rebuilding started 100 years later and the church continued to be embellished and restored, in Gothic and flamboyant styles, over the succeeding centuries. Many of the finer works were donated by merchants who grew rich during Dieppe's

Ivories

Ivory was big business in Dieppe during the 17th century. Consignments of the exotic tusk were brought from India and Africa to this north-western corner of Europe and here, in the tight grey back-streets of the port, a busy cottage industry would fashion this primeval tooth into an assortment of elegant and expensive paraphernalia. There were at one time 350 craftsmen in Dieppe producing —as an old document up in the museum recounts—"every kind of curio in ivory: carved, engraved, fluted and fretworked cases; open work snuff boxes and other snuff boxes worked in all manners; shuttles and bobbins for Ladies; knives, earpicks, baskets, reels and trumpets; ordinary crucifixes and fine crucifixes of all sizes; figures of saints mounted on pedestals and other figures to decorate chimney-pieces; all sorts of fans, cut and carved in every style; snuff boxes with the customer's own arms or initials; beads and billiard balls, dice-boxes, backgammon pieces, chess and domino sets...". Most of the craftsmen were Protestants and, suffering sectarian discrimination towards the end of the 17th century, many left Dieppe. The ivory industry declined, but its history and examples of the workmanship are displayed in the port's museum.

Solid, austere Dieppe castle has a panorama over beach and town. Once part of ancient fortifications, it was later the governor's residence; now it is a museum.

great maritime age. There is a frieze, which was salvaged from Jean Ango's town residence on quai Henry IV, depicting Dieppois' discoveries in the Americas. There are interesting shops in the lanes of Saint Jacques' square.

Dieppe's other main central church, Saint Remy, is off rue de la Barre, the continuation of Grande Rue after place du Puits Sale. It dates from the early 16th century and houses an 18th-century organ which is said to be one of the finest in France.

Dieppe's flint and sandstone **château** stands impressive and dominant upon a cliff at the western end of town.

Remnants of the early medieval castles which stood here have been incorporated in the present 15th–17th-century structure. In those days, the château served as the official residence of the governors of Dieppe; now it is a museum. On display is a fairly eclectic set of collections, including local maritime curios, pre-Columbian pottery from Peru, 19th-century Dutch paintings and, most sensational of all, the "Dieppe Ivories".

Opening times: 10.00a.m. to 12.00 p.m. and 2.00–6.00 p.m. daily; closed on Tuesdays between mid-September and mid-June; tel: 35-84-14-76.

Dieppe to Le Tréport

The white cliffs of the Alabaster Coast are a feature of the shore between Dieppe and le Tréport, some 30 km (19 miles) up the coast, and even beyond into the department of Somme.

Le Tréport, along with Dieppe, was France's first and foremost seaside resort. Furthermore, the Parisian holiday-makers, who came here in their droves each summer, sought out new locations along the coast between the two resorts for their novel fad of sea-bathing.

From Dieppe's downtown, head east, crossing the drawbridges over the inner ports and following Grand Rue du Pollet for the main D925 le Tréport road. Turnings to the left off the D925 lead to small resorts.

A few kilometres out of Dieppe is Puys, which can be reached from Dieppe more directly by way of a minor road from the town, where Alexander Dumas died in 1870 and where his son, Dumas fils, continued to live; Lord Salisbury, England's conservative prime minister in the late 1800s, also holidayed here. A monument remembers the Canadian commandos, who landed at Puys and died during the failed attack on Dieppe in 1942.

Minor roads running parallel to the D925 link the small resorts, many of which, like Puys, were damaged during the War. Next is Belleville-sur-Mer, followed by Berneval-sur-Mer, Saint Martin-Plage and, incongruously, the EDF nuclear power plant. Beyond is Biville-sur-Mer and then Criel-sur-Mer, with its 17th-century château, on the River Yères. The roads cutting inland along the river pass through pretty

A view from the cliffs at le Tréport across the border into Picardy and its resort of Mer-les-Bains.

countryside and villages towards Grandcourt. On the far side of the river mouth is Criel-Plage and the neighbouring resort of Mesnil-Val from where the D126e runs along the cliff-top to the Calvaire des Terrasses. Here, at the Calvary, there are splendid views along the coast, out to sea and down over le Tréport and across to Mers-les-Bains and Picardy on the far side of the River Bresle. A road leads down through the residential district of town to the port itself; alternatively, if you are feeling particularly energetic, there is a 378-step stairway.

Le Tréport

Le Tréport, at the mouth of the Bresle, has long been a port. The silting of its river reduced its importance. However, its transformation into a seaside resort in the middle of the last century saved it from further decline and, at the same time, gave it new life and character.

King Louis-Philippe, who would summer at nearby Eu (*see* page 96), enjoyed spending time in le Tréport and with him came his guests, including Queen Victoria. The stamp of royal approval gave le Tréport credibility. Furthermore, le Tréport, along with Dieppe, is the closest sea-town to Paris, and with the opening of the Paris–le Tréport railway in 1875, the ease of travelling from capital to coast was greatly enhanced.

Le Tréport is essentially a small resort, and it is still very active and popular in summer. However, the fashionable no longer favour the place. Style has been replaced by candy-floss, and the atmosphere is now far more

*L*e Tréport may not have the chic of Deauville, but once the morning mist has lifted the beach will be as crowded as any in Normandy.

easy-going than self-conscious. Unlike on the *planches* at Deauville, it would be pointless worrying about what to wear as you wander the promenade backing le Tréport's pebble beach.

Fish, too, continues to be an important source of revenue in le Tréport. The fishing boats moor at quai François 1er, the fisherwomen sell their men's catch in the nearby market and the restaurants along the quay's pavement serve up delicious fresh fish dishes.

A hill rises above the quay upon which stands the upper town and its 16th-century church of Saint Jacques, which is particularly impressive for its hanging keystones. From up here, the stairway ascends the cliff to the Calvaire des Terrasses.

The Bresle Valley

The River Bresle, rising in eastern Normandy, forms the northern border of the province: it is the division between the flat monotonous plains of Picardy and the rich rolling farmlands of Normandy.

Eu

It is 4 km (2½ miles) by road from le Tréport up the Bresle to Eu, a town long associated with the "big" royal occasion. Duke Rollo built the original fort here in the 10th century and died in it in 933. Duke William married his Matilda within these ramparts in 1050 and, in 1064, conferred here with Harold about the destiny of the English crown. Louis XI burnt the castle, and the town, in 1475, fearing its capture by the English in the event of their invasion. In the 1840s, and before his flight to England, King Louis-Philippe, the Citizen King, used to pass his summers in Eu and, on two occasions, had Queen Victoria as his guest.

Work on the present Renaissance **château** was started in 1578 by Henry de Guise, though it was not completed until almost a century later by the "Grande Madamoiselle", the cousin of Louis XIV. Later the château was acquired by the Orleans family and by King Louis-Philippe. Fire in 1902

*T*he life of William the Conqueror is very much part of Normandy folklore. Plaques throughout the land commemorate his presence: in Eu he married Matilda.

caused much destruction; however, the château has been restored and now serves as the Town Hall and a museum. Various apartments are on display, including rooms decorated by Viollet-le-Duc in the 1870s, and period furniture, dinner sets, portraits, Queen Victoria memorabilia, and a 1900's

96

bathroom. There is also an exhibition of Bresle glassware, mainly perfume bottles, and various implements used in the trade (see below). The lovely gardens, part formal, spread out behind. *Opening times*: 10.00a.m. to 12.00 p.m. and 2.00–6.00 p.m. daily except Tuesdays from the Saturday before Palm Sunday to the first Sunday in November; tel: 35-86-44-00.

The splendid Gothic church of **Notre Dame and Saint Laurent** is dedicated to Saint Lawrence O'Toole, the 12th-century primate of Ireland, who died in Eu. He is buried here and his *gisant*, recumbent figure on a tomb, is said to be the oldest in France. The church, which dates back to the 12th–13th centuries has been destroyed and rebuilt on several occasions. It houses some fine pieces of religious art and has a 19th-century restored crypt. The Counts of Eu are amongst those entombed.

Other noteworthy mausoleums are those of Duke Henri de Guise, the aptly named elusive aristocrat, and his wife Catherine de Cleve, which are in the 17th-century College Chapel of the old Jesuit college down rue du College. It was founded in the 16th century by the duke as a protest against Protestantism. The lavish marble tombs, fashioned by some of the finest sculptors of the day, represent the de Guises.

On to Blangy and Aumale

The D49 runs south-east along the Bresle valley from Eu to Blangy and on to Aumale, a total of 42 km (26 miles). Just out of Eu, a narrow road leads right, off the D49 and up and into the Forest of Eu. The route along the narrow forest roads, occasionally passing through countryside and villages and dipping down to the pretty neighbouring valley of the Yères, is a longer but better way than the busier D49. Grandcourt, just out of the forest and on the Yères is a pleasant enough place to aim for. Then turn back through the forest along the D149 and head, via the manor and church of Rieux, to Blangy.

In these forests, small scattered communities have been making glass since the Gallo-Roman era. In the 15th century, the local glass barons, families such as Caqueray, le Vaillant, Brossards, Bongars, evolved under the auspices of the Counts of Eu. With the opening of the Paris–le-Tréport railway line, which runs its latter stage alongside the Bresle, in 1875, many of the *verrières* re-located down in the valley. Today, the Bresle's glass factories constitute an important industry and are particularly well known for their *flacons à odeur*, scent bottles, which are produced for the famous Paris perfume houses and for export. Some of the traditional glass-making methods are being revived as small specialized cottage enterprises.

Busy **Blangy**, badly damaged by the Germans in 1940 and rebuilt without much beauty, straddles the N28 thoroughfare, a main north–south avenue for tourists and truckers travelling to, and from, the northern Channel ports. Henry IV stayed in the Manoir de Fontaine, by the river; open on request from the local *syndicat d'initiative*.

It is a fairly pretty 22 km (14 miles) stretch from Blangy to Aumale: even prettier is the parallel road on the Picardy side of the river. The

*A*n extravagant bridge
spans the River Yères, a
forgotten trickle flowing through
the heart of Seine-Maritime.

14th–15th century moated château of
Rambures is in Picardy: across the
Bresle at Nesle-Normandeuse; up the
steep valley slope on the far side and
across the flat plains to the château.

*G*lass making has long
been a tradition in the Bresle
valley and the manufacture of
the flacon à odeur, the scent
bottle, for the top Paris perfume
houses is the local speciality.
This flacon is a Christian Dior
design.

Flacons à Odeur

Visits to the glassworks can be arranged direct or through the local *syndicat d'initiative*. **Blangy-sur-Bresle**: Verrerie Waltersperger on the outskirts of Blangy; tel: 35-93-52-48.

Romesnil: on the edge of the forest between Blangy and Nesle-Normandeuse. The old glassworks by the hunting pavilion built by Prince de Dombes was closed in the 1980s.

Nesle-Normandeuse: founded in 1882, the glassworks specialize in decorative crystal and perfume bottles; tel: 35-86-04-68.

Le Courval and Guimerville: early 17th-century glassworks with its old le Courval factory on the edge of the forest, and the newer Guimerville plant in the valley below (a further plant is at Gamaches on the other side of the river between Blangy and Eu). Perfume bottles are made under the Verrières du Corval mark; tel: 35-93-55-33.

Vieux Rouen: the glassworks were founded here in the late 19th century; the original workers' cottages provided by the factory still allow staff housing at nominal rents.

Aumale: a division of Boralex where they make phials and bottles for the pharmaceutical industry; tel: 35-93-42-09.

Aumale, straddling the Bresle and two provinces, escaped the extensive war devastation suffered by Blangy. Timber-framed houses still line the long central market and, at the far end, stands the Gothic–flamboyant church of Saint Pierre and Saint Paul.

M odest châteaux by quiet streams, local history in forgotten valleys; Manoir de Fontaine on the Bresle at Blangy once provided a bed for Henry IV.

Henry IV was wounded by an arquebus during the Battle of Aumale on 5 February 1592. The later French monarch, Louis-Philippe, used to pass through Aumale, and Blangy, on his way to Eu; he had one of the town's gates destroyed so as to accommodate the width of his entourage; he made his fourth son the Duke of Aumale.

A narrow brown house on a hairpin bend with rooms for the slim.

On to Neufchâtel-en-Bray

Two stretches of main road from the Bresle meet at Neufchâtel-en-Bray: the 25 km (15 miles) of N28 from Blangy and the 22 km (13 miles) of N29 from Aumale. Typical Pays de Bray farmlands and villages lie within the triangle of these three market towns. An alternative route from the Bresle valley to Neufchâtel is the D60, west off the D49 at Vieux Rouen:

The road proceeds through Aubeguimont to Richmont. Here the 3 km (2 mile) high street, the village is little else, leads to the right; beyond is Saint Leger-en-Bois—with its leaning church spire—and the larger Foucarmont with its concrete church tower serving as a conspicuous landmark, on the main N28. However, continuing on the D60, one passes through the Basse Forêt d'Eu and open undulating countryside for 17 km (10 miles) before reaching Neufchâtel-en-Bray.

Neufchâtel-en-Bray

Neufchâtel, literally meaning New Castle, gained its name from the fortifications built here by Henry Beauclerk in the 12th century. Subsequently, it gave its name to the piquant cheese produced in the surrounding countryside.

France's Henry IV razed the "new castle" in the late 16th century; much of the rest of the town was destroyed during the War. The 13th–16th-century church of Notre Dame, with its slate-covered spire, belfry and porch, has been restored, while most other buildings were beyond repair and had to be entirely rebuilt. Pays de Bray is one of

The Bondon de Neufchâtel

The rich, sharp, salty *bondon de Neufchâtel*, produced in the Pays de Bray since the early years of the Norman dynasty, is the oldest of Normandy's cheeses. The *Neufchâtel* gained particular prestige in 1035, after Hugues I of Gournay levied a special tax, the *Dime des Frometons*, on the successful cheese-making enterprizes of the Abbey de Sigy. Its popularity soon spread across the Channel to England where it was served in the taverns during the Middle Ages. At the turn of the 18th century the town of Neufchâtel-en-Bray—from where the cheese earned its name—was holding three large dairy markets a week when the whole place reeked of the pungent-smelling cheese. Folklore also proudly claims that Napoleon took a fancy to the locals' prize produce after he was presented with a basket of the ripe cheeses; hence the expression *Neufoleon Bondoparte* denoting a small, powerful *Neufchâtel*.

Today, Fromagerie l'Hernarut and Fromagerie Lefebvre Isidore on rue des Abreuvoirs in Neufchâtel are the main producers of the cheese. However, scattered deep in the countryside of Pays de Bray are some three dozen individual farmers who continue to craft the Neufchâtels using the traditional methods of their forefathers.

Monsieur and Madame René Binet and their 17 brown and white Normandaise cows live in the village of Saint Leger-aux-Bois, 25 kms north of Neufchâtel. For the past 32 years, Binet —like eight generations of his family before him—has been making the *Neufchâtel* cheese. Twice a day—in the morning and early evening—Binet gathers his cows, and milks their heavy udders. Down in his small dark, dank cellars, the milk is poured into large

Every morning, Madame Binet shapes the Neufchâtels.

buckets and after adding the "vaccine"—by crumbling a small amount of cheese into the milk—it is left to curdle for 24 to 36 hours. The curds are then strained through a fine cloth, to rid it of excess liquid, and finally pressed and kneaded before being smeared in salt and moulded into the classic *Neufchâtel* shapes: the cylindrical *bonde* (from where we get *bondon*) and the rectangular *briquette*—both weighing 100 g (3½ oz)—and the heart-shaped *angelot* and the *double bonde*, both of which weigh 200 g (7oz). Each Normandaise is able to convert her daily consumption of lush pasture into about 20 litres of milk—a lower quantity, though, creamier, than the milk production of the more common black and white Hollandaise cow—and, with each litre, the farmer creates 150 g (5¼ oz) of cheese.

The *Neufchatels*—white, slightly soft, covered with a *croute fleurie* (a flowery rind) and containing 45% *matière grasse*—are stacked and left in the cellar to mature for at least six days, after which time they are ready for consumption. Compared to the soft, mild Camembert—the "younger" but better known Normandy cheese—the *Neufchâtel* has a firm touch, a crumbly coarse texture and strong taste.

The morning's work over, Binet reached down to a lower shelf in a dark corner and produced a withered, wrinkled yellowish-brown *briquette*. Holding it delicately between thumb and forefinger, he explained in a reverential whisper that the cheese had been allowed to mature for a month. He breathed its strong aroma in deeply and quietly nodded his head in satisfaction. He uncorked the bottle of chilled, fizzy home-brewed cider—cider, the drink of Normandy, or a fruity red wine such as a Côte du Rhone, should accompany a *Neufchâtel*—and cut a thin slice of cheese, offering it on his knife.

Packed and labelled, Binet's Stacks of Neufchâtel cheeses are ready for delivery.

The initial taste of a mature *Neufchâtel* is powerful as it stings the tongue, palate and throat; a rough earthy flavour fills the mouth, but this is slowly replaced by a rich, though dry, creamy taste of cheese. Gulp a draught of cider and the effervescent liquid sparkles in the mouth, tingling every tastebud. For a few seconds, one breathes, touches, tastes the orchards and pastures of Normandy. It is a remarkable sensation.

The cheeses are collected several times a week by the regional distributor who takes them to shops in Neufchâtel and other local towns. Each cheese bears a label indicating its origins— "René Binet, Saint Leger-aux-Bois"— and the stamp of the *comite national des appellations d'origine des fromages* (CNAOF) as an indication that the cheesemaker is approved and that his produce is of high standard.

While the farmers follow the various CNAOF guidelines, each has inherited through his family his own idiosyncratic ways of making cheese. These quirks give individuality to the cheeses. And so, to an expert, a "René Binet" is distinguishable from the "Henri Bloquel", or a "Patrick Chevalier", or a "Claude Monnier" or any of the other *Neufchâtels* crafted by the other "Neufchâtel artisans".

Now, though, the EC bureaucrats in Brussels are laying down new legislation. Directives to be issued over the next years will require Binet to modernize his 6 m (6.5 yd) x 2 m (2.2 yd) cellar. His damp, mouldy brick walls will have to be recovered, the floor has to be re-tiled, wood surfaces must be replaced by zinc. Furthermore, the *paille de seigle*—the rye straw—upon which the cheese is traditionally placed to enhance its maturing, will also have to go for hygenic purposes.

Binet may well close down rather than conform to these guidelines. His fate is, after all, inevitable. His four grown sons, like so many of their generation, have no interest in farming and have quit the land to find work in the towns. And so Binet, now in his late fifties, is contemplating selling his cows and taking early retirement.

Information about the Neufchâtel is available from:

Syndicat de Defense et de Qualité du
    Fromage de Neufchâtel
Hôtel de Ville
BP 40
76270 Neufchâtel-en-Bray
and
Groupement Feminin de Developement
    Agricole du Pays de Bray
1 place du Général de Gaulle
76440 Forges-les-Eaux

Potato Soufflé Neufchâtel (6 people)

6 medium potatoes
150 gm *Neufchâtel*
3 eggs
2 soup spoons cream
50 gm butter

Place scrubbed and pricked potatoes in the oven for 45 minutes. Halve and scoop out the pulp. Mash together the pulp, *Neufchâtel*, egg yolks, cream and butter. Season with salt and pepper to taste. Add whisked egg whites if desired. Fill the potato skins with the mixture and place in the oven for a further 15 minutes.

Factory produced cheeses tend to dominate the shelves; however, the fresh hand-made farm cheeses will always take pride of place.

the main sources of dairy produce for Parisians and it is as the "Dairy Capital of Bray" that Neufchâtel is best known.

Neufchâtel remembers its traditional past in its **Musée de J B Mathon et André Durand**. Pottery from Martincamp, crockery from Forges-les-Eaux, furniture, glass, iron work and other traditional crafts typical of the Pays de Bray, as well as an eclectic collection of items such as a 13th-century bible, enamelled cross and canons of the National Guard, are exhibited in a restored 16th-century house. An old

*T*he Loire-styled
*Château de Mesnières, a
structure incongruous to this
part of the country.*

cider press and mill are in the back garden. *Opening times*: 3.00–6.00 p.m. daily except Mondays in July and August and Saturday and Sunday afternoons during the rest of the year.

West and South of Neufchâtel-en-Bray

North of Neufchâtel, 5 km (3 miles) away on the D1 Dieppe road, is Mesnières-en-Bray. Entrance to its **château** is down to the left, towards the railway line. The castle at Mesnières stood at the junction of what were known as the royal roads between Paris and Dieppe, and Rouen and Eu. With such a location and high profile, it courted danger and, indeed, it was destroyed by the English during their Agincourt campaign in 1415.

Louis de Boissay rebuilt this, his family home, in the early 16th century.

Buttonhole of Bray

The geological phenomenon, La Boutonnière de Bray, the Buttonhole of Bray, was a side effect of the creation of the Alps. As violent terrestrial agitation in the Tertiary Era conceived the Alps, the Earth's crust rumpled and rippled and here, in this pocket of Normandy, these turbulent motions produced a high crest, a mountain, which over the subsequent eons, has been eroded to reveal different stratas of soil. And today, there remains the unique lip and dip of the Buttonhole of Bray. This feature is best appreciated from various viewpoints in the region and these are incorporated in a tour of the Neufchâtel and Forges-les-Eaux regions (*see* below).

His contractors were instructed to flank the château and its wide fantail stairway with two massive 28 m (59 ft) high towers. This was of the style much favoured by the Loire aristocrats, to whom he was related. Several rooms, including the stag gallery with its row of stag busts and the maproom with fading 17th-century paintings on wood panelling, and the chapels are open to the public. In the early 19th century, the château was used as an orphanage, soon becoming, as it still is today, the Catholic boarding school of Saint Joseph. *Opening times*: 2.00–6.00 p.m. Saturdays and Sundays from Easter to All Saints' Day. Tel: 35-93-10-04.

S aint Beuve-en-Riviere, a typical Normandy village with its church, a primary school, a bar-restaurant, a cluster of houses and little else.

Cross the railway line and continue along the D97 through Autrecourt to Fresles with its medieval church, Pommérval and the Forêt d'Eawy are just to the west (*see* page 114), and then south on the D114 through Bully, Esclavelles, Massy, Sainte Geneviève to the main D915 from where there are views over the Buttonhole of Bray. There are pockets of pretty countryside to the west.

About 5 km (3 miles) southwards along the D915 there is a turning, the D102, to the left (just beyond and to the right is Roncherolles-en-Bray with its 13th-century church). Take the D102 through Bois de l'Abbaye: the remains of the 12th-century abbey, and a road 6 km (4 miles) to Forges-les-Eaux, are on the right; further along on the left are Mont Grippon and the medieval church and chapel at le Rosière. By the junction with the D35 is the 16th-century château at Treforêt, modified in the last century, and nearby the chalybeate springs and well of Saint Maur, an ancient place of pilgrimage. The D35 leads the 10 km (6 miles) northwards back to Neufchâtel.

Alternatively, cross the road to Mesnil-Mauger with its "three-roofed" church and panorama. One minor road, northwards, leads past an old manor farm and through Hodeng before joining the D135; from here, it is 7 km (4 miles) to Neufchâtel with the dovecot of Bouelles on the right.

Or, from Mesnil-Mauger, take the D120 east to Louvicamp, once site of an ancient church, whose relics are now in the church at Mesnil-Mauger; there are good views from Louvicamp. Continue on the D120, passing Mont Benard (231 m, 252 yd), the source of the Epte and divider between it and the Bethune, to le Thil-Riberpre where there is a medieval church.

From here, bear left along the D83 to Gaillefontaine. General Hoche lived here, his residence still stands; also, near this small town, are relics of the priory of Clair-Ruissel and a late 19th-century château; an old fort stood on nearby Mont Roti before its destruction in the 15th century.

Some 8 km (5 miles) west of Gaillefontaine is Forges-les-Eaux.

About 16 km (10 miles) to the north, along the D135, is Neufchâtel. *En route* is Saint Maurice, with its 11th-century church and old château's farm, and Beaussault with its restored medieval church, 16th-century manor and the remains of an old fort and priory.

Forges-les-Eaux

Here at Forges-les-Eaux, in the bottom of the Buttonhole of Bray, the valleys of the Andelle, Epte and Bethune radiate in three different directions. In Gallo-Roman times, the local community crafted iron. The industry thrived for centuries, but by the 16th century, the waters rather than the minerals had become the town's trade. The belief that the iron-rich chalybeate springs at Forges-les-Eaux had medicinal properties drew the fashionable and ill the 115 km (71 miles) from Paris to this small and pleasant spa. Parks were created, providing the convalescents conducive areas for strolling. The most notable of those to take the waters here were Louis XIII, his queen, Anne of Austria, and Cardinal

Richelieu. They spent part of the summer of 1632 in the resort, as it was hoped the waters would be the very tonic Anne required to trigger her fertility.

Forges-les-Eaux is still an active spa town, with gambling at the casino being the town's indulgence; in 1919, it enjoyed extra patronage from the Parisians after casinos within 100 km (62 miles) of the capital were closed. The gardens Louis and his entourage wandered through are open to the public and you can take the invigorating waters from the "Grotto". The façades on either side of the avenue des Sources are from Louis XV's hunting lodge near Versailles—casino side—and from the 17th-century Carmelite Convent at Gisors. In the centre of town, behind the Hôtel de Ville, there are three small museums.

Musée la Résistance which recounts the locals' activities in the region during the Second World War. *Opening times*: 10.00 a.m.–12.30 p.m. and 2.30–6.00 p.m. daily.

Musée des Faïences exhibits the celebrated crockery and pottery made in Forges-les-Eaux between the late 18th and late 19th centuries. *Opening times*: 10.00–11.30 a.m. and 2.00–5.00 p.m. on working days except Mondays.

Musée des Maquettes displays models depicting local rural life. *Opening times*: 2.00–5.30 p.m. during the summer season.

T hough famed for its dairy farms and apple orchards, Normandy is a land of mixed agriculture with wheat being an important staple.

East of Forges-les-Eaux

Take the D915 Gournay-en-Bray road out of Forges-les-Eaux. After the château on the right, 4 km (2½ miles), a turning to the left, the D41, leads to la Poterie and Saumont where there is a 16th–18th century church and chapel. Continuing along the D41 there is the 17th-century manor house of la Poterie between the railway and river. Beyond is Haussez and Courcelles, both with medieval churches.

Bear north-westwards for the views from the D61 and the village of Saint Michel-d'Halescourt, with its medieval church. Continue eastwards to the D135 and Mondesville and Grumesnil,

The solid, not too ostentatious residence of a village farmer-landowner.

with its 13th–18th century church. And then north to Villedieu, with its medieval church and farm which once belonged to the Knights Templar and subsequently to the Knights of Malta.

Return westwards via Haucourt, on the fringe of the Buttonhole of Bray and site of an old château owned by the powerful Mailly-Haucourt family, and to les Noyers with its medieval church.

From les Noyers re-cross the D135 and bear left at the D156. The old church of Longmesnil is along a turning to the right, and continue to Pommereux with its medieval church and remains of a home of the former Comte de la Poterie. Beyond, is la Bellière with its medieval church of Saint Laurent. It is a few kilometres from here back northwards to Forges-les-Eaux.

South of Forges-les-Eaux

Head south out of Forges-les-Eaux on the D921 and cut through the edge of the Forêt de Bray: a forest of 800 hectares (1,976 acres) which was eight times as big in the Middle Ages. Bear right after 3 km (2 miles) to take the D61, past the residence of Baron d'Haussez, minister of Charles X in 1830, and up to la Ferté, on the rim of the Buttonhole of Bray; there is a good view from up here. A fortification once stood on this hill; now, though, the village's proud historical sight is a 16th-century Henry IV house which was brought here and re-assembled in the late 1960s. The old church at neighbouring Saint Samson has been restored.

Continue westwards along the D61 past an 18th-century manor, and across the River Andelle to Rouvray-Catillon with the 17th-century château of Catillon. And then south along the D13 via Bethencourt, with its dovecote, to Sigy-en-Bray with its 12th-century church and abbey of Saint Martin. A few kilometres to the west is Bois-le-Borgne with its dovecote and chapel, while to the east, along the D41, is the canton centre of Argueil, with its church and 16th-century château. The "Road to Rouen" is to the south-west (see below).

However, Fry, with its church of Saint Martin, its manor and dovecote, is just to the south of Argueil. Continue southwards along the D128 via la Mystacrie and la Vente to Saint Laurent where there is a manor and the remains of a 12th-century priory founded by Huges de Gournay, an assistant to Henry Plantagenet. Beyond take the D57 left to Beauvoir-en-Lyons. From here, from the church of Saint Nicolas, there is a fine view to the east, with the cathedral of Beauvais visible on a clear day; the ruins of a fort are near the church.

North of Beauvoir-en-Lyons, the D1 and then the D241 lead through the Forêt de Mont Robert (121 m, 232 yd) to Hodeng with its 13th–16th century church and on to Hodenger, where the original church was built by English monks who came here after William's conquest of England. Beyond is the junction of la Vierge next to Mésangueville with its restored 13th-century church of Saint Nicolas. Northwards, roads lead via Saint Samson and la Poterie back to Forges-les-Eaux.

There are villages to the east of the Beauvoir-en-Lyons–Hodener line with heritage of local interest: Brémontier, with its church; Merval, with its dovecote; Bellozanne, with its abbey; Dampierre and Beauvreuil with their châteaux and churches. From Beauvreuil it is 7 km (4 miles) to Gournay-en-Bray.

Raconteur Par Excellence

Henri René Albert Guy de Maupassant, born in 1850 the son of a wealthy stockbroker, is Normandy's best-loved raconteur, storyteller. As an aspiring writer he mixed with the contemporary stars of literature, such as Flaubert and Zola, who at first thought of him rather discardingly as a nice enough, simple, athletic young chap rather than an author with a future. However, it was Guy de Maupassant's natural, unpretentious style which won him popularity. His straightforward tales—sketches of people and social situations he saw around him—give a very human insight into everyday life using Normandy as the stage.

Gournay-en-Bray

Gournay-en-Bray, on the River Epte and also on the traditional "Normandy–France" frontier, has long been a rival of Gisors 25 km (15 miles) downstream (*see* page 301). Gournay is another Bray cheese town and it was here, in 1850, that a farmer's wife created the Petit Suisse blend of cheese from the produce of her Swiss cow herd. Like Neufchâtel, Gournay is a dairy centre for the Paris market.

Also like Neufchâtel, Gournay suffered bombing in 1940; however, its 12th-century church of Saint Hildevert survived relatively unscathed. Interesting amongst its features are the carved statues of human figures: early examples of such work.

To the east of Gournay, roads cross over into the department of Oise, while, to the south, the D915 leads to Neuf-Marche, into the department of Eure and on to Gisors. Roads to the west, the main N31 and the D916, cut through the edges of Forêt de Lyons (*see* page. 314).

Roads to Rouen

The N13 passes through rich forest, and about 12 km (7 miles) out of Gisors there is a 40 m (131 ft) high beech, the *Hêtre de la Buonodière*, off the road to the left. Continue through la Feuillie, with its slim church spire, and la Haye, with the pretty D238 leading north to the Andelle valley, and on to châteaux at Vascoeuil (*see* page 314) and Martainville (*see* below) before the final stretch to Rouen city, a total of 50 km (31 miles) from Gournay.

South-west of Argueil and Fry is le Mesnil-Lieubray with its 16th-century château and dovecote. Continue through Nolleval west to Morville-sur-Andelle, with its church and dovecote, and the confluence of the Andelle and Heron. The château of Vascoeuil is a few kilometres downstream, while to the west, beyond Elbeuf-sur-Andelle and in neighbouring Crevon valley, is Ry.

Flaubert is said to have used Ry as the role model for "Yonville", the village in *Madame Bovary*. And Delphine Couturier, wife of the local Doctor Delamare, was apparently the inspiration behind Madame Bovary herself. Plaques commemorating Flaubert, and some of his characters and scenes from the book, have been placed around Ry. There is also a museum, the **Musée d'Automates**, in an 18th-century ciderie where *Madame Bovary* is further represented. *Opening times*: 11.00a.m. to 12.00 p.m. and 2.00–7.00 p.m. Saturdays to Mondays and holidays from Easter to November; open daily in July and August tel: 35-23-61-44.

About 6 km (4 miles) up the pretty Crevon valley is Blainville with its flamboyant church and remains of a medieval castle.

From Ry continue along the D13 the 4 km (2½ miles) to Martainville and its bulky brick and stone château built for Jacques le Pelletier, a wealthy Rouennese merchant, in 1485. Great towers are attached at the four corners of the château, and Gothic designs embellish window frames and the impressive chimney stacks which sprout

*N*ormans set out the chairs and eagerly await the arrival of the Tour de France through their town.

Following Rivers Upstream from Dieppe

strangely from the rooftops. Today, the grounds, which include a grand 16th-century pigeon coop and 18th-century barn, are open to the public. And within the building is the **Museum of the Traditions and Arts of Normandy**, where there are reconstructions of life in the last centuries with period furniture in rooms dominated by vast fireplaces and heavy timber beams. *Opening times*: 10.00 a.m. to 12.30 p.m. and 2.00–6.00 p.m. (5.00 p.m. during winter) daily, closed Tuesdays; tel: 35-23-44-70.

From Martainville, the N13 continues west for 10 km (6 miles) to Darnetal, a suburb of Rouen, before reaching Rouen itself.

The Eaulne Valley

Quai de Carénage leads across the inner ports east towards the D925. The D920 branches inland to Envermeu, with its Gothic church, and Londinières, with old statues in its church. Both market towns are on the River Eaulne. From Londinières, roads cross the river and cut through the predominantly beech Forêt de Hellet to the parallel valley of the Béthune. The D1314, the most significant of these roads, is the most direct route to Neufchâtel-en-Bray.

The Béthune Valley

Having crossed the inner ports by the way of quai du Carénage, bear right down rue J Brunel and pick up the D1 for the 36 km (22 miles) to Neufchâtel. The route follows alongside the River Béthune and roads off it lead into Bray farmlands and forest. A turning to the right, 5 km (3 miles) before Neufchâtel, runs down to the château at Mesnières (*see* page 104).

The Scie Valley

Avenue Gambetta leads south out of Dieppe to join the main N27 Rouen road.

The N27 meets the Scie at Saint Aubin-sur-Scie. Just to the south is the 16th–17th century **château of Miromesnil**. A grand avenue of beeches leads to the house with its imposing façade decorated with pilasters topped by urns. Guy de Maupassant is said to have been born here in 1850, though Fécamp was more likely his birthplace, and some of his effects are on display. Also on show is the memorabilia of various aristocrats who owned the place. There is a 16th-century chapel in the gardens with notable wood carvings. *Opening times*: 2.00–5.30 p.m. from May to mid-October daily except Tuesdays; tel: 35-04-40-30.

*T*he crisp red apple is better for eating than for brewing.

Apple Compensation

Without suitable land to grow vines the Normans are unable to produce their own wine. A grave deficiency and misfortune in a land such as France, one would imagine. Not so. For on this soil which bears no grape, there flourishes the apple. And where there is the apple there is, at least in Normandy, cider. This fermented apple juice—the *elixir vitae* of the Normans—comes fizzy, still, sweet, dry, home-made and factory-made, and traditionally accompanies most meals and all occasions.

There are minor châteaux a few kilometres further south at Aubermesnil and Ecorcheboeuf; the latter, on the Scie, has an old cider press, open to the public. Continue upstream along the D3. This is rich cider country and there is a **ciderie** at Anneville-sur-Scie. The cider produced here is marketed under the Duche de Longueville label, a brand commonly seen in shops around Normandy; visits to the plant are possible, and there is also a display of traditional equipment used in the making of cider. Hourly tours from 9.00–11.00 a.m. and 2.00–4.00 p.m. from mid-June to mid-September; tel: 35-83-32-76.

The canton centre of Longueville, with its church and ruins of a 12th–16th-century castle, is further upstream. The D3 continues south to Auffay. The apple orchards of Saint Crespin are to the right, while those of le Catelier, in the pretty countryside which divides the Scie and the Varenne, are to the left.

The Cideries Mignard are at Auffay and one of their labels is the *Cidre Jacques de Toy*. Cider is sold on the premises throughout the year and the plant can be visited during the cider-making season between 10 October and 10 December; tel: 35-32-81-01. Also at Auffay is the Jaquemart, a glockenspiel.

The D48 runs east of Auffay the 10 km (6 miles) to Belloncombre on the Varenne; a road off to its right leads to the Louis XIII château at Bosmelet, open on request from May to October; tel: 35-32-81-07, 4 km (2 miles) from Auffay.

The Scie peters out soon after Auffay, but the D3 continues all the way to Rouen. About halfway is Clères, site of a zoo wild-life park in the surrounds of the much built-upon medieval château. Creation of the **zoo** got under way in the 1920s and it features, particularly, waterfowl amongst its 450 species of birds. *Opening times*: daily from mid-March to late November; tel: 35-33-23-08. There is also the **Car and Military Museum**, where some of the earliest automobiles and bicycles are displayed; military vehicles are also on show. *Opening times*: daily through the year; tel: 35-33-23-02.

From Clères, the D3 continues its pretty route across the River Cailly and through Forêt Verte to the suburbs of Rouen.

Along the River Varenne

La Pénétrante leads south out of Dieppe in the direction of the small town of Arques-la-Bataille, 7 km (4 miles) out of Dieppe, with its 16th-

*T*he old woodmen's wigwams constructed from branches and twigs still provide shelter in the forests.

century church of Notre Dame. Nearby are the ruins of its castle, on a rocky spur with views over the river and forest beyond.

The war-battered castle of Arques was built originally by Duke William in the early part of the 11th century. Henry Beauclerk strengthened the fortifications in the 12th century, as did others during times of belligerence over the following centuries. However, the most famous contest was in 1589 when the newly crowned Henry IV, with 7,000 soldiers and a substantial arsenal secure in the castle, took on and beat the Duke of Mayenne, a seasoned campaigner with over three times the force.

The D154 runs along the west bank of the Arques. After 6 km (4 miles), a road leads up to le Bois-Robert from where there is a good view over the countryside. However, continuing along the river, the road crosses to the east bank at Torcy-le-Petit and Torcy-le-Grand, small villages straddling the Varenne, and proceeds to Muchedent, with its medieval church, and on to Bellencombre, Rosay and Saint Saëns on the upper reach of the river.

East of the Varenne spreads the **Forêt d'Eawy**, 6,600 hectares (16,300 acres) predominantly beech woodlands. Minor roads lead through the dense and lovely forest: for example, the D97, which can be picked up from either Bellencombre or Rosay, leads to Pommérval.

The main Neufchâtel–Rouen route, the N28, bypasses Saint Saëns. Alternatively, there are several cross-country routes to Rouen. One possibility is the D12 to the village of Cailly. From there you can follow the pretty course of the River Cailly into Rouen.

Alabaster Coast: Dieppe to Fécamp

Rue du Fg. de la Barre and the connecting D75 leads westwards up and out of Dieppe. Just out of town, and on the right of the road, is the **Museum of 19 August 1942**. On that date, two years before the Normandy Landings, a contingent of Canadian soldiers attempted to capture the Germans, Freya Radar which was situated here. The mission failed. The museum, in an old blockhouse, recounts the incidents and displays War memorabilia. *Opening times*: 10.00 a.m. to 12.00 p.m. and 2.00–6.00 p.m. daily from April to October.

Beyond, there is a view down over Pourville-sur-Mer. This was one of the places where the Canadians landed on that fateful August day; much damage was caused during the ensuing fighting. Resorts with more character lie further along the coast.

The road runs through Pourville-sur-Mer before turning inland and up to Varengeville-sur-Mer. The village itself is not by the sea, but there is a lane down to Port-l'Ailly, a short beach, with no facilities, wedged between cliffs.

On the left side of the road at Varengeville is the **Renaissance Manoir d'Ango**, which was built in the 1530s by Italian designers, with the quirkiness of their style, as a country home for Jean Ango. Here Ango, the great Dieppe shipping tycoon, would entertain the influential of the day. Lavish

parties there may have been, but the relative modesty of the manor, in comparison to the vast extravagant châteaux elsewhere, is part of its appeal; the dovecote, though, is unusually decorative. *Opening times*: 2.00–6.30 p.m. daily from April to 10 November and weekends and holidays during the rest of the year; tel: 35-85-12-08.

Villas, not unlike detached Surrey residences in England, lie surrounded by their neat gardens in the woods to the right of Varengeville. The picture is reminiscent of the English middle-class home counties. Indeed, the house at **Parc de Moustiers**, along one of the lanes, was built by the English architect Sir Edwin Lutyens in 1898. Its lovely 9 hectare (22 acre) garden is also more English than French and it is at its most spectacular in late spring when the splendid rhododendrons are in blossom. *Opening times*: 10.00 a.m. to 12.00 p.m. and 2.00–7.00 p.m. daily, except Sunday mornings, from Easter until All Saints, Day; tel: 35-85-13-19.

The unusual Manoir d'Ango at Varengeville is one of the few legacies of Jean Ango, Dieppe's great 16th-century shipping tycoon.

Temporary exhibitions are held in the house.

The lane proceeds to the small medieval church of Saint Valery which is spectacularly situated by the edge of the cliff with views along the coast towards Dieppe. Graves are crammed close together, and amongst the famous buried here is Cubist Georges Braque (1882–1963) whose stained glass, the Tree of Jesse, is in the church. Braque, who grew up in Le Havre, bought a house in Varengeville in 1930.

The D75 continues along the coast from Varengeville. A pretty detour to the right leads to Vasterival and the Ailly lighthouse and rejoins the main

road just before the small resort of Sainte Margueritte-sur-Mer with its medieval church. Beyond is the mouth of the Saone and the resort of Quiberville. The road following alongside the river is a picturesque route into the interior of Normandy. Along the way is the 15th-century manor of Gourel near Branchy; at Hermanville, on a tributary just to the east, there is the church of Saint Martin, while at Auppegard, a couple of kilometres beyond, there is the church of Saint Pierre.

The next of the small resorts is Saint Aubin-sur-Mer by the mouth of the Dun. Again the riverside road is a way

A graveyard with a view. The church at Varengeville, perched on the cliffs near Dieppe, has a splendid panorama of coast and sea.

*S*ir Edwin Lutyens, the architect of the British Raj who created the grandeur of New Delhi and designed such monuments as the Cenotaph in Whitehall, built a house in Varengeville which is today surrounded by Parc des Moustiers and its English gardens.

into the interior and 3 km (2 miles) upstream along the D237 is Bourg-Dun. The village's large and impressive church of Notre Dame is a mixture of fine examples of Romanesque, flamboyant and Renaissance workmanship. Veules-les-Roses is 7 km (4 miles) to the west along the D925; halfway along is la Chapelle-sur-Dune with its medieval lepers' refuge.

Typically hemmed in by cliffs, **Veules-les-Roses** is one of the more attractive mid-sized resorts along the Alabaster Coast. While the pebble beach is little different to others, the village behind is charming; its church of Saint Martin, dating from the 13th century, has interesting features, such as spiralling columns and a timber-framed roof.

The larger Saint Valery-en-Caux is 8 km (5 miles) on. This town is very much a port, mainly fishing, as well as a resort. The beach is flanked by the

*A*ugust in Veules-les-Roses: after a long lunch the family takes its siesta on the beach.

Falaise d'Amont on the east and the Falaise d'Aval on the west. Paths lead up to the summits of both. The latter is more spectacular and monuments up here are dedicated to the French 2nd Cavalry Division and the 51st Highland Division in commemoration of action during the retreat to Dunkirk in 1940.

The coast road, the D79, continues past the Paluel Nuclear Power Station to Veulettes-sur-Mer, another small resort. Legend has it that a large town once stood here at the mouth of the Durdent. But its citizens were sinful and so God raised the seas and drowned them in their streets. The town was lost to the ocean floor and subsequently the new Veulettes was built. Its medieval church, on a hill slope, is safe from any future heaven-inspired inundations. Some 9 km (5½ miles) inland, on the D10 along the pretty Durdent valley, is Cany-Barville.

An Excursion Inland from the Alabaster Coast

Just east of Veulettes-sur-Mer, the D10 leads up the Durdent valley, the old pilgrimage chapel at Janville is left at Paleul, for the 9 km (5½ miles) to the canton centre of Cany-Barville. Just beyond is the village of Barville, with its pretty church, and, on the Durdent, the château of Cany.

The mid-17th-century **château** was the extravagant work of François Mansart, the creator of Balleroy, to a commission by Pierre le Marinier. The drive spans the moat, the forecourt leads to the crescent-shaped double stairway. The red brick and stone façade is dominated by the generous number of windows. The interior is still furnished with 17th–18th-century pieces and the Flanders tapestries are well worth seeing. *Opening times*: 10.00 a.m. to 12.00 p.m. and 3.00–6.00 p.m. daily except Fridays and the fourth Sunday in July from July to October; tel: 35-97-70-32.

Continue up the Durdent. There are dovecotes along, or just off, the valley at Grainville-la-Teinturiere, at Bieurville near Bosville, at Mont Morel near le Hanouard, at Auffay (also with a 15th–16th château), at Petit-Veauville near the village of Hericourt-en-Caux.

Pigeons Lose Privileges in the Revolution

Dovecotes, *colombiers*, can be found throughout Normandy, but there is a significant concentration of them in this region.

The construction of dovecotes dates back to the Roman occupation and became the entitlement of the Norman feudal landlords during the medieval age. These stocky towers were usually round, though sometimes square or polygonal, and often had elaborately designed brick and stone work and, typically, tiled pepper-pot roofs. They were the splendid homes of pigeons. More importantly, they were symbols of the aristocrats and symbols which led to disquiet amongst their subjects. As soon as the peasant sowed the seed each season, the pigeon, protected by decree, swooped down to freely take its fill. Thus the poor suffered at the expense of the satiation of their lords' pets. There were protests, with demands for the closure of *les colombiers* during certain periods of the year and, with the arrival of the Revolution in 1789, the privilege of the dovecotes, and the immunity enjoyed by the pigeons, came to an end.

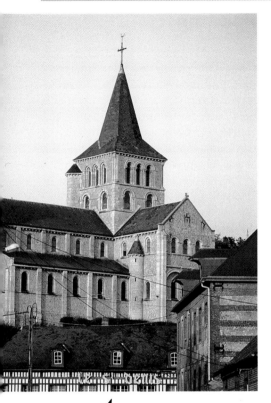

A large well-kept solid church dominates the village of Hericourt-en-Caux. It is a common sight in rural Normandy, though congregations are virtually non-existent.

Hericourt-en-Caux is a junction of minor roads. Eastwards, the cross-country D149 covers the sometimes monotonous flats of Pays de Caux. Near the town of Doudeville are châteaux at Galleville and le Fresnay. At 10 km (6 miles) to the south is Yvetot (*see* page 148).

Westwards, the D149x leads to Fauville-en-Caux via la Chaussée, with its dovecote, and on to Bolbec. However, from Frauville-en-Caux, continue along the D228 (there is another dovecote off to the right at Bennetot) to Benarville, with its old fort, and on the D99 to Bailleul.

The mid-16th century Renaissance **château of Bailleul**, the central portion cramped within chubby corner towers, was built by Bertrand de Bailleul. His grand ancestor was a knight alongside William at Hastings.

Subsequent forefathers founded a college at Oxford—Balliol—and ascended to the throne of Scotland in the 13th century. The château is set in neat gardens surrounded by thick forest. Masters hang in the period-furnished interior, and there is a relief of the *Adoration of the Magi* in the château chapel. *Opening times*: 10.00 a.m. to 12.00 p.m. and 2.00–6.00 p.m. daily from 15 June to 15 September; weekends and holidays from Easter to 15 June and 15 September to November. Tel: 35-27-81-39.

Left along the D10, just north of Bailleul, is Goderville and, 16 km (10 miles) beyond, Montivilliers and le Havre (*see* page 146). About 4 km (2.5 miles) to the right is the junction with the D28 which, to the left, leads a pretty course to Fécamp. However, continue east, and then north along the D17, to Valmont.

Another knight from Hastings, Robert d'Estouteville, who is featured in the Bayeux Tapestry, was head of another famous Normandy family. The Estoutevilles built their castle on the spur above the present village; the Romanesque keep survives, though other sections of the châteaux are Renaissance.

Valmont's **Benedictine abbey** was originally built in 1169, though it underwent drastic restoration in the 14th and 16th centuries. Today, the abbey is largely in disrepair, though the fine Lady Chapel has survived and is particularly impressive. There is a figure and the tomb of the draconian Nicolas d'Estouteville, who, according to local legend, founded the abbey as a penance for a catalogue of misdeeds. The abbey, a section of the **château** and the gardens, including the leisure park, can be visited. *Opening times for abbey*: 10.00 a.m. to 12.00 p.m. and 2.00–6.00 p.m. daily except Wednesdays and Sundays (open on Sundays from May to October); tel: 35-29-83-03. *And for the château*: 2.00–6.00 p.m. daily in July and August and during weekends and holidays from April to July and September to late October; tel: 35-29-84-36.

Eastwards from Valmont the D150 threads a pleasant path the 11 km (7 miles) to Fécamp, while westwards the D10 leads back to Cany-Barville via Gerponville with its old farm of Grandes Portes.

Beyond Veulettes, the coast road twists and dips a particularly scenic route across wooded valleys and down to tiny resorts before straightening out for the approach to Fécamp. Along the way is Sassetot-le-Mauconduit where the 18th-century château, and former residence of Empress Elizabeth of Austria in the late 19th century, is now a hotel, though the park can be visited (tel: 35-28-00-11). Above Fécamp is the chapel of Notre Dame-du-Salut, for centuries a place of worship for sailors and from where there are views along the coast.

Fécamp

Fécamp is the largest settlement between Dieppe and le Havre. It has its past, and the historical relics to prove it. However, it is a working town and port and, as a resort, it lacks the charm, intimacy and pleasantness of the smaller seaside places along the coast.

The Precious Blood is the origin of Fécamp's greatness. After the Crucifixion, drops of Christ's blood were put into a container which was wedged in a fig tree trunk and thrown out to sea. The trunk floated to Fécamp and the blood became the subject of veneration. A monastery was constructed in the mid-7th century to house this holy treasure. It was destroyed by the Vikings, but the blood survived.

Duke Richard I the Fearless founded la Trinité Abbey Church in the 10th century as a shrine for the Precious Blood. This was elaborated upon by his son, Duke Richard II the Good, who built a Benedictine abbey at the turn of the 11th century and housed in it an order of monks he brought from Dijon. The abbey prospered and, as word of its magnificence spread, the abbey, with its blood, became Normandy's main place of pilgrimage until attention turned to Mont-Saint-Michel *(see* page 252).

Not much remains of even the ruins of the early abbey. However, opposite the old site, a short walk east of the town centre along rue A Legros and rue A-P Leroux, is **la Trinité**. The church is huge: its 127 m- (416 ft-) length makes it one of the longest in France. It is not Richard I's structure, that was destroyed by lightning, and

Large, though otherwise not so imposing, the great church of la Trinité houses the holy Precious Blood which has drawn pilgrims to Fécamp for centuries.

the present church, or cathedral as it is now, dates back to the 12th–13th century with frequent additions added during later centuries.

The result is a hybrid of various styles from different ages; the same can be said of the collection of religious art contained within. The overall effect, though, is impressive, not least because the finest craftsmen of the times were employed to work on it. It is a monument of great significance, as la Trinité still serves as a mausoleum for Duke Richard I and his son, and a home for the Precious Blood which continues to draw pilgrims, especially on the Tuesday and Thursday after Trinity Sunday.

The Brother's Benedictine

Brother Bernardo Vincelli, a local Benedictine monk, used to gather flowers and herbs during his wanders over the hilltops around Fécamp, and these he would blend for his own amusement into a variety of potions. Then in 1510 he hit upon his magic formula—a "medicinal brew" for those of poor health compromising 27 ingredients—which warmed the heart, spun the head a little and made all who drank it rather happy. Vincelli's recipe was lost when the monastery library was ransacked during the French Revolution, but in 1863 a local historian discovered it written on a piece of paper and—realizing this monkish panacea would appeal to more than just the sick—initiated the mass production of the "Benedictine" liquor. The distillery and museum, recounting the history of Vincelli's concoction and including a display of the crucial 27 herbs, is housed in a 19th-century Gothic–Renaissance pile in downtown Fécamp.

A monk concocted "Benedictine" in the 16th century. Now the liqueur is mass-produced in this vast ornate Gothic–Renaissance-style 19th-century monument in downtown Fécamp. A "high church" distillery if ever there was one.

The **Municipal Museum** is on rue A Legros, 300 m (328 yd) on the way back to the centre. Ceramics—from Rouen, elsewhere in France and beyond—are a main exhibit, with babies' feeding bottles providing a curious display; an ivories room was opened in 1989. Fécamp has long been a fishing port of significance and it is France's cod city. Its trawlermen have traditionally caught their cod off Newfoundland and a variety of other fish from waters closer to home. Times, though, have changed and, as long-distance trawling has waned, Fécamp has started to trade in other merchandise. Fécamp the port is still documented in the museum. Traditional Normandy life, religious art, local paintings are amongst the other exhibits. *Opening times*: 10.00–11.30 a.m. and 2.00–5.00 p.m. daily except Tuesdays; tel: 35-28-31-99.

At the end of the road, and across place Charles de Gaulle, is place Saint Etienne with its restored 16th-century church, Saturday market and tourist office.

O ld man inspects modern art outside Benedictine distillery.

The Benedictine Distillery is ½km (⅓ mile) further east, a 19th-century neo-Gothic–Renaissance building. While Fécamp's cod fishing may only be known to Frenchmen, its "Benedictine" is famous universally.

The **museum** here describes the history of Benedictine; other galleries show pieces salvaged from the early abbeys of Fécamp, as well as collections of ivories, enamels, wrought iron and other special exhibitions. *Opening times*: 9.00–11.30 a.m. and 2.00–5.30 p.m. daily from early April to early October; closed at weekends during the rest of the year; tel: 05-28-00-06.

Rue du Domaine leads down from the distillery to quai Berigny and its harbour. To the right, deeper in town, are the busier wharves of Bassin Freycinet, while to the left is the yacht marina with the beach and the boulevard Albert Ier stretching to the left at the entrance to the sea.

On to Etretat

Follow rue des Forts eastwards from la Trinité for the D926, the main road towards Rouen. Just out of Fécamp, the D150 and the D28, off the D926 to the left and right respectively, offer the more pleasant riverside routes into the Pays de Caux.

As for the main coast road, the D940, it bends inland to les Loges, on the northern fringes of a pretty quarter of countryside, before turning seaward to Etretat. The minor road, the D211, which runs closer to the shore is preferable. It branches to the right off the D940 soon after Fécamp and leads down to the small resort of Yport and then up to Benouville. Opposite, offshore, is the Aiguille de

Belval, a rock pillar rising from the sea, which gives a hint of what to expect at Etretat just beyond.

Etretat

The coast's chalk cliffs reach their dramatic climax at Etretat. The small town lies in a hollow, indeed, below sea level, coddled between two chalk hills. Headlands flank its gently curved pebble beach like two massive sentinals. What makes these particular cliffs so extraordinary is the way Nature has, over eons, carved spectacular shapes out of the rock face.

To the right is Falaise d'Amont: a stairway, 180 steps gouged out of the stone, leads up the hill. Up at the top is the seafarers' chapel of Notre Dame-de-la-Garde, with the carved dolphin gargoyles, from where there are splendid views across Etretat to Falaise d'Aval. Nearby, the arrow-shaped Nungesser and Coli Memorial shoots skywards. It commemorates the two aviators who set off on 8 May 1927 to become the first to fly non-stop from Paris to New York. Locals waved and cheered them on from this cliff-top as they flew overhead. They were the last to see them. An exhibition recounts the events. From here, it is possible to walk the few kilometres along the cliff to Bénouville.

Falaise d'Aval to the left of the beach is more remarkable. Once again, a path leads to the top, past an old German gun house and the golf course, to the summit at 85 m (279 ft). Wind and sea have hollowed out a portion of rock to create a high-vaulted arch resembling, in profile, an elephant's trunk hanging in the water; standing guard is a 70 m (230 ft) rock pillar. Beyond is a small bay below the sheer cliffs and, at the far end, is another sculptured arch, the Manneporte, the "Great Gate". The views from these cliff-tops looking down over the rock shapes are magnificent.

It is possible to continue to walk to Cap d'Antifer and its lighthouse. It is another 2 km (1 mile) to the village of Bruneval, both it and Cap d'Antifer are linked to Etretat by a longer road route. General de Gaulle laid a monument here to commemorate a daring joint British parachutist–French Resistance operation which destroyed a vital German radar placement at this point on 27–28 February 1942. The mission was completed successfully, and the British escaped on naval vessels waiting offshore. It was one of the first such raids on the European mainland after the Dunkirk evacuations.

It is a further 3 km (2 miles) along a pretty road to Saint Jouin. Besides its beach the arm of a long mole stretches out into the Channel. This is the Havre–Antifer petroleum terminal, where supertankers off-load their oil which is then pumped along a 27 km (17 miles) pipeline to le Havre. It is a couple of kilometres from Saint Jouin to the D940, the main Etretat–le Havre road.

Accounts of Etretat by 19th-century writer Alphonse Karr attracted aristocrats, other writers, musicians and a host of artists to Etretat. The small fishing village was transformed into a fashionable resort. Nonetheless, the drama of the seascapes, the shapes of the rock, the light breaking through the clouds reflecting the brilliant white

*M*arie *Harel, mother of the Camembert.*

of the cliff faces continued to serve as inspiration. Monet painted Etretat; once a wave engulfed him and his easel and carried away with it an unfinished masterpiece! Matisse, Dufy, Braque were amongst the many other artists to work here. Guy de Maupassant wrote in Etretat and, in 1879, Offenbach took refuge in the resort to compose his "Tales of Hoffman"; both have streets named after them.

The town itself is still given over to tourism, but it is not as fashionable as it was in the past. With the creation of Deauville, the smart crowd began to take their custom down the coast, leaving behind the legends of their stay; many villas were to be knocked down during the German occupation. Neither does much remain of the fishing community, though some of the old boats have been specifically converted, as a tourist attraction, into the curious sheds known locally as *caloges*. Les Halles, the covered market, has been rebuilt as an arcade for shops. During the First World War it served as a hospital for the British and Allied troops. 549 were to die here from their wounds. The Romanesque church of Notre Dame, on the way into town, dates from the 11th century and is a surviving feature of Etretat's more ancient past.

Etretat to Le Havre

It is 30 km (18 miles) from Etretat to downtown le Havre along the D940. It is a relatively dull stretch. The D39 heading inland to Cirquetot gives an opportunity to see a bit of the countryside; writer André Gide (1859–1951) was married, lived for a while and is buried just to the north of the village

at neighbouring Cuverville. From Cirquetot, the D79 heads south towards Notre Dame Du Bec, with the castle of le Bec dating from the 12th century, and down the River Lézarde through Epouville, with Manéglise and its small Romanesque church off to the left, to Montivilliers on to the outskirts of le Havre (*see* page 156).

(*see* page 156)

Rouen

Like all great cities, Rouen breathes its past, present and future. The colonizing Romans absorbed the existing settlement and renamed it Rotomagos, but it was Rollo, ex-Viking and first of the Norman dukes, who, infusing the place with his enthusiasm, gave it the solid foundations for future greatness. Rollo was christened Robert in Rouen; he made the city the capital of his duchy and developed it as an inland port. Furthermore, as a bridging point across the Seine and splendidly placed on this river avenue between Paris and the sea, Rouen was bound to succeed.

Success attracts proportionate disaster, and a measure of a great city is its ability to resurrect itself after calamity. Indeed, destruction can clear the stage for fresh inspiration. Philippe-Auguste, having won the formidable Château Gaillard from John Lackland in 1204, moved downstream and captured Rouen after an 80-day siege. The Rouennais picked themselves up from the rubble and, under the French king, they and their city prospered.

Disaster was repeated in 1418, during the Hundred Years War, when Rouen, as the centre of Normandy

126

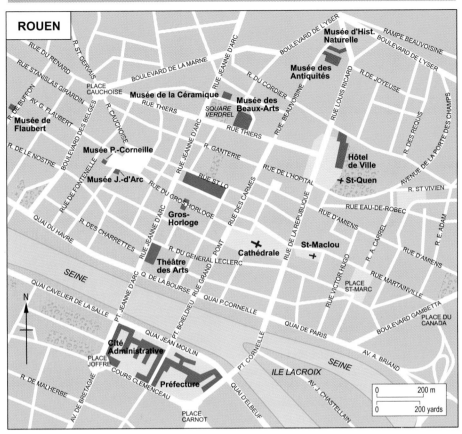

ROUEN

Musée d'Hist. Naturelle
RAMPE BEAUVOISINE
BOULEVARD DE L'YSER
RUE DU RENARD
R. ST GERVAIS
BOULEVARD DE L'YSER
RUE STANISLAS GIRARDIN
BOULEVARD DE LA MARNE
RUE JEANNE D'ARC
R. DU CORDIER
Musée des Antiquités
R. DE JOYEUSE
RUE LOUIS RICARD
PLACE CAUCHOISE
Musée de la Céramique
RUE THIERS
SQUARE VERDREL
Musée des Beaux-Arts
R. DES REQUIS
DE BUFFON
AV. G. FLAUBERT
R. CAUCHOISE
RUE BEAUVOISINE
AVENUE DE LA PORTE DES CHAMPS
Musée de Flaubert
BOULEVARD DES BELGES
RUE THIERS
R. DE LE NOSTRE
Musée P.-Corneille
RUE JEANNE D'ARC
R. GANTERIE
Hôtel de Ville
RUE DE L'HOPITAL
+ St-Ouen
R. ST VIVIEN
Musée J.-d'Arc
RUE DE FONTENELLE
RUE ST LO
RUE DES CARMES
RUE EAU-DE-ROBEC
R. E. ADAM
QUAI DU HAVRE
R. DES CHARRETTES
RUE DU GROS HORLOGE
Gros-Horloge
RUE DE LA REPUBLIQUE
RUE D'AMIENS
R. A. CARREL
RUE D'AMIENS
SEINE
R. DU GENERAL LECLERC
PONT
Cathédrale
St-Maclou
+
RUE MARTAINVILLE
Théâtre des Arts
Q. DE LA BOURSE
RUE GRAND
RUE JEANNE D'ARC
QUAI P.CORNEILLE
RUE VICTOR HUGO
PLACE ST-MARC
N
QUAI CAVELIER DE LA SALLE
PT. BOIELDIEU
PT. JEANNE D'ARC
QUAI JEAN MOULIN
PT. CORNEILLE
QUAI DE PARIS
BOULEVARD GAMBETTA
PLACE DU CANADA
Cité Administrative
PLACE JOFFRE
COURS CLEMENCEAU
SEINE
AV. A. BRIAND
R. DE MALHERBE
AV. DE BRETAGNE
Préfecture
QUAI D'ELBEUF
ILE LACROIX
AV. J. CHASTELLAIN
PLACE CARNOT

| 0 | 200 m |
| 0 | 200 yards |

T own plan of Rouen.

and the heart of the resistance, was ruthlessly besieged to the point of starvation by the English. Joan of Arc, the young peasant girl who saw a vision and rallied her countrymen against the old enemy, was captured at Compiègne and brought to Rouen for trial in 1430. Trumped-up charges of heresy levelled by a French court led to her death at the stake the following year. Twenty years on an investigative body headed by the pope declared Joan had been wrongly sentenced. Thus Joan gained official status as a martyr and, with her canonization and recognition as patron saint of France in 1920, she won posthumous compensation for the injustice. Rouen has adopted Joan as one of their own, and here she is remembered and revered.

In 1449, Charles VII recaptured Rouen from the English, and the place subsequently emerged as a flourishing Renaissance city. However, it was to suffer in the mid-16th century during the Wars of Religion when the Protestants ransacked the streets; and again, in 1685, when the revocation of the Edict of Nantes persuaded

127

Cast an eye above the modern shop windows and you enter the Rouen of a bygone time, a city that Flaubert, for example, would recognize from his childhood.

Rouen's Protestants to count their losses, quit the city and emigrate.

Rouen grew wealthy on textiles in the 18th century and, as it did so, it attracted other industry as well as the arts and the fashionable. It evolved as a rich and cultured city.

Rouen, like so many Normandy towns and cities, suffered its severest damage during the bombings of World War II. Post-War reconstruction, notably the modern port (the fifth busiest in France) and industrial facilities, has enabled Rouen to keep abreast of the times. There is an air of prosperity in the city, and of youth, thanks partly to the university, and feeling is as much for the future as it is for the past. One expects, or at least hopes for, Normandy, a province with such a heritage of history, the arts and commerce, to have a great city which reflects its richness. Normandy has such a city in Rouen.

Rouen straddles a curve of the Seine. The downtown old quarter of the city is on the north side, though it is away from the river. The best places to appreciate the Seine are from above, from the chalk spurs flanking the city. Arriving from the east, there are viewpoints looking down over the Seine and Rouen from the suburbs of Bonsecours, from the basilica, and Côte Sainte Catherine. On the west side of the city, the views are from Canteleu.

Though much of Rouen was razed during the War, enough did survive in reasonable enough condition to be restored. The old quarter, characterized by narrow lanes lined with 15th–18th century half-timbered houses, remains most intact around the magnificent cathedral of Notre Dame.

However, survivors of the past are scattered in the lively downtown beyond the shadows of the cathedral.

Most of what is worth seeing in Rouen can, and should, be covered on foot (many streets are pedestrianized; there are central multi-storey car parks). The place du Vieux-Marché is a suitable starting point for a tour.

The place, at the western end of the centre, has always been very much a public square where gatherings were held and executions conducted. This was where Joan of Arc was burnt in the summer of 1431. The square had to be re-created after the War and today it is dominated by the modern grey, slate-covered church of Joan of Arc and the 20 metre (65 ft) Cross of the Rehabilitation which honour Joan, Rouen's and France's symbol of defiance and truth. Like most daring designs, the bizarre-shaped church courted controversy when it was completed in 1979, but then it is fitting that

Joan of Arc is represented by something stronger than the conventional. The beauty of the church's interior is easier to appreciate, and is all the finer for the inclusion of panes of 16th-century stained glass. There is also a statue of Joan by the church and a museum, in the cellar of a house on the south side of the place, provides her biography through various displays.

Several 16th–18th-century houses, some restaurants, line much of the place and this makes the centrepiece appear all the more incongruous. Just to the west, down rue de la Pie, is **Museum Corneille** in the house where Pierre Corneille (1606–84) was born and where he lived most of his life. Here the distinguished writer is remembered. Half a kilometre further west, on rue Lecat, is the house where Gustave Flaubert was born in 1821. His father was a surgeon and this was his official residence; on display are family mementoes and early 19th-century surgical implements. *Opening*

*N*arrow rue Gros Horloge, the historic thread through the heart of Rouen, links place du Vieux Marché with cathédrale Notre Dame.

Father of Drama

Pierre Corneille, the son of a lawyer and himself a graduate of law, gained his reputation as a dramatist with the support of Richelieu. He drew his characters from classical mythology and history and sought the tragedy within the person rather than that imposed by exterior forces. Corneille is often described as the forerunner of modern French drama. His popular, fast-moving *Le Cid* (1637)—an adaption of Guillen de Castro's *Mocedades del Cid*—did not please his patron as it did not comply with the "rules" of the French Academy, and subsequently Corneille faded from the public eye.

times: there are guided tours around both the Corneille and Flaubert museums; the former is closed on Tuesday and Wednesday mornings, while the latter is closed on Sundays and Mondays.

South of the place du Vieux-Marché, on the place de la Pucelle d'Orléans, is Hôtel de Bourgtheroulde, one of Rouen's grand ornate mansions rather than the more typical half-timbered houses, which was built early in the 16th century. This was the time of transition, from Gothic–flamboyant to Renaissance, and the styles of design can be clearly identified in the architecture of the building.

Walk east of place du Vieux-Marché and you enter rue du Gros-Horloge, a pedestrian lane, Rouen's "High Street", which links place du Vieux-Marché to place de la Cathédrale. The silhouette of the spires of Rouen's great cathedral, the goal at the end of the road, can be seen at the far end.

Rue du Gros-Horloge is today, as it was in the past, Rouen's busy shopping street. The crowds, the bustle, the hawkers pack the long, narrow thoroughfare providing a modern version of a medieval scene. The old timber-framed houses line parts of the way and further evoke the past. The Gros-Horloge, the Great Clock, itself is supported by an arch which spans the road.

Originally it was at the top of the adjoining belfry. But people got fed up with craning their necks skywards and, in response to demands, it was removed to its present place in 1527. Since then the splendid golden Renaissance dial has become the conspicuous symbol of the city and a popular rendezvous in the heart of Rouen. It still chimes 9 p.m., once the hour of the curfew. The belfry, dating from the 14th century, can be visited, and a ticket bought here also permits entry to the Museum of Fine Arts and le Secq des Tournelles (see page 65). *Opening times*: daily except Tuesday and Wednesday mornings from Palm

The 16th century one-armed Gros-Horloge, a typically extravagant Renaissance timepiece, has long been the symbolic —and near enough actual— centre of Rouen.

Sunday to the second Sunday in September. A collection of ancient clocks and bells are on display and there is a fine view from the belfry across the city.

From the Gros-Horloge, it is 200 m (124 yd) to the place de la Cathédrale and the cathedral of **Notre Dame**, which is one of the world's great Gothic constructions.

The place is dominated by the imposing west front, a study which obsessed Monet as he strove to capture it on canvas in its many lights. The monument has absorbed more artistic talent than any other in Normandy. Masons spent the Middle Ages, from 1145 to 1514, building the cathedral; and since then craftsmen have been adding to and restoring the original structure constantly. Even now a team is painstakingly repairing the damage caused during the last War.

The Saint Romanus Tower on the left of the west façade dates from the 12th century and has a 9,500 kg (20,904 lb) bell. The 16th-century Butter Tower, on the right, was provided for by the local bourgeoisie and has a 55-bell carillon. Its sponsors felt they could not forego the rich Normandy dairy products for Lent; so they made their offer to the church in return for the lifting of the dietary sanctions during this traditional period of fasting.

The Saint John and Saint Stephen doorways flank the central doorway, on the left and right respectively, and depict the martyrdom of the two saints. The central doorway is the work of Roulland le Roux who was the cathedral's master craftsmen in the early 16th century; its tympanum, destroyed and restored in the 17th century, depicts the Tree of Jesse.

Inside, the early Gothic nave is magnificent for its size, strength and simplicity. The lantern tower soars to a remarkable 51 m (167 ft). Its spire, such a feature on the Rouen skyline, rises to 151 m (495 ft) making it the tallest in France. Made of cast iron it replaced the 16th-century spire in 1876. On the left side of the transept is the ornate Booksellers' Stairway leading to a balcony; the Booksellers' Doorway leads out into the Booksellers' Court, so-called because booksellers used to gather here.

Again, the beauty of the 13th-century chancel lies in its cool simplicity of design. The stained glass spans seven centuries, with 13th-century glass in the ambulatory and modern Max Ingrand glass in the Joan of Arc chapel. Next to the chapel, the decorated 14th-century Calende Doorway, flanked by 13th-century towers, leads out to the southern side of the cathedral.

Appropriately, the cathedral houses the tombs of some of Normandy's great historical figures: Rollo, William Longsword, Richard the Lionheart are amongst those buried here. The casket containing the heart of France's Charles V was discovered in the crypt during excavations in the 1940s. The most ornate sepulchre is the tomb of the cardinals of Amboise, fashioned in 1515 according to a Roulland le Roux design; the two prominent cardinals, George I and George II, uncle and nephew, are shown kneeling in obeisance to the Christian virtues which are represented in the panels of the tomb.

Also of particular note here in the Lady Chapel is Jean Goujon's alabaster and black marble tomb of Louis de Brézé, the Seneschal of Normandy in the early 16th century, who is represented as the warrior of truth upon his mount. Diane de Poitiers, his widow and later famous as the mistress of Henri II, is featured mourning her late husband.

The tourist office, operating from a fine Roulland le Roux Renaissance house in place de la Cathédrale, organizes guided tours around the cathedral and the old quarter.

Starting from the Saint Romanus Tower, walk down the alley into rue Saint Romain, which runs along the north side of the cathedral to the church of Saint Maclou. This is Rouen's finest "old", Renaissance to 18th-century, street. The core of the downtown shopping quarter spreads into the area to the left. Just beyond Notre Dame is the 15th-century archbishop's palace where Joan of Arc was tried. Across the main rue de la République is place Barthélémy and the delightful church of Saint Maclou, an outstanding example of Gothic–flamboyant architecture built between 1437 and 1520, which has also undergone a long restoration programme after the bombings of 1944. The splendid carved doors are attributed at Jean Gujon, one of the great Renaissance craftsmen.

Rue Martainville leads along the north side of the church. Here, there are the characteristic lop-sided half-timbered houses, some have been converted into good local restaurants. Off to the left, 184–186 Rue Martainville, is the Aître Saint Maclou, a cloister and medieval plague cemetery built in the early 16th century. Death is depicted in the macabre, though sometimes comical-looking, carvings of skulls and bones. The bombs somehow spared the cloister; today, its buildings are used by the School of Fine Arts.

Double back to rue Damiette which leads off from the north-west corner of Saint Maclou. This is another of Rouen's famous old "half-timbered streets". The narrow rue Damiette with its antique shops runs north to Place Du Lt Aubert, a pleasant terminus for dark lanes. The district to the right, along rue Eau-de-Robec, was once a bourgeoise quarter which degenerated into an area of ill repute. Redevelopment has pulled it from its unsalubrious past and the waters of the Robec, which have long flowed along the street, have been incorporated into the

A grey and white cat blends in well with the stone- and wood-work of the Aître Saint Maclou, Rouen's medieval plague cemetery.

Rouen's magnificent Saint Ouen rises above the half-timbered houses of rue Saint Roman.

new design. The interesting Museum of Education, housed in a former brothel at the end of rue Eau-de-Robec, gives us an idea of schooling in the past. *Opening times*: afternoons except Sundays and Mondays.

From place du Lt Aubert, it is a short walk northwards to the huge Gothic church of **Saint Ouen**. Work on this, Rouen's other great church, commenced in 1318 and continued, sometimes sporadically, for nearly 200 years. This was the site of one of Normandy's first abbeys; its destruction and the fall of later churches cleared the way for the building of the present Saint Ouen. Approaching from the south side, you enter through the Marmouset Doorway with its fine gable and statues of saints and kings above. The interior is rated as one of the most perfectly proportioned examples of Gothic architecture in the country. Splendid are the windows, impressive in size and decorated with 14th-century stained glass; the exception is Max Ingrand's contemporary glass depicting the Crucifixion. Here too, in Saint Ouen, is one of France's largest organs. Gardens enclose the east end of the church, and from here the exquisite flying buttresses are best appreciated.

On the other side of Saint Ouen is place General de Gaulle and the Hôtel de Ville. The main rue Louis Ricard leads north, passing the Lycée Corneille—which boasts Corneille, Flaubert, Maupassant amongst its illustrious alumni—to Saint Marie Fountain where it bifurcates. On the left side of the road, opposite the fountain, are gardens and a 17th-century convent which now houses the **Musée des Antiquities**. The museum has a rich and varied collection: Roman remains from Lillebonne, Normandy's premier Roman site, including the celebrated mosaic of Apollo chasing Daphne; medieval religious art, some brought across the Channel by the English during their occupation; a range of other crafts including ivories, enamels, bronzes, glassware, furniture and tapestries from home and abroad which all help to make the museum the best-endowed of its kind in Normandy. *Opening times*: 10.00 a.m. to 12.00 p.m. and 2.00–5.00 p.m. daily except Wednesdays; tel: 35-98-55-10.

Next door is the **Museum of Natural History** which presents Normandy's flora and fauna, as well as its ethnography. *Opening times*: same hours as the Museum of Antiquities, though its days of closure are Mondays, Tuesdays and Sunday mornings. From here, either head south along rue Beauvoisine, turning right along rue Beffroy for the Museum of Fine Arts, or return to place General de Gaulle.

The busy rue Thiers leads westwards from the place General de Gaulle to the Museum of Fine Arts (Musée des Beaux Arts). Alternatively, take the parallel rue de l'Hôpital, from opposite Saint Ouen, which leads into rue Ganterie, with its shops and half-timbered houses, and turn right at allée Delacroix for the museum.

The **Museum of Fine Arts** houses the works of Normandy's artists such as Gericault and Poussin; works by artists inspired by Normandy, such as Monet, there is one of his paintings of Rouen cathedral, and other Impressionists; works portraying distinguished Normans, notably the portraits by Jacques-Emile Blanche (1861–1942) of his contemporaries in the literary field.

The local theme is one dimension of the museum. Also displayed are French, Dutch, Flemish, Spanish and Italian masters, including works by Caravaggio, Velazquez, Corot, Teniers and Ingres. Indeed, the museum's outstanding prize is the *Virgin and the Saints* an altarpiece painted by Gerard David in 1523. Furthermore, the museum's large collection shows the progression of trends from 16th-century religious art, through Impressionism to the Dada–Surrealism movement, with examples of works by Marcel Duchamp and others, and works by contemporary artists. *Opening times*: 10.30 a.m. to 12.00 p.m. and 2.00–6.00 p.m. daily except Tuesday and Wednesday mornings; tel: 35-71-28-40. A multiple ticket entitles entry to the belfry (*beffroi*) by the Gros-Horloge (*see* page 131) and the Museum of Wrought Iron (le Secq des Tournelles).

Beyond the Museum of Fine Arts, on rue Faucon on the northern side of square Verdrel, is a 17th-century house which is now the home of the **Museum**

As in towns and cities throughout the country, Rouen has its patches of dust where the good citizens can play boules, the national pastime.

Though much restored, Rouen's Law Courts reveal Renaissance decor at its richest.

of Ceramics. Rouen is famous for its ceramics and in particular for that of the Rouen Faïence.

Some 6,000 pieces of ceramics, local, French and foreign, are exhibited and include the ornate Louis XIV and Louis XV Rouen china. *Opening times*: the same as the Museum of Fine Arts; tel: 35-07-31-74.

Tour Jeanne d'Arc, a *donjon* built by Philippe-Auguste in 1204, is in rue du Donjon, a couple of streets north of the Museum of Ceramics. Here Joan of Arc was detained and tortured prior

Bourgeois Tableware

The art and popularity of *faïence*—ceramics made of compound clay glazed with a tin-based enamel—flourished in Rouen between the 16th and 18th centuries. The perfect blend of Normandy earth—a heavy red clay with a light sandy soil—which forms the basis of Rouen *faïence* undergoes rigorous preparation before shaping and firing. These were the ceramics—elaborate crockery and other tableware typically with pastoral scenes painted in blue, green, yellow, red upon white backgrounds—found in the solid bourgeois and aristocratic households.

to her immolation; an account of this episode and history of the tower is on display. *Opening times*: 10.00 a.m. to 12.00 p.m. and 2.00–5.00 p.m. closed Wednesdays; tel: 35-98-55-10.

Le Secq des Tournelles is in the former church of Saint Laurent behind the Museum of Fine Arts. It displays an extraordinary and extensive collection of metal work, some 12,000 pieces, which dates from the 3rd century and includes locks and keys, buckles, cutlery, decorative railings, statues, signs, tools and much, much more. *Opening times*: the same as the Museum of Fine Arts.

Next to le Secq des Tournelles is the 15th-century church of Saint Godard with its fine stained glass.

Roads south of this cluster of museums lead back to rue du Gros-Horloge. Take allée Delacroix and follow its continuation to the Palais de Justice. Go through its gateway into the large courtyard. The Renaissance building, once the House of the Exchequer, has an exquisitely crafted, and much restored, façade. Beyond is the rue aux Juifs, so-called because this was the site of a medieval synagogue. Rue du Gros-Horloge is a couple of minutes' further on. Rouen's great clock is just to the right: continue down the road for place du Vieux-Marché; to the left is the cathedral.

Elbeuf and Environs

Rouen south of the Seine, still part of the Seine-Maritime department, is contained within a tight meander. And beyond the city, stretched along the curves of the southern bank of the Seine, is the industry which gives Rouen much of its present *raison d'être*. What has not been engulfed by urban and factory developments, notably the Forêt du Rouvray and the Forêt de la Londe, has been slashed by autoroute and route national.

All the same, it is not all grime. Follow quai d'Elbeuf, on Rouen's south bank, up the river and join the D18, and continue through the suburbs and along a pretty reach of the river to Roches d'Orival; there is a path up to the rocks from where there is a view over the Seine. The road continues along the chalk face to Orival, with its 15th-century church, and on to the old textile centre of Elbeuf, which is now dominated by the more modern 20th-century industries. However, the churches of Saint Jean and Saint Etienne, Gothic and Flamboyant respectively, are of note, not least for their 16th-century stained-glass windows. Elbeuf's **Natural History Museum**, with exhibits from a wide range of nature including pieces of rock and stuffed animals, also has displays relating to local history. *Opening times*: Wednesday and Saturday afternoons; tel: 35-81-00-99. Roads continue into the department of Eure.

However, double back and after Orival the D64 bears left through forest across the neck of the meander and dips under the autoroute to the Château of Robert-le-Diable. The origins of the castle date back to the 11th century, though, typically, it was frequently subjected to destruction and reconstruction over the centuries. The origins of its name are less clear, though "le Diable", "the Terrible", is said to be a reference to Robert the Magnificent, William the Conqueror's father. Today, the ruins are most impressive for their dramatic location high above the bend in the river and for its views along the Seine. Unfortunately, traffic thunders along the autoroute behind and the south bank of

Château de Robert-le-Diable, the silent ruined castle of William the Conqueror's father, stands between time. Below, flows the Seine, an ancient avenue; behind, cuts the autoroute to Paris.

the Seine is dominated by a car factory and other plants. The castle houses the **Viking Museum**, there is a replica of a *drakkar* longboat, and retraces the Viking–Norman history. *Opening times*: daily from March to November; tel: 35-23-81-10.

Descending through the forest from the château's perch, there is Moulineaux—and its medieval church with 13th-century stained glass—to the right and la Bouille down to the left by the river.

La Bouille, which can be reached by various roads from downtown Rouen, is on a scenic bend of the Seine and is at the division between the urban sprawl and the countryside, with the feeling being more for the latter than for the former. Indeed, the Rouennais have long been coming to the pretty village for a day's outing or for a weekend lunch, and restaurants maintain a high standard to keep their clientele. Monet, too, would spend time here and maybe Flaubert, who lived up the river at Croisset, used to take a break at la Bouille. A ferry links la Bouille with Sahurs on the far bank, from where the road continues downstream or back, through Croisset, to Rouen.

Proceeding down the Seine on this, the south side, the next meander is hardly populated at all, and the D64 leads to a point opposite Duclair; there is a ferry. Alternatively, the D265 cuts across the meander's neck to Yville-sur-Seine, with its 18th-century château. There is a road which leads a couple of kilometres up-river to the ferry point for la Mesnil-sous-Jumièges. The next meander contains the Forêt de Brotonne.

La Route des Abbayes: Rouen to Jumièges

Monasticism developed in France in the 6th century and monks, with a sensible eye for serene beauty, selected the scenic banks of the Seine as their home. The abbeys they built became the centres of learning and religion and prosperous pillars of the community. Then the Vikings arrived in the 9th century. In their *drakkars* (longboats) they ventured up the Seine, their avenue of pillage, ransacking the shores as they pushed ever deeper into France. The monks abandoned their monasteries, their riches and even their lives to the barbarian sword from the north. Only after Rollo the Viking had discarded brute force and paganism in favour of settlement and Christianity in AD 911 did the ravages cease and did the monks re-emerge to practice their faith openly.

A route along the right bank, the Route of Abbeys, follows the serpentine curves of the lower Seine from Rouen to le Havre.

Heading westwards out of Rouen take quai du Havre, along the north bank of the Seine, which links with quai G Boulet, which, in turn, leads to the D982. The road ascends to Canteleu, with its 18th-century château and views down over the Rouen and the river, and then cuts through Forêt de Roumare to Saint Martin-de-Boscherville. Alternatively, bear left before Canteleu along the riverside D51 for Croisset and Pavillon Flaubert.

In 1843, 22-year-old Gustave Flaubert was struck by a mystery nervous attack. He gladly abandoned his law studies in Paris and "retired" to an estate bought by his doctor father at Croisset. Here, in virtual solitude, he dedicated his life to writing, producing such works as *Madame Bovary*. The house was sold after his death in 1880, though, in 1905, the "Friends of Gustave Flaubert" managed to buy the *pavilion* which was on the edge of the residence's grounds. Today, this is a museum housing the effects of Flaubert the writer. *Opening times*: 10.00 a.m. to 12.00 p.m. and 2.00–5.00 p.m. daily except Tuesday and Wednesday mornings; tel: 35-36-43-91.

The road follows the bend of the river downstream to Val-de-la-Haye, where there is a monument commemorating the return of Napoleon's corpse to France, and to Sahurs on a pretty stretch of the river opposite la Bouille, a ferry point, on the far bank. Childless Anne of Austria, wife of Louis XIII, prayed at Sahurs' chapel of Marbeuf and promised to bequeath a silver statue should she be blessed with a baby. She subsequently gave birth to Louis XIV, le Roi Soleil, and so she sent a figure, the exact weight of the newborn heir to the throne, to the chapel. The statue was lost, and possibly melted down, during the Revolution.

Downstream 4 km (2½ miles) is Saint Pierre-de-Manneville and the Manoir de Villers; and a further 3 km (2 miles) on, at Quevillon, is the 17th-century château of la Riviere-Bourdet, which is locally dubbed the "Versailles of Normandy". A few kilometres beyond this is the abbey church of Saint Georges at Saint Martin-de-Boscherville.

The bland façade of Saint Georges hides one of the finest Romanesque churches in Normandy. Enter and, on a clear day, one is struck by the light pouring through the windows which further brightens the interior as it reflects from the clean white stone. The eight bays lining the nave are classic Romanesque and their purity, enhanced by the relative lack of incongruous, obtrusive later additions to the church, give the place a rare and refreshing unity and crispness.

The Monastery

The plan of the monastery is generally standard. In the centre is the square cloister—a courtyard enclosed by four galleries; running along one side of the cloister is the abbey church; along another side are rooms such as the chapter house and other daytime functional quarters; the refectory constitutes another side, and the dormitories or cells make the fourth side.

In the latter half of the 11th century, Raoul de Tancerville, chamberlain to Duke William, founded an abbey at Saint Martin-de-Boscherville on the site of old pagan temples. It, and its church of Saint Georges, was enlarged and developed by his son in the early 12th century, who replaced his father's Saint Augustine monks with a group from the Saint Evroult Benedictine order. A piece of black marble near the altar marks the grave of Antoine, the 19th abbot, who died in 1535. Saint Georges thrived, but was never one of the large or great monasteries. This was fortunate, for the church was later overlooked by the destructive forces of the Revolution after locals hastily reclassified it as their village parish

Lightness, purity, serenity, the simple emotions felt in the empty abbey church at Saint Martin-de-Boscherville.

church of Saint Martin. The monks were ousted, though, and little was left of the abbey itself. Remains of the **12th-century chapter house** can be visited, and it is most notable for its elaborate arches adorned with carvings. *Opening times* to the abbey grounds: 10.00 a.m. to 12.00 p.m. and 2.30–6.30 p.m. daily except Tuesdays from April to October; tel: 35-32-01-32. The church itself is public and can be visited throughout the year free of charge.

Rejoining the D982, continue to Duclair, with its 12th-century church of Saint Denis—with its Gallo-Roman columns, medieval statues from Jumièges and Max Ingrand stained glass—and its reputation for tasty ducks. Then bear left, following the meander, along the D65, via le Mesnil-sous-Jumièges and its 13th-century manor, to Jumièges.

The D43 leads 10 km (6½ miles) north to Barentin, an industrial town up the River Austreberthe. The valley is spanned by a brick viaduct, a bridge for the Paris–le Havre railway. Along with Barentin's industry, there is its art. This ranges from sculpture by Rodin to a 14 m (46 ft) polystyrene replica of the Statue of Liberty which found a home here after the filming of *Le Cerveau*.

Jumièges

The skeletal remains of the great abbey at Jemièges are sufficiently extensive for one to appreciate the awesome size of the structures which once stood here. The impact of the place may be all the more spectacular for being ruins: walls, towers, arches seem to soar to greater heights without roofs to distract from the impressive elevation. Enough of the ground plan is visible, and by allowing the mind's eye to fill in the gaps, one develops a picture of this magnificent medieval abbey.

Caneton Rouennais

The ducklings used by chefs in *caneton Rouennais,* Rouen's celebrated dish, are traditionally reared in Duclair. They are a special breed—a hybrid of wild and domestic duck—and they suffer their unfortunate fate through strangulation or suffocation so that the blood is retained to enhance the flavour of the meat (hence its other name *canard au sang*). From slaughterhouse to kitchen where the duck is roasted, stuffed with its liver and squeezed of its blood—which is then used in the sauce—garnished, decorated and finally proudly presented as Rouen's prize palate pleaser.

The earliest monastery at Jumièges was built in AD 654 by Saint Philbert. It was destroyed effectively over a period of 10 years in the mid-9th century by the invading Vikings. Seventy-five years later, and some 15 years after the Nordic pagans had undergone their remarkable transformation to become Christ-worshipping Norman citizens, Duke William Longsword reconstructed the abbey and housed within it a group of Benedictine monks. During the following century, Jumièges gained prominence and several of its order secured senior posts across the Channel. Abbot Robert, for example, won the confidence of Edward the Confessor and was chosen as Archbishop of Canterbury.

The Revolution and its aftermath at the turn of the 19th century heralded the final collapse of the abbey after

A view of the transept and nave of the church of Notre Dame. A magnificent skeleton of one of Christendom's great medieval abbeys.

centuries of prosperity. The last of the monks were more or less evicted, and the man who bought the abbey, fired by a mentality as damnable as that of the Vikings, set about pulling the place apart for its stone building blocks.

What remains are sections of the church of Notre Dame including its façade, flanked by 43 m (141 ft) high towers; the immense nave, enclosed by 27 m (89 ft) high walls and part of the transept supporting a watch-tower. Adjoining it at its southern end is the old storeroom which leads into an area once occupied by the cloisters at the centre of which is an old yew tree. At the far end are the remnants of the sacristy, the chapter house, the entrance to the ruined 10th-century church of Saint Pierre and the Charles VII passage which linked Notre Dame to the smaller Saint Pierre.

The **abbey complex** is set in a park; at the eastern end is the neat 17th-century abbey house and, in contrast to the churches, it is very much intact and sports a fine new roof. *Opening times* of the abbey: 9.00 a.m. to 6.30 p.m. daily from 15 June to 15 September; 9.00 a.m. to 12.00 p.m. and 2.00–5.00 p.m. weekdays except 1 May and closing at 12.30 p.m. and 6.00 p.m. at weekends from 1 April to 14 June and 16 September to 30 October; 10.00 a.m. to 12.00 p.m. and 2.00–4.00 p.m. weekdays, except national holidays, and closing at 1.00 p.m. and 5.00 p.m. at the weekends from November to April; tel: 35-37-24-02.

The parish church of Saint Valentin was built in the 11th–12th centuries by the monks, though the choir and large ambulatory were added in the 16th century when it was proposed that this would become the new abbey church; subsequently, religious pieces from Notre Dame were brought to Saint Valentin where they remain today.

Jumièges to Saint Wandrille

A few kilometres north of Jumièges is Yainville, with its medieval church, and, back on the D982, the old shipyard town of le Trait and, 5 km (3 miles) on, the abbey of Saint Wandrille off to the right.

Alternatively, there is the route via the Forêt de Brotonne: Port Jumièges, a ferry point, lies on the opposite bank of the river from the Abbey of Jumièges; nearby, there is good view across to the towers of the abbey. Enclosed within the meander, which is part of the Seine-Maritime department and Parc Régional de Brotonne, is the Forêt de Brotonne. Besides the D313, not far from Port Jumièges, is the Chêne à la Cuve, the curious "four-trunked oak" and, a walk beyond, there is also a famous beech. Minor roads and footpaths lead deeper

---

"Parc Regional de Brotonne"
Straddling the beautiful lower meanders of the Seine, Parc Regional de Brotonne covers 40,000 hectares (98,800 acres) in the departments of Seine-Maritime and Eure. The park was conceived in the mid-1970s with the aim of protecting—and presenting—the nature and traditions within the area it encompasses. Much of the park is wooded, notably by the Brotonne Forest on the south bank, and contains the abbeys of Jumièges and Saint Wandrille, the town of Caudebec-en-Caux, château Etelan, the Mannevilles Nature Reserve and numerous walks, nature trails, craft and folklore museums.

into the thick forest. The D313 leads northwards towards Pont de Brotonne, a 1,280 m (4,200 ft) bridge which was opened in 1977 and spans the Seine 50 m (164 ft) above the waters. Back on the north bank, and to the right of the bridge is Saint Wandrille.

Saint Wandrille

Young Count Wandrille and his bride received the call of God on their wedding day and, turning their backs on the world, they immersed themselves in solitude and prayer. And in AD 649, Wandrille, who was later canonized, founded the monastery which new bears his name here in the lovely Fontenelle valley a couple of kilometres from the Seine.

Wandrille's monastery, originally known as the Abbey of Fontenelle, experienced a history similar to that of the Jumièges abbey. A renowned seat of learning and residence for scholars, where the classic *Epic of the Abbots of Fontenelle* was written in 831, the monastery was razed by the Vikings in the mid-9th century only to be resurrected by Norman dukes in the 10th century. The respect, or at least tolerance, the Benedictine monks and their religion received from the outside secular world for long periods over the following centuries, was particularly badly damaged by the Revolution.

And, at the turn of the 19th century, the monastery, flushed of its inhabitants, fell into decay. Fate in the post-Revolution era was relatively kind to the Saint Wandrille abbey. Instead of becoming a quarry of ready-made stone building blocks like Jumièges,

*T*hrough history abbeys have suffered attacks as severe as those experienced by military strongholds. Saint Wandrille's still shows its scars.

indeed, a rich corpse for the carrion, it was converted into a textile mill. The monastery was later owned for a short time by an Englishman, the Marquis of Stacpoole, and at the end of the 1800s the monks re-appeared, though their stay was also only brief.

In 1906, Saint Wandrille's reverted, once again, to temporal ownership, namely to Maurice Maeterlinck, the

After a turbulent history the fugitive Benedictine monks are back at Saint Wandrille. The 14th–15th-century cloisters are a refuge from the outside world.

147

Belgian writer and 1911 Nobel Laureate, before reoccupation by the Benedictines in 1931. Today, Saint Wandrille's continues as an active monastery and the monks support themselves through making and selling furniture polish and various crafts.

Visitors can wander through the outer gardens, but quiet is requested. Entrance to the "inner sanctum" is through the grand 18th-century Porte de Jarente and only on a guided tour. The site is dominated by the well-maintained 17th–18th-century monastery buildings. There are ruins of the old abbey church, but they are not as dramatic as those of Notre Dame at Jumièges. The 14th–15th century cloisters suffered far less with war, fire and time but only one of the four galleries is open to the public.

As for the "new" church, it was an enlightened moment in 1969 when the monks decided to procure a medieval barn, disassemble it, cart it 50 km (30 miles), re-erect it here in their grounds and consecrate it as their place of worship.

Opening times: guided tours of the cloisters: 11.30a.m., 3.00p.m. and 4.00p.m. on Sundays and holidays and only the afternoon times during weekdays; Mass, with Gregorian chant, held in the church at 10.00a.m. on Sundays and holidays and at 9.30a.m. during the weekdays; vespers at 5.00p.m. on Sundays and holidays, 5.30p.m. during weekdays (Thursdays 18.45); tel: 35-96-23-11.

A short walk from the main abbey complex, and built on the site of a more ancient shrine, is the uncharacteristically shaped 10th-century chapel of Saint Saturnin.

Yvetot

The series of lanes threading through the countryside north of Saint Wandrille offer a prettier route to Yvetot than the main D490. Through some historical quirk, according to folklore, the town was the free state of Yvetot and enjoyed the independent status, legislative autonomy and its own king for 400 years until the Revolution. The concrete church of **Saint Pierre**, built in the mid-1950s, has some of the finest examples of Max Ingrand stained glass.

Here, too, in this once-important cotton town, there is a collection of European and Eastern ivory pieces and ceramics displayed in the **Hôtel de Ville**. *Opening times*: 8.30–11.30 a.m. and 1.30–5.00 p.m. daily except Sundays, closed on Monday mornings and Saturday afternoons. Also there is a collection of traditional farming implements and domestic utensils at the Museum of Pays de Caux. *Opening times*: 9.00 a.m. to 12.00 p.m. and 2.00–6.00 p.m. daily from June to September and afternoons from Easter to All Saints' Day; tel: 35-95-03-69.

At Allouville-Bellefosse, a village 6 km (3½ miles) south-west of Yvetot, there is a 1,300-year-old oak tree and, nearby the **Museum of Nature** where dioramas are used to introduce the local flora and fauna and the effects of pollution on the region. *Opening times*: 10.00 a.m. to 12.00 p.m. and 2.00–7.00 p.m. daily; tel: 35-96-06-54. Further west is Gruchet-le-Valasse and Bolbec.

The "Seine route" continues the few kilometres from Saint Wandrille to Caudebec-en-Caux.

Caudebec-en-Caux

The *mascaret*, a tidal bore, used to whip up the Seine and crash over the river bank here at Caudebec. That was before ways were engineered to quell this dramatic riverian phenomenon. The Seine regularly claimed its victims, most notably Victor Hugo's daughter Leopoldine downstream at Villequier (see below). Man, though, was always a more destructive force. Braced to face assault during the Hundred Years War, the people of Caudebec were unable to prevent their town falling to the English in 1419; 30 years later Caudebec was liberated and experienced intermittent periods of prosperity over the following centuries before suffering terrible damage during the Second World War.

Fortunately, the flamboyant church of Notre Dame—the older church fell apart during the English occupation—remained relatively unscathed amongst the rubble. The 15th-century church bears carvings from low down to the top of its exquisitely crafted tower, the workmanship moved Henry IV of France to pronounce it "the most beautiful chapel in the kingdom". Within, the organ, various-statues and the stained-glass windows—mostly dating from the 16th century—are of particular note.

The **13th-century Templars' House**, towards the Seine from the church, down rue Basin, also survived the War and now houses the local history museum; special collections, including firebacks and lapidary, are also displayed. *Opening times*: 3.00–6.00 p.m. daily from June to September and weekend afternoons in April, May and October; tel: 35-96-00-21.

Another museum, the **Seine-Maritime Museum**, recounts the life and navigation along the Seine and includes, in its boat shed, the last *gribane*, a late 19th-century cargo sail boat, used on the river. The museum is on avenue Winston Churchill, on the way out of town. *Opening times*: 2.00–6.30 p.m. daily in July and August and daily except Tuesdays from March 15

A band of medieval minstrels welcome visitors into Caudebec's church of Notre Dame.

to November; open weekend afternoons in November and December; tel: 35-96-27-30.

Villequier

From Caudebec-en-Caux, the D81 leads the 4 km (2½ miles) to Villequier. The tranquil riverside town has a lovely setting, with its waterfront promenade hemmed between a gentle curve of the Seine and a row of old half-timbered residences. Villequier did not suffer the destruction, or the reconstruction, of this century, as did the more prominent Caudebec. Victor Hugo and his family often stayed here as guests of Auguste Vacquerie. Vacquerie's bourgeois 19th-century mansion, one of the corniche's smarter houses, is now a museum.

Leopoldine's letters and other effects are displayed and her fate is recounted in the **Victor Hugo Museum**. Hugo memorabilia is also exhibited and includes his *Contemplations*, some of the lines of which were inspired by Leopoldine's death. *Opening times*: 10.00 a.m. to 12.00 p.m. and 2.00–5.30 p.m. daily except Tuesdays (also closed Monday during the winter) and open until 6.30 p.m. from April to October; tel: 35-56-78-31.

*W*riter Auguste *Vacquerie's home at Villequier was made famous by a greater literary figure, Victor Hugo, who would holiday here with his family. Today the house is the Hugo museum.*

The Bore that Killed Leopoldine

The strong tide forces its way into the mouth of the river and—as it crashes against and overpowers the natural flow of the river—it creates a wave, or bore, pushing upstream. Such was the phenomena on the Seine before man built devices to quell *la mascaret,* as the bore is known in Normandy. However, there was a time when the menace of *la mascaret* was all too real. On 4 September 1843, Leopoldine, Victor Hugo's newly wed 19-year-old daughter, her husband and two relatives were boating on the river at Villequier when *la mascaret* rushed upstream, upturned their vessel and drowned all four of them. The unfortunate group are buried at the local church, where Victor Hugo was also laid to rest.

Villequier to Lillebonne

Continuing along the D81, bear left at Norville along the D281 for the late 15th-century Gothic–flamboyant château of **Etelan**. Built on the site of an older castle, it has been owned by various prominent Frenchmen; Voltaire was a regular guest in the 18th century. The view to the south is over the marshes, which reach down to the Seine, and of the thick Forêt de Brotonne on the far bank. *Opening times*: 2.30–6.30 p.m. daily except Tuesdays from 15 July to September; tel: 35-39-91-27.

The road continues through Saint Maurice-d'Etelan towards Notre Dame de-Gravenchon and Lillebonne. Just before Lillebonne, at Mesnil-sous-Lillebonne, there is a collection of Pays de Caux fossils and minerals displayed at the small 12th–16th-century church of **Saint Anne**. *Opening times*: 2.30–6.30 p.m. daily except Tuesdays from May to October; tel: 35-38-30-52.

Lillebonne

For Normandy, Lillebonne's fame came early. After Julius Caesar conquered Gaul, Juliobona-Lillebonne developed into a prosperous port. Duke William gathered his nobles here at his castle, rebuilt in the 12th–13th century, but now in ruins, to brief them before the attack on England. Did he appreciate that Caesar, the other great conqueror of England, may have done the same at this spot some 1,100 years before? The decline of the town was due to the silting of the bay leaving old Juliobona high, dry and redundant.

One hundred years ago Lillebonne regained prominence when textile mills were built in the area and even today is a busy satellite of le Havre. But it is as Normandy's most famous Roman centre that Lillebonne is best known and the ruin of its 2nd century AD amphitheatre, which, it is estimated, could seat some 10,000 people, is the most significant Roman remain of its age so far discovered in the province; furthermore it is the best example of an amphitheatre north of the Loire. The **Municipal Museum** houses archaeological finds from the Gallo-Roman era, as well as furniture, chinaware and other artefacts collected from Lillebonne's later history. *Opening times*: 2.30–6.30 p.m. daily except Tuesdays from May to October and weekends and holiday afternoons from October to May; tel: 35-38-53-73. The 16th-century church of Notre Dame is notable for its 55 m (180 ft) high spire.

Bolbec and on to Le Havre

Bolbec is 7 km (4 miles) to the north. *En route* is the **abbey of Valasse** at Gruchet-le-Valasse. Matilda, daughter of Henry Beauclerk, founded the Cistercian abbey in the 12th century. Some of the early Gothic architecture has survived its turbulent history, though the main façade is 18th century. Conferences and exhibitions are held in the old abbey. *Opening times* for the public are limited: 2.30–5.30 p.m. on the second and fourth Sundays from April to November; tel: 35-31-03-02.

From the market town of Bolbec, the busy N15 heads west for le Havre. After 6 km (3½ miles) a turning to the right leads the few kilometres to the château of Filières near Gommerville.

Surrounded by a moat, the white-stoned **château of Filières** dates part from the 16th century and part from

Mustard on the rampage. A bumper crop near Lillebonne engulfs a lonely tree and obscures the view of the manor house.

lon, can be visited. *Opening times*: 10.00 a.m. to 12.00 p.m. and 2.00–5.00 p.m. daily in July and August and on Wednesdays, weekends and holidays in the afternoons from Easter to All Saints' Day; tel: 35-20-53-30.

The Approach Roads to Le Havre

Continue westwards on the D31 for the old wool town of Montivilliers on the outskirts of le Havre. The abbey of Saint Sauveur was founded by Saint Philbert in the 7th century and the monastery was to spawn the town of Mostiervillier, meaning "monastery estate", which subsequently became Montivilliers. In the 11th century, the abbey was essentially a nunnery and received healthy patronage as ducal sisters took their oaths and joined the establishment. The Romanesque abbey church dates from around 1100, though it was added to during later periods of prosperity. The more recent of the two naves was built in the 16th century, after Saint Saveur became the parish church and required more space to accommodate the increase in congregation.

A walk away is the **charnel house**, with the remains of a 16th-century gallery, and a cemetery. *Opening times*:

the 18th century. However, plans by Marquis de Mirville to further enhance his home in the late 1700s were doomed never to come to fruition due to the Revolution, a time when aristocrats thought it prudent to keep a low profile. The gardens were landscaped in the 17th century and one of the main features is the "Cathedral", an avenue lined with beeches with boughs spreading to create a tunnel. Some rooms, including the Chinese sa-

Below the Tancarville bridge a man keeps one hand on his fishing line and the other on his beer.

8.00 a.m. to 12.00 p.m. and 2.00–5.00 p.m. daily except Sunday afternoons; tel: 35-30-17-95.

It is a pretty route alongside the River Lézarde the 7 km (4 miles) to the château of le Bec, near Notre Dame-du-Bec. In the other direction is downtown le Havre.

Alternatively, pick up the D982 from Lillebonne for the 7 km (4 miles) to Tancarville and its château and bridge. Overlooking the Seine from the cliffside, the château was built on the medieval ruins of the castle belonging to Raoul of Tancarville, chamberlain to William the Conqueror; the old Eagle tower still stands. In contrast, the nearby Tancarville suspension bridge is one of Normandy's great 20th-century monuments.

Four years in construction, the long-awaited bridge at Tancarville was finally opened in 1959 and thus, for the first time, the banks of the Seine below Rouen were linked. Invaluable to transport, the splendid bridge, suspended 50 m (164 ft) above the river, must be the most important 1,400 m (1531 yd) stretch of road in Normandy. There is a toll for vehicles. Across the bridge is the Marais Vernier.

Autoroute 15 (no toll) leads from the bridge into le Havre. Alternatively, it is possible to pick up minor roads running parallel. Along the way is Saint Jean-d'Abbetot, a medieval church with fine murals, and, on the outskirts of le Havre, the château d'Orcher at Gonfreville.

On a cliff high over the Seine estuary, the original 11th-century castle served as a defence and lookout. Indeed, the **château** has a splendid vantage from the 600 m (656 yd) long Terasse d'Orcher. Like a number of fortifications around Normandy, it was part demolished in flight in the 14th century and rendered it useless to the victorious English. Most of the present structure dates from the 18th century and rooms are decorated in the fashion of that era. *Opening times*: The park is open from 9.00 a.m. to 5.00 p.m. daily except Thursdays; the château is open from 2.00–6.00 p.m. daily from early July to mid-August; tel: 35-45-45-91.

Continuing to le Havre, you pass through Harfleur, another port of the past. It was the Gallo-Roman port of Caracotinum and later thrived from the 9th to 16th centuries. The many battles fought over Harfleur between the French and English, including Henry V's capture of it in 1415, indicates the extent of its importance. But then the silt clogged the waterways and attention shifted. Now Harfleur has been swallowed up by le Havre's industrial zone. Its fine flamboyant church of Saint Martin, with its 83 m (272 ft) high bell tower, is a conspicuous relic of a more glorious past. The **Priory Museum**, a 16th-century sailors' inn, recounts Harfleur's illustrious history. *Opening times*: 3.00–6.00 p.m. Wednesdays to Saturdays; mornings also on Sundays; tel: 35-45-40-62. Roads from Harfleur lead to downtown le Havre.

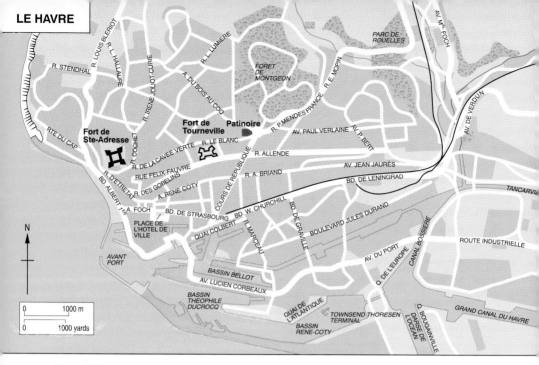

Le Havre

T own plan of le Havre.

Francisopolis evolved in the 16th century, as nearby Honfleur and Harfleur slowly choked on excessive silt and faded as the region's prominent ports.

The new port, on the northern lip of the Seine estuary, was christened after King Francis I, though the rather more prosaic name of le Havre, *havre* meaning harbour, was soon adopted. Its position at the gateway of the avenue to the heart of France was always bound to give le Havre a high profile. And so it did. Le Havre became the country's major commercial trans-Atlantic link. And, during the latter part of the 18th century, provisions exported from here furnished the Americans' independence movement against the British.

Le Havre prospered, though it was constantly beset by calamities—a succession of attacks and natural disasters—the most frightful being the Allied assault in September 1944 against the Germans who had held the port stubbornly after Normandy and Paris had fallen. The destruction was extreme and le Havre subsequently earned the dismal epithet "Europe's most damaged port". But after every setback, le Havre has taken two steps forward. And, today, the newly built port is flourishing. Only Marseilles handles a greater quantity of France's trade.

The architect Auguste Perret (1874–1954), a champion of the concrete structure, was given the job to resurrect le Havre after the War. The results have received mixed reactions: one man's "inspired modern urban design" is another man's "cold, characterless cityscape". Le Havre is a chequerboard of long straight boulevards, most notably the main wide, tree-lined avenue Foch. What the city is not, is "quaint old Normandy", and for this reason most tourists pass le Havre by.

The autoroute from Tancarville leads into le Havre's western outskirts, and continues as a boulevard right through the centre of the city, with each successive section of its road taking a different name. First, boulevard de Leningrad, the boulevard Winston Churchill, followed by boulevard Strasbourg which leads to the huge place de l'Hôtel de Ville, which, with its giant town hall, constitutes the heart of le Havre; finally, the smart avenue Foch continues on the far side of the square to Porte Océane and the beach.

The district to the right of the boulevard de Leningrad stretch is Graville, a quarter with little to recommend it save for its abbey. A place of Christian worship has existed here since the 7th century and, from a humble sanctuary, there evolved an abbey. History dealt its usual hand of mixed fortune over subsequent centuries. What is left today is the 11th-century church of Saint Honorine and a fine collection of medieval art which is housed in the nearby **Priory Museum.** *Opening times:* daily except Mondays and Tuesdays. There are good views over towards the Seine estuary from by the church.

Le Havrre's downtown is around place de la Hôtel de Ville. Rue de Paris leads southwards through the main shopping area of quartier Moderne. Off to the left is Bassin du Commerce, an inner harbour, with its attractive

Pont de la Bourse footbridge; to the right is Espace Niemeyer, an arts–leisure complex designed by Oscar Niemeyer, and, a few blocks beyond, the church of Saint Joseph.

The church, a spectacular concrete offering from Perret, is dedicated to those who died in 1944. The octagonal tower dominates the building and the surroundings. The stained glass on the walls of the square structure allow a colourful light into an otherwise severe interior.

Continue down rue de Paris and on the left you will find Notre Dame, a cherished memory from the past. Built in the 16th–17th century, the Gothic–Renaissance church was one of the few survivors of the 1944 debacle. And in a street beyond is the **Natural History Museum**, housed in the old law courts, whiich will be of particular interest to birdwatchers since birds are a main feature. *Opening times*: 10.00 a.m. to 12.00 p.m. and 2.00–6.00 p.m. on Wednesdays, Saturdays and Sundays, afternoons only on Mondays and Fridays and closed on Tuesdays; tel: 35-41-37-28.

A block further on is a drawbridge crossing the neck of Bassin du Roi, the original port, to the quarter of Saint Francis, site of 16th-century Francisopolis. This, if anything, is le Havre's "quaint old Normandy" and the Old Havre Museum in a restored 18th-century house on rue Jérôme Bellarmato, near the church, recounts the history and traditions of the city; open daily except Mondays and Tuesdays. The Bassin du Commerce with its footbridge is just to the north.

Rue de Paris concludes at quai Southampton where fishermen set up

Le Havre had to be rebuilt after the Second World War. The view looking westwards across Bassin du Commerce is of a modern city: the Pont de la Bourse, Espace Niemeyer and, behind, the tall tower of Saint Joseph.

stalls. To the left, and in front, spreads le Havre's huge port complex. There are guided tours around the harbours; for further information contact the tourist office at the town hall. And to the right, along the waterfront, is the splendid glass–metal **André Malraux Museum of Fine Art.**

The purpose of the design was to conjure with light and thus provide the most suitable ambience for the different displays. On show are the works of the great local artists. Raoul Dufy (1877–1953) was born in le Havre, and the museum exhibits its unique collection of his paintings. Honfleur boy Eugène Boudin (1824–98), the father of Impressionism and a great influence on young Claude Monet, worked for a while in le Havre. In his later years, Monet would say that he "owed everything to Boudin". Works by Boudin, Monet, Renoir, Jongkind, Manet,

Sisley and other Impressionists are on display. There is also 16th–19th-century Flemish and Italian art. *Opening times*: 10.00 a.m. to 12.00 p.m. and 2.00–6.00 p.m. daily except Tuesdays; tel: 35-42-33-97.

Opposite the museum is the communications tower, the semaphore, with a cluster of tugs below. Continue northwards along the waterfront boulevard Clemenceau and you will pass the marina and reach Porte Océane, with avenue Foch off to the right, and the beach. The corniche leads on to Sainte Adresse, le Havre's pleasant resort suburb.

On the way, up on the right behind the beach, is the old fort of Sainte Adresse from where there is a magnificent view over city, sea and coast. Sainte Adresse proper is at the end of the beachside drive. From place Clemenceau a road twists up to Pain de Sucre, a memorial to General Lefèbvre-Desnouttes, who died at the sea in 1822, from his grieving wife. The sailors' church of Notre Dame des Flots is nearby and beyond is the merchant navy's maritime school. There are extensive views from the coast road up here on the headland.

159

Wide Sand Beaches, Rich Pastures and the Fattest of Cheeses

Scurrying home to Spain after the Armada, the *Salvador* smashed into rocks off Normandy and sank, giving its name to this stretch of coast. *Salvador* was subsequently corrupted to Calvados. These shores were evocatively named Côte de Fleurie and Côte de Nacre—the Flower and Mother of Pearl coasts—and resorts like Trouville and Deauville sparkled in the sands. The Allies code-named these beaches and landed here on D-Day. Here is Normandy at its lushest—mellow pastures, plump cows and creamy cheese.

Caen

Caen, on the banks of the Odon near the confluence with the Orne, was no more than a modest settlement during Gallo-Roman times. And so it remained until William the Conqueror graced it with his presence and his funds. The city is said to have been William's favourite and it was here he planned his other great "conquest": the winning of Matilda.

The courtship was brusque with Matilda, William's cousin and the

A farmer brings his calf to market in the boot of his Deux Chevaux.

daughter of the Count of Flanders, rebuffing the duke's proposals by announcing she would rather take the veil than marry a bastard. Insulted, but undeterred, the headstrong William rode to Lille where he roughed up the petite Matilda, pulling her around a chamber by her plaits. The outcome of this encounter was the marriage of the couple at Eu in 1050. William was as obsessed with victory in love as he was in war.

The image of William, the burly bruiser, is softened by his genuine affection, and faithfulness, towards Matilda. Their love won through the severest of tests. Being cousins, their marriage was deemed illegal by the Vatican and they were excommunicated. Nine years later the able

CALVADOS

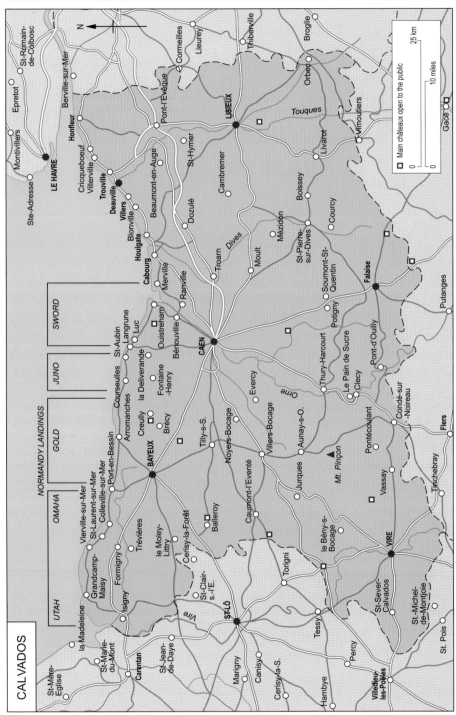

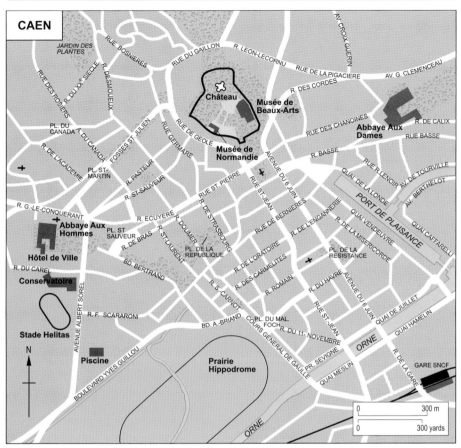

Town plan of Caen.

Lanfranc, William's influential high priest, persuaded the new pope to have the couple reinstated into the fold. In celebration of this reunion with church, William built the Abbaye aux Hommes and Matilda the Abbaye aux Dames.

Booty brought back by William from England after his conquest in 1066 financed work on the abbeys. Caen's quarries furnished the building material, the same creamy white stone which had been used in the construction of the Tower of London's White Tower and Canterbury Cathedral. Matilda was buried in her abbey in 1083 and William in his four years later. The abbeys still stand, in the east and west of Caen respectively, and are a legacy of a happy marriage of a turbulent man.

English money fashioned Caen, and Englishmen later influenced the shaping of the city. In 1346, Edward III

Map of the Calvados region.

163

Caen's Beautiful Briton

Eton, Oxford, followed by a commission in the smartest of regiments thanks to the influence of his friend the Prince of Wales (later George IV). Such was George Brummell's background when at the age of 20 he inherited £30,000, left the army as a captain and set up residence in the heart of Mayfair. A snappy dresser—hence his nickname "Beau"— and a wit, he became an essential invitee at any high society party. He was, indeed, the *arbiter elegantiarum* of his time. However, his extravagance and penchant for gambling dragged him into debt and in 1816 he fled to Calais to avoid his creditors. By now his life was irrevocably in decline and a spell as British Consul in Caen from 1830 to 1832 was just a pause in his decay. He did time in prison in 1835 and was later interned in a charitable institute, Le Bon Sauveur, due to attacks of paralysis. And here he died in 1840 aged 62. Grandson of a shopkeeper, son of a man made good, Beau Brummell, doyen of fashion, died a sad, forgotten man in a Caen poor house.

captured Caen on his way from Cotentin to Crécy. Subsequently it was lost to the French, but retaken by Henry V in 1417 after Agincourt; the English remained for 33 years during which time the Duke of Bedford founded Caen University. Four hundred years later Beau Brummel, doyen of early 19th-century fashion, took refuge here, introducing his particular brand of Englishness on to the Caen scene; he, like others of the 19th-century English community, is buried in the city's Protestant cemetery. And the British army was back again when, in the summer of 1944, they set about expelling the Germans from Caen.

It was hoped that Caen, 12 km (7½ miles) from the sea, would be liberated on D-Day itself. It was not to be. After bitter fighting, the city was eventually won by the British and Canadian forces on 9 July.

Caen had been 75 per cent destroyed. The city was rebuilt in a light and attractive style using Caen stone and, today, it contrasts with many Normandy towns which were reconstructed hastily from the ashes of the War in a grey, dour, drab design.

Reduced to Rubble

A reporter's account in the English *Daily Telegraph* on 10 July 1944, the day after the liberation of Caen by the Allies:

"It was hard to tell where Caen began. Whole areas of the town have been obliterated by bombing and shellfire.

It was barely possible to recognize whether a particular heap of churned dust was once a house. It was impossible to pick out the lines of the streets. Imagine a pleasant and prosperous country town lying in rolling, fertile country on the other side of an almost Arcadian river. It raises spires and towers heavenwards. It is the very picture of contentment. Now see the same town after the masonry of its buildings has been ground, not only to fragments, but even to fine white dust. Heaps of such dust cover large sectors of Caen. Above them rise shattered, shambling ruins. Here is a corner of the house with some few splintered sticks of furniture poking irrelevantly outwards, or the pudding-like solidity of a mattress. Elsewhere is the debris of what have been a dining room table and chairs, though one cannot be certain. Everywhere rubble, rubble, rubble and bare matchstick trees in what were once gracious gardens. That is what large-scale bombing and shell-fire does in modern war."

The castle has always been the heart of Caen. Its solid, medieval ramparts surrounded by, and enclosing, neat lawns are still the city's focal point. William started building the château fort in 1060, though it was his son, Henry Beauclerk, who constructed the great keep in 1122. Fifty years later, Henry II met with a legate in the castle to hear the pope's condemnation of Thomas à Becket's murder. The castle was continually strengthened over the following centuries, and as a garrisoned citadel it was able to withstand Edward III when he captured Caen, though it did capitulate to Henry V. More recently, restoration of the castle had to be made after the damage caused by the fighting in 1944. There are good views from the ramparts over the city below.

The 14th-century Porte des Champs, on the east side, is the oldest gate, but the main entrance to the castle compound today is through the Porte sur la Ville on the south side. To the right, on entering, is the modern building of the **Fine Arts** (Beaux Arts) **Museum** which has a fine collection of 15th- to 20th-century European paintings, with the 17th-century French and Italian paintings being of particular note; some of the Italian masterpieces are here thanks to Napoleon and his men who plundered them during their campaigns. Also displayed are engravings, porcelain and furniture. *Opening times*: 10.00 a.m. to 12.00 p.m. and 2.00–6.00 p.m. daily except Tuesdays and holidays; between 1 October and 15 March the museum closes at 5.30 p.m.; tel: 31-85-28-63.

Opposite the museum is the St George's chapel which dates back to the 12th century, and beyond, on the far side of the herb garden, is the old

---

No Escape for the Bourgeoisie

With a head and heart filled with sentimental dreams of Byronic love, the young convent-educated Emma Rouault, daughter of a reclusive farmer, married the local doctor, Charles Bovary. Any hopes Emma may have had for a life of romance and gaiety were quickly suffocated by the intense banality and boredom of the provincial existence she was sucked into by her marriage to the dull Charles.

Flaubert, himself a man of good middle-class stock, had an obsessive dislike of the bourgeois, those, according to him, "who have a low way of thinking", and as a young author he compiled a dictionary attacking the *idées recues* (accepted ideas). It took Flaubert five years to write *Madame Bovary* which he subtitled *Moeurs de Province* (Provincial Customs). Passionate Emma, stifled by the oafish habits of her doting Charles and the small town ways and self righteousness of Yonville, wildly throws herself into secret love affairs with the local squire and then the lawyer's clerk. It is like a desperate scream in the bourgeois drabness. For a while she lives her romantic dreams, but they are of course illusions. Her lovers desert her, her clandestine extravagant lifestyle pulls her ever deeper into debt and finally she poisons herself.

When *Madame Bovary* first appeared in *Revue de Paris* in 1856 it offended public sensibilities and Flaubert, the editor and the publisher were all put on trail on a charge of immorality. They were acquitted. Asked once who Emma Bovary was based on, Flaubert answered enigmatically, "Madame Bovary is myself". Maybe there is a little bit of Emma Bovary in all of us.

*P*orte sur la Ville, the "town" entrance into Caen castle, the city's cream stone centrepiece.

Governor's House, now the **Museum of Normandy**. The museum recounts the evolution of the Norman culture, supported by archeological finds and the implements of traditional trades and crafts. *Opening times* are the same as the Fine Arts Museum; tel: 31-86-06-24.

North of the Governor's House is the exchequer and then the remains of the keep, both dating from the time of Henry Beauclerk. Beyond the walls lies the university campus.

Outside the ramparts, and facing the Porte sur la Ville, is place Saint Pierre and its 13th–16th-century church. The famous spire, erected in 1308, tumbled after suffering a direct hit from the

British navy during the fighting of 1944; it has been replaced and the nave, which was also damaged by the shell, has been repaired. Traditionally, Saint Pierre has enjoyed custom and donations from Caen's wealthy bourgeois class. Once the Odon flowed past the *chevet* of the church, along what is now boulevard du Maréchal Leclerc, and worshippers would row to service. However, this, like other stretches of waterways, has long been covered. The ornate Renaissance embellishments inside the church, especially at the eastern end, reflect the wealth of its 16th-century patrons and contrast with the older more modest Gothic decor.

A further legacy of the 16th-century bourgeoisie to survive 1944 is the now restored Hôtel d'Escoville, across the road from Saint Pierre. Built by Nicolas Le Valois d'Escoville in the 1530s, its lavish adornments, as seen in the inner courtyard, reveal something of the ostentation of the Caen merchants of this period. The house is now the tourist office.

Caen's main shopping, hotel and restaurant area is immediately to the west, south and east of place Saint Pierre; several of the thoroughfares are now pedestrian precincts.

Follow rue Saint Pierre south-west. Numbers 52 and 54 are 16th-century

The 14th-century tower of Saint Peter's tumbled, smashing much of its Church's nave as it fell, after suffering a direct hit in 1944. The present spire was constructed after the War.

half-timbered houses; the former being the **Postal and Telecommunications Museum** which provides a history of mail and communications. *Opening times*: 10.00 a.m. to 12.00 p.m. and 2.00–6.00 p.m. Tuesdays–Saturdays from 16 June to 15 September; 1.30–5.30 p.m. Tuesdays–Saturdays from 3 April to 15 June and 16 September to 10 November; it is closed from 1 January to 2 April; tel: 31-50-12-20. Beyond is the Gothic–Renaissance church of Saint Sauveur, also called Notre Dame de Froide Rue, at the junction of the old rue Froide, which is now an attractive shopping mall.

Rue Saint Pierre leads into rue Ecuyère—rue aux Fromages on the right is a passage to place Saint Sauveur with its smart 18th-century buildings—which in turn opens out into the place Fontette. On the right is the sombre Palais de Justice. Turn to the left and into place Louis Guillouard; to the east is the rather dilapidated church of Vieux Saint Etienne and the Notre Dame de la Glorietta behind it. Westwards is a view of the **Abbaye aux Hommes**, the impressive 18th-century façade of the monastery, now partly occupied by the Town Hall, and, to its right, the splendid eastern end and spires of Saint Etienne.

Work on Saint Etienne, the abbey's church, was started in 1066, in Romanesque style, consecrated in 1077 and completed in the 13th century, in Gothic style. The church's aspects of northern Italian style were probably the influence of Lanfranc, the first abbot, who was from Lombardy. The austere 11th-century Romanesque west front is dwarfed by its twin towers, which rise as solemn as the façade, but become more fanciful as they peak into their 13th-century Gothic spires; the northern one being the more elaborately worked of the pair. The original lantern tower in the centre of the church collapsed in 1563, its replacement dates from the 17th century.

There is a chill inside William's sepulchre: you are surrounded by space, simplicity and strength. All that remains of the Conqueror is one of his thigh bones, a pitiful relic of such a great man.

There may not be much of William in body, but there is in spirit. Local folklore maintains that Saint Etienne will always be safe while the English monarchy, the line initiated by William, still has its throne. So strong is this belief that, during the battle for Caen in 1944, citizens took refuge in the church and, indeed, they and the building were left virtually unscathed.

Work on the imposing present monastery buildings, attached to the south side of Saint Etienne, were begun by master builder Brother Guillaume de la Tremblaye in 1704. One hundred years later they were opened as the imperial *lycée* and so they remained until 1965 when they became the **Hôtel de Ville**. The buildings are open to the public and tours depart daily on the hour from 9.00 a.m. to 5.00 p.m. with the exception of 1.00 p.m.; tel: 31-30-42-01. The visit includes: la salle de lecture et de detente, now an exhibition hall; le "Chauffoir"; la salle du chapitre, now a registry office for marriages, with its Louis XV

Revenge Against the Defenceless Dead

Providence did not grant William peace even in death. The king had died in Rouen, but the bringing of his body to Caen for burial was delayed. The funeral was without pomp and fanfare, but not without event. First its sanctity was shattered by a fire. Then by a local called Asselin, who stood up and started abusing the dead William for having evicted his father from his house, so as to allow construction of the abbey on this spot. Asselin demanded compensation. He had his price and wanted immediate payment. The assembled prelates and nobles dug deep, gave him what they had to keep him quiet and promised to make up the difference later. This incident over, William's bloated, presumably unembalmed, body burst with the bowels spilling their contents, emitting a vile stench which no amount of aromatic incense or fragrant petals could disguise. Furthermore, the gravemaker had miscalculated William's uncommonly large stature, and the monks, having hastily gathered the reeking corpse, had to unceremoniously bundle and squeeze it into the undersized sarcophagus.

Some 500 years later, the Huguenots desecrated William's tomb during the destructive Wars of Religion. However, his bones were retrieved and restored to the grave. Only, though, to be filched again by the irreverent revolutionaries in 1793 who chucked the lot into the river, all except for William's femur, which must have escaped their notice, and now lies in the rightful place in Saint Etienne as the sole remnant of the man who did so much to shape medieval Christendom. Engraved on his tomb is the epitaph: *Hic Sepultus Est In Victissimus Guillelmus Conquestor, Normannlae Dux, Et Angliae Rex, Hujus Le Domus, Conditor, Qui Orbit Anno M.LXXXVII.* In further remembrance to William, the town of Hastings, which owes its fame to him, donated two panels of choir railings on 2 July 1927, to mark the Conqueror's 900th birth date.

The cloister garden, the oasis at the heart of the monastery, at Caen's Abbaye aux Hommes.

oak woodwork; la sacristie; le vestibule, with its stairway and wrought-iron banisters; le refectoire; le cloître, from where there is a good view of the south side of Saint Etienne; le "Parloir", oval-shaped and with notable woodwork; and the great salle des gardes, dating from the 14th century.

At the southern end of these buildings is the **Musée de la Nature**, housed in the former abbey bakery, where Normandy's nature, a garden of medicinal herbs and reconstructions of traditional rural scenes are presented. *Opening times*: 2.00–5.30p.m. Mondays–Fridays from April to September and Wednesdays only during the low season; tel: 31-30-43-27.

A short walk north-east of Abbaye aux Hommes, just beyond rue Bicoquet, is Saint Nicolas, a parish church built by the monks of Saint Etienne in the late 11th century. This is Romanesque architecture almost at its purest: a tower was added in the 15th century; the more recent renovation has been in the original style. The cemetery is also worth a wander. And to the north, quite a way beyond and *en route* to the Caen Memorial Museum, is the pleasant **Jardin de Plantes**, originally created in the 17th century by a professor of the university medical faculty, with over 2,000 species of plants (tel: 31-86-28-80) and, on the other side of rue Bosnieres, the heavily stained-glassed 1950s church of Saint Julian.

East along rue Montoir Poissonnerie, between place Saint Pierre and the castle, one reaches rue de Chanoines. Up on its left is the Quartier du Vaugueux, an attractively restored pedestrian zone with small cafés and restaurants. Matilda's Abbaye aux Dames is at the quiet top end of rue des Chanoines and, above and away from the downtown, it does not receive the attention given to the brother abbey.

Matilda's abbey church of la Trinité is still predominantly Romanesque, though there have been subsequent additions and alterations, notably its 18th-century spires and the façade, making it more adulterated than her husband's Saint Etienne. None the less, the large nave and much of the architecture, though recently restored, is original and Matilda's bones, entombed under black marble in the chancel, have enjoyed the peace denied to William's. The couple's daughter Cecile was ordained the second abbess and this started a trend amongst the nobility: 46 abbesses of La Trinité were to come from aristocratic families, each one gaining the title Madame de Caen.

Annexed to the church is the monastery which, like that of Abbaye aux Hommes, was constructed in the 18th century to a design by Guillaume de la Tremblaye. Caen's Hôpital General had been founded in 1655 and, in 1823, it was transferred to the **Abbaye aux Dames**, remaining here until 1984; today the old monastery is the home of the Regional Council. Daily tours of the building are at 2.30 and 4.00 p.m.; tel: 31-06-98-98. Visits include: Le cloître, similar to that at the Abbaye aux Hommes; la lavatorium; la salle du bureau; la salle des abbesses, with portraits of two aristocrats from

its order, Anne de Montmorency (1554–1588) and Marie-Aïmée de Pontecoulant (1787–1792), who was the older cousin of Charlotte de Corday; le grand vestibule, with its stairway; the formal gardens. Much of the furniture and art was dispersed during the confusion of the Revolution and hence the buildings present a relative lack of decor.

The nearby ruins are of Saint Gilles, the 12th-century church for the abbey neighbourhood.

Beyond the west–east axis of central Caen—Abbaye aux Hommes, Castle and the place Saint Pierre-Abbaye aux Dames—lies the rest of the city. South of the place Saint Pierre is the Saint Jean district which was severely damaged during 1944. The predominantly flamboyant church of Saint Jean originates from the 14th century, though it had to undergo restoration after Henry V's rampage through Caen in 1417 and then again after the Allies' invasion. On one side of the church is place de la Résistance and a statue of Joan of Arc which once stood in Oran, but was politely returned to the French after the Algerians had gained independence. On the other side is the house where the young Charlotte de Corday d'Armont stayed before travelling to Paris to kill Marat on 13 July 1793; four days later she was guillotined.

Continuing southwards you reach the Orne, with the racecourse and the gardens of the Prairie lying a short distance upstream, and, over the bridge, are the 12th-century church of Saint Michel and the railway station. Caen was built on the banks of the Orne, the Odon and their tributaries; canals were also constructed and the city was

Death in the Bath

In the aftermath of the storming of the Bastille in 1788—the start of the French Revolution—there emerged two rival factions: the Girondin, the "federalists" who drew support from the middle classes and refugee nobles, and the Montagnards, the more radical left-wing republicans who had the sympathies of the artisan and lower classes. By 1793, the Montagnards, with Robespierre, Danton and Marat amongst its leaders, dominated the National Convention, having ousted the Girondins whom they now set out to purge. The Committee of Public Safety under Robespierre rounded up the opposition for the guillotine. The reign of terror had begun: Louis XVI was executed in January, his Marie Antoinette was killed in October. Caen became a lair for the "federalist" movement, and one of their young supporters was Charlotte Corday, a convent girl of noble descent from a village near Sées. In the summer of 1793, she travelled to Paris where she gained an interview with Jean Paul Marat under the pretext of supplying him with names of dissidents. Marat, submerged in his theraputic bath was easy prey. Cordat read her list of "enemies of the state", but, as Marat thanked her for her co-operation, she drew out a dagger and stabbed him to death. Charlotte Corday was convicted of murder by the Revolutionary Tribune and guillotined in place de la Revolution on 17 July 1793, 10 days before her 25th birthday.

dubbed the "Venise Normande". But behind this alluring image lurked the sinister reality: the unsanitary standards of the waterways led to frequent outbreaks of typhoid, as well as cholera, smallpox and the plague.

Today, many of the old channels have been covered or filled in.

T he simple, elegant exterior of Memorial Museum at Caen. Nowhere is the War for the liberation of France and Europe more effectively told than here.

However, in 1857 the Bassin de Saint Pierre was inaugurated, along quai Vendeuvre to the east of Saint Jean, at the same time as the newly created 12 km (7½ mile) long canal which ran alongside the Orne to the sea. Caen is a centre for the steel industry, iron ore deposits have been mined in the region for ages, and the canal helped boost the city's trade. In 1930, it was France's 7th port, today it is 12th.

On the north-east outskirts of Caen is the Memorial, the Museum for Peace; it can be reached by Bus 12 from the city centre.

Caen, one of the most tragic victims of 1944, was an appropriate place to found **Le Memorial**, "**Un Musée pour la Paix**", a war museum dedicated to peace. Built in the 1980s, the spectacular long, rectangular building made from Caen stone contains a stunning exhibition of design and display recounting the two World Wars. Film, sound, photos, documentation and a wide range of War relics are used to maximum effect to drum home the events of 1939–44 in superbly graphic fashion. It is an extraordinary history lesson taught with the aid of hi-tech and slick presentations. The museum and its gadgetry is as much on show as the exhibition, "the history and the horror of the War", which they display.

A visit to the Memorial should be a prelude to a tour of the Normandy landing beaches. Indeed, the museum will give an understanding of the way Normandy as a whole was occupied, destroyed and rebuilt. It gives meaning to the memorials to the dead in every village and the surfeit of drab, characterless buildings which had to be

---

"Lest We Forget . . . "

Of all the museums in Normandy commemorating "The Summer of 1944" *Le Memorial* is the best, the most sophisticated and the most comprehensive. In different stages it relates: the period between the two World Wars; the crisis of 1929, the rise of Hitler and the build-up to the Second World War; the fall of France, the Vichy government and the Resistance and life under occupation; the war itself with footage of battles fought around the world; the D-Day landings and the Battle of Normandy; "Hope", a film, the projection of more recent wars, the fragility of peace and the defence of liberty against aggressors. The exhibits portray the destruction and misery of it all and the joy amongst the sorrow of achieving freedom. Captions and books are in various languages, including English, and in the foyer there is usually an exhibition drawing attention to current wars.

---

erected cheaply and quickly in the aftermath to accommodate the numerous homeless. A minimum of 2 hours should be allowed, as there are film-showings at regular intervals; the ticket office shuts 1½ hours before closing time.

Opening times: 9.00 a.m. to 7.00 p.m. daily; 9.00 a.m. to 10.00 p.m. from June to September. Closed during the first two weeks of January. Address: Esplanade Dwight-Eisenhower; tel: 31-06-06-44.

Côte Fleurie

Avenue G Clemenceau, running just to the north of the Abbaye aux Dames, leads east out of Caen to join the D515 Ouistreham road. At Bénouville, the

D514 crosses the Orne over Pegasus Bridge and bends towards the coast: to the evocatively named Côte Fleurie, the Flowery Coast, a gentle often sandy sweep of shore stretching from the Orne to the Seine. The road meets the coast at Merville-Franceville Plage, an important German gun post which was captured during the early hours of the Allied offensive in June 1944 (there is a War museum open during the summer), and continues on to Cabourg.

board. The original neat, ordered, geometric street-plan still exists. The promenade runs alongside the large sandy beach. Halfway along the Casino, the Grand Hotel and a roundabout constitute a focal point from where the avenues and boulevards radiate.

The trend for beach bathing remains as popular as ever, but the desirability of particular resorts is never so certain. The chic are notoriously fickle and, over the years, many of Cabourg's smart clientele have moved on to

Cabourg

Beach bathing became the vogue for the fashionable French in the middle of the last century. The pioneering developers of seaside resorts targeted Côte Fleurie and, in 1860, the plans to create Cabourg were on the drawing

With the trend of seabathing came the desire for a holiday home at a resort and hence the rise of the "terraced chateaux" such as this at Cabourg.

patches of sand elsewhere in France, indeed, further up the coast, Europe and the world. Nonetheless the old villas stand and an aura of charm and style, albeit rather faded, still hangs over the resort. Marcel Proust first came to Cabourg as a child in 1881 and he returned many times after, staying as a guest at the Grand. His *A l'Ombre des Jeunes Filles en Fleurs*

Grand Recluse

Marcel Proust, the son of a Catholic doctor and Jewish mother, was born in the Paris suburb of Auteuil in 1871. He was a sickly, asthmatic child and, because the blossoms in the garden caused him particular anxiety, his parents used to take him to Cabourg or Trouville for the summer holidays; here—away from the sweet scent of flowers—he would happily watch the "jeunes filles en fleur" playing on the beach.

As a young author, he mixed with Paris society and an intellectual clique including the likes of Anatole France. However, the Normandy coast served him as inspiration and the Balbec of *Within a Budding Grove* was based on Cabourg.

In 1906, after the death of his parents, Proust, the bachelor-socialite, became a recluse. He would rarely venture from his cork-lined room at 102 Boulevard Haussemann in Paris. While staying at the Grand in Cabourg, he would rent the rooms above, below and beside his own so as to avoid the noise and smell of others; apparently he would retire to bed fully clothed, even wearing his gloves.

During these long hermetic years Proust wrote *Remembrance of Things Past*—the initial task took from 1905 to 1912, though he spent the following ten years expanding the works. Proust died in 1922 while working on *Cities of the Plain*.

---

gives an insight into the elegant turn of the century Cabourg, which can still be imagined if you look behind the veneer of the modern souvenir shop. And, in memory of their most famous regular, locals named their waterfront corniche promenade Marcel Proust.

Dives-sur-Mer

The Dives divides Cabourg from Dives-sur-Mer. The two towns, linked by a span of a bridge, are hundreds of years apart. In the 11th century, Dives-sur-Mer was a busy port and it was here on 12 September 1066 that Duke William gathered his army and set sail for Saint Valery-sur-Sommes before they crossed to England. Marketing William is not uncommon in places claiming an association with him. Here in Dives-sur-Mer there is Le Village d'Art Guillaume le Conquerant, a picturesque 16th-century posting inn *relais de poste* which is now a craft centre selling William souvenirs amongst its wares. Henry IV, Alexander Dumas, Madame de Sevigne, Dives-sur-Mer's clutch of more recent celebrities, are amongst those who lodged at the inn over the centuries.

William's senior knights, the town's other names of note, were listed in 1862 in the great church of Notre Dame. This was a popular place of pilgrimage between the 11th century and the Wars of Religion. Fishermen had pulled up a statue of Christ from the local waters; the figure, of mysterious origins, was finally housed in the church and drew huge crowds of devotees. A stained-glass window in the north transept tells the story. Part of

Les chevaux de trot— *the trotters, or the chariots as they are nicknamed—at Cabourg offer an alternative to the big races up the coast at Deauville.*

the 11th-century Notre Dame remains, though most of the present church dates from the 14th and 15th centuries. Across rue Gaston Manneville from Notre Dame is the long and splendid 15th–16th century timber-framed Halles, the market place.

The "sur-Mer" of Dives is rather outdated: William's port silted up long ago and the town looks to local industry instead of the sea for its revenue. "Dives" did not develop along the expanding coastline and now the resorts of Cabourg to the east and Houlgate to the west dominate this stretch of Côte Fleurie.

The best route to Houlgate is eastwards from Notre Dame onto the D45 and then off to the left on the minor D45a for a kilometre or two to Houlgate.

Houlgate, Villers-sur-Mer, Touques

Houlgate, smaller, less well known and traditionally less fashionable than Cabourg does, though, have its impressive sandy beach, promenade and a casino. On the far side of the resort, a road climbs les Vaches Noires (the Black Cows), a wedge of dramatic cliff between Houlgate and the next resort of Villers-sur-Mer. There are extensive views along the coast. Alternatively, for a full frontal view of the cliff face wait until low tide and walk along its base, approximately 5–6 km (3½ miles) to Villers-sur-Mer.

Of a similar size as Houlgate, Villers-sur-Mer also has the salient features of these Côte Fleurie resorts: long, wide, sandy beach, seafront promenade and a casino. Fossils which have fallen from les Vaches Noires are displayed in the local **Museum of Paleontology** (open through the day in July and August and for shorter hours during the rest of the year; tel: 31-87-01-18.

The beach and the coast road continue to the smaller joint resorts of Blonville-sur-Mer and Benerville-sur-Mer. Behind rises Mount Canisy from where the vista encompasses a long stretch of the coast. This is pretty and just below, to the east, is the River Touques. Attractively set on the far side of the valley, and with a fine vantage of its own, are the ruins of castle **Bonneville**, William the Conqueror's home (tours on the weekend afternoons from mid-March to mid-October; tel: 31-88-00-10); from up here William could keep a protective eye on the port of Touques, a kilometre or so downstream.

Touques' maritime days ended with the silting of the river. Like the larger Dives-sur-Mer, it can boast William's patronage and visits from historical figures, such as Thomas à Becket who blessed the church which now bears his name. The fine and older 11th-century church of Saint Pierre is now ignored and deconsecrated. Touques as a whole has suffered a similar fate: the advancing coastline has literally pushed the town into the background and, with the growth of the splendid Deauville-Trouville resort conurbation on either side of the river's mouth, Touques has fallen further and further into the shade.

A warm summer's afternoon and a rendezvous at a pavement café is an essential part of the daily curriculum.

Deauville and Trouville

Deauville and Trouville, at the Touques' mouth on the west and east bank respectively, together constitute Côte Fleurie's prize bloom. It, and more particularly Deauville, blossoms beautifully but briefly. The Deauville season commences in July and concludes on the fourth Sunday in August with the running of the Grand Prix: the great culmination of the racing calendar. During this short period, Deauville flowers as colourfully, as fragrantly and as elegantly as any resort in France. But even as the horses are being led back to the stables after the final race, the fashionable are on their way back to Paris. Deauville quickly fades, and remains in its more usual state of quiescence, except for conferences and occasional races, until the following July.

The Deauville Grand Prix—the annual horse race held on the fourth Sunday in August—is the climax of Normandy's social calendar.

Trouville's discovery precedes that of Deauville. A small fishing community lived undisturbed along the beach in the mid-19th century. Artists, in search of solace and light, came here, and their paintings, rather like today's exotic travel photos, advertised an enchanting world. These were the early days of the Second Empire. Beach bathing had caught on at Dieppe and le Tréport and, in 1852, a new resort with casino was established at Trouville. High society holidayed here; the lower ranks of the fashionable took note and followed suit. The hype has worked ever since and much the same trend continues today.

*T*rouville the fishing village, another face of the town which is better known for its casino and as a smart holiday resort.

Deauville evolved later, apparently in response to the high rents demanded in Trouville. Ironically Deauville is now the more expensive of the two twins. The main features both share are the casinos and the stretches of long, sandy beach with the *planches*, the wooden board promenade where people wander to see and be seen, which of the two naturally depends on who you are. Purpose-built Deauville, the more stylish, expensive and extravagant of the two, has its marina, two racecourses and a greater chic image to boast and maintain.

On to Honfleur

The high D513 coast road east of Trouville, congested in summer, passes the villas half hidden by clusters of trees and overlooks the Seine estuary with its oil refineries off le Havre. Some 6 km (3½ miles) on is the small resort of Villerville, which, after the *metroporesort* of Deauville–Trouville, is without style though refreshingly modest and more "Normandy" in

A late evening stroll along the planches at Deauville. A quiet moment on Normandy's most fashionable catwalk.

character. Just beyond is the often-photographed ivy-covered 12th-century church at Cricqueboeuf. Soon after, the D62 to the right leads to the 18th-century gardens and château of Barneville, while the coast road continues by the beautiful Côte de Grâce to Honfleur, a total of 15 km (9 miles) from Trouville.

Côte de Grâce is a splendid prelude to Honfleur. From the Calvary and from nearby Mont Joli, there are excellent views over the Seine estuary and also over Honfleur and the coast. The chapel of Notre-Dame-de-Grâce, with the venerated statue of Our Lady, has long been a place of pilgrimage for all those embarking across the seas from Honfleur. Côte de Grâce is within reasonable walking distance of the port below.

Honfleur

Honfleur is its old harbour, le Vieux Bassin. The colourful fishing boats and yachts are wedged closely together at their moorings; overlooking them are the tall, narrow, slate-hung, timber-beamed houses squeezed together along quai Sainte Catherine; opposite, on the quai Saint Etienne, are stone buildings, including an old church and former prison; a short, narrow channel, spanned by a drawbridge, leads to outer waters and on one side stands the 16th-century Lieutenance, which was once the residence of the Governor of Honfleur and served as part of more extensive fortifications.

The small, rectangular Vieux Bassin is the heart of Honfleur and the old town clusters tight around it. The

accounts of Honfleur's significant seafaring history. Today, the neighbouring old prison houses the Folk Art Museum where traditional local Normandy crafts are exhibited. The overall scene is very picturesque. Replace some of the modern boats with older vessels, clear away the tourists and the picture of 17th–18th-century Honfleur is untainted.

Honfleur's importance dates back to medieval times and for a long time it was the object of contention between the French and English. However, Honfleur's glory developed later, when it became a favoured base for mariners during the great seafaring era of the 16th and 17th centuries.

These were pioneering days. A Frenchman, Jacques Cartier, had claimed Canada for his king and country in 1535. Few took much interest in this new territory, until, early the following century, it was deemed worthy of colonization. In 1608, Samuel de Champlain was despatched from Honfleur to formerly colonize Canada. This he did, establishing the settlement of Quebec. Four thousand Normandy folk, primarily Percherons followed to start a new life in Canada. Indigenous Indians attempted to resist the occupation and, in 1665, French soldiers were sent to protect the settlers. Furthermore, to ensure that French stock really did take root and survive, Louis XIV sent boatloads of hardy lasses, "the king's daughters" as they were nicknamed, across the Atlantic to marry the colonizers. Old Quebecois families trace their origins back to Normandy and Honfleur was a principle port from where their forefathers departed to the New World.

The view from here, the steps by the Lieutenance, is of Honfleur's Vieux Bassin, one of the most picturesque scenes in Normandy.

houses along quai Sainte Catherine retain their period façades, though they have now been converted into cafés, restaurants and galleries. The church on quai Saint Etienne is now the Maritime Museum with model ships and

Indeed, Honfleur, like Dieppe up the coast, became a gateway to the American colonies and in 1668 Louis XIV had a new harbour, Vieux Bassin, built to cope with the traffic; it was enlarged further in the following century. It is not difficult to picture the prospective settlers, sailors, adventurers, merchants and the assortment of other characters scurrying along the tight quaysides. Then in the 19th century, the commercial shipping was moved to the newly created Bassin de l'Est and the Vieux Bassin was left to local crafts.

Honfleur's attraction extends beyond the Vieux Bassin and the maritime. The old character is also in the lanes behind quai Sainte Catherine.

According to local legend, all the stonemasons were occupied fully in reconstruction during the aftermath of the Hundred Years War. So the local shipwrights took it upon themselves to build a stop-gap church out of wood in order that they would have somewhere to thank God for ridding them of the English. The temporary, and beautiful, 15th-century church of Sainte Catherine is still there and, in this part of the world, it is a unique example of a wooden church. Its belfry, wooden in structure, stands alongside. Religious art carved from wood by locals are in both church and belfry.

The light along the Normandy coast attracted artists, and in the 19th century Honfleur became a colony for French and foreign painters. It remains so to this day. Another local story relates the tale of Eugène Boudin (1824–1898), the son of an Honfleur pilot, who developed his untutored talent for painting through capturing the surrounding landscapes in a unique style. He would meet with fellow artists such as Jongkind, the young Monet and others over cider at "la mère Toutain" at the farm of Saint Simeon—on the road to Trouville and now a restaurant. It is said from these discourses and the subsequent experimenting there arose "Impressionism". The "School of Honfleur", with some works by Boudin and his contemporaries and the canvases of later artists inspired to come and paint this corner of Normandy, is displayed at the **Eugène Boudin Musuem**. The museum is a short walk from Sainte Catherine's along rue de l'Homme-de-Bois and left on rue du Roi Albert 1er; traditional local furniture and costumes are also displayed here. *Opening times*: mornings and afternoons except Tuesdays; closed on weekday mornings from October to mid-March; closed January to late February; tel: 31-89-16-47.

The quarter behind quai Saint Etienne, l'Enclos, once was surrounded by the old fortifications. The stone and timber-framed houses have been restored. Local exhibitions are held in the former Salt Stores (salt for preserving was stocked here) and the cafés, too, often hang the work of aspiring artists. Beyond is the church of Saint Leonard, the other side of the gardens opposite the bus stop, with its attractive 16th-century façade.

Across the Seine estuary from Honfleur is the industry of le Havre. Honfleur's own relatively modest industrial zone is on the eastern side of town. This is bypassed by the Pont de Tancarville road as it exits from Honfleur; immediately after, the road enters the department of Eure.

The Impressionists Declare War on Beauty

In 1872 Claude Monet painted the view from his room in le Havre. It was a harbour scene in the pink of dawn. In the foreground he placed a dark crude silhouette of a rowing boat and in the background only the vaguest of outlines revealed the wharves; all was enshrouded by the hazy blue mist of morning. As this was his own personal interpretation of the scene, and not a true depiction, Monet ended up calling his painting *Impression, Soleil levant* (Impression, Sunrise).

Earlier artists, notably England's J.M.W. Turner, had sought to capture the atmosphere rather than the likeness and their works had inspired, amongst others, Eugène Boudin, the quintessential outdoor artist and master of moody sky and seascapes. Boudin, a Honfleur man, met and influenced the aspiring young Monet and pointed him down a path away from convention, along a route which would lead to a new genre of art: Monet and a group of avant garde painters sought to capture the light and feeling of a scene as they perceived it; the form of the subject matter became secondary, the precise outline of a shape was of little consequence; brush strokes, previously concealed, now became a feature; working on the canvas "on location", rather than in the studio with the help of sketches, became the routine. The idea was to catch the light—that glint of sunshine on the water—to feel the atmosphere, to breathe the scene. The fact that the end result was not a picture postcard image was irrelevant.

During the late 1860s, Monet and his artist circle would meet on Fridays at Cafe Guerbois at 9 avenue de Clichy in Paris to discuss their work and plan projects. Amongst the group were Bazille, Cezanne, Degas, Morisot, Pissarro, Renoir, Sisley and, besides the painters, there were various other artists, including the photographer Nadar: the pseudonym for Felix Tournachon. As a group they named themselves the *Anonyme Co-operative des Artistes peintres, sculpteurs, graveurs, etc.* (Co-operative Society of Painters, Sculptors, Engravers, etc.) The art of this clique shocked the establishments Salon of the French Academy who refused it exhibition. So Nadar offered his studio as a gallery.

The exhibition was not held until 1874. On 15th April Nadar's second floor rooms on 35 boulevard des Capucines were opened, revealing to Paris society 165 works by 30 of this new breed of artist. Amongst the paintings was Monet's *Impression, Soliel levant*. Ten days later the critic Louis Leroy reviewed the show in *le Charivari*, entitling his article "The Impressionists' Exhibition". He ridiculed the art and quoted one visitor's comment of Monet's painting, "The first sketch of a wall-paper is more finished than that seascape!". Another said that these artists had "declared war on beauty". Leroy's term "Impressionist", derived from the title of Monet's painting, stuck as the name for this movement of artists.

The Impressionists held seven further exhibitions over the next 12 years. Members came and went—Monet, for example, exhibited at only five of the shows. In its strictest sense, the "Impressionists" refers to the original artists of the group or, sometimes, to those whose works were displayed over the years; more loosely and popularly it applies to all the exponants of the genre of Impressionism.

Impressionism was the break from classical art; it was a breath of fresh air. Furthermore, it was the revolution against convention which paved the way for the development of modern art this century. From Impressionism arose Divisionism, or Neo-Impressionism, founded by Seurat, a movement including Van Gogh and Gauguin, and this is in turn preceded Fauvism. From these roots evolved Cubism and other increasingly abstract art. These were the new radical styles to shake the art world.

Monet, the grand old man of Impressionism, died in 1926 aged 86. The

Impression, soleil levant, by Monet. Critics at the time joked that the painters of this genre loaded a pistol with different coloured tubes of paint and fired it at the canvas, finishing off the "masterpieces" by signing their names.

art scene had changed drastically since those early days of Café Guerbois. Impressionists in their "declared war on beauty", are regarded as the very epitomy of beauty. And the 200 paintings the desperate and impoverished Monet sold in 50 franc lots in 1867 would now be worth many millions of pounds.

East of Caen

The Marshlands

The main eastbound route out of Caen is the A13 autoroute to Pont l'Evêque and beyond. Running parallel is the N175 and along this road is the British cemetery and the metal craft workshops of Sannerville. Further on, some 13 km (8 miles) out of Caen's outskirts, is the canton centre of Troarn with the nearby ruins of its 13th-century abbey. Just beyond is the River Dives and an area of fenland in what was once the river's estuary. These flatlands, appropriately nicknamed la Petite Hollande, have marshland flora and fauna and, though sliced by autoroute and route nationale, they are in themselves an empty quarter. Le Route des Marais, the Fenland Route, dips into the region, but really to appreciate this unusual corner of the countryside one should abandon the car and take to foot across dike and hedgerow.

From Troarn, take the D95 northwards to Bures-sur-Dives and the edge of Bavent. A road to the right leads to Bricqueville, Robehomme and footpaths venturing deeper into the fens. A twisting lane continues north of Robehomme, following the course of the Dives the few kilometres to the D27. Alternatively, from Bavent remain on the D95 to Varaville. In 1057, Duke William defeated a French army at the Battle of Varaville. His victory was attributed to the changing tide which rushed in and drowned the enemy soldiers, leaving their king stranded high and dry on the hillock of Brucourt.

About 6 km (3½ miles) north of Varaville along the D513 is Cabourg and the coast. However, continue east on the D27 across the marsh and River Dives and bear left along the D45b for Grangues. From here, head southwards to Criqueville and its château and on, beyond the autoroute, to Putot-en-Auge with its chapel and manor; the manor, like the nearby manors of Beauquemare and Saint Germain, is not open to the public. Continue, a road to the left leads to Beuvron-en-Auge, on the D49 to Brocottes and its chapel and to Ham by the Dives and overlooking the fens.

Over the Dives is Saint Pierre-du-Jonquet, Saint Ouen-du-Mesnil-Oger and Janville before the final couple of kilometres back to Troarn.

Cider Country

Immediately to the east of La Route des Marais is La Route du Cidre in the lush Calvados region of the Pays de D'Auge. Continue along the N175—the east–west avenue from Caen—to Dozulé, 11 km (7 miles) beyond Troarn, and bear right 5 km (3 miles) along the D85. From here, an avenue leads to Clermont-en-Auge with its chapel and view over the valleys of the Vie and Dives with the *bocage* beyond. 3 km (2 miles) to the south-west is the attractive village of Beuvron-en-Auge with its half-timbered manor and other well-maintained, old buildings. Continuing southwards on the D49, one passes Victot, with its château and stables, and then bear right on the D16 and follow on to the N13 for Crèvecoeur-en-Auge.

T he manor-château of Victot. Decorative brickwork covering the walls with geometrical designs is a common feature of the stately homes in this quarter of Calvados.

A castle stood at Crèvecoeur in the 9th century, defending the road between Caen and Lisieux, the latter being only 17 km (10 miles) to the east along the N13. The present "château complex": manor house, farm, lodge, dovecote, chapel and a moat into which visitors can dangle a line, dates from between the 12th and 15th centuries. It was restored in the 1970s and houses the **Schlumberger Museum of petroleum research and Normandy architecture**. The Schlumberger brothers were inventors and pioneers in oil

drilling techniques from Alsace who worked in the region earlier this century. *Opening times*: 12.00–8.00 p.m. daily in July and August; 1.00–7.00 p.m. daily except Wednesdays in April, May, June and September; 2.00–6.00 p.m. on weekdays in March and October; tel: 31-63-02-45. A few kilometres further south, up a turning off the D16, is the Mont de la Vigne with its views, manor and ruins of a medieval castle (gardens open on Sunday afternoons from April to October and on Monday afternoons during the rest of the year). There are other manors a short distance beyond.

However, return northwards and from Crèvecoeur take the D101 5 km (3 miles) to Cambremer, the local canton and cider centre. Selected farmers around here are awarded the "*Cru de Cambremer*" for the excellent cider, *pommeau* and calvados that they brew. Farms with a sign displaying this

A most characteristic Normandy sight: the brown and white Normandais cow in an orchard, biting apples from the tree.

distinction invite passers-by to sample, and perhaps buy, home-made produce; a list of such outlets is available from the tourist office. East of Cambremer minor roads form a twisting route via Grandouet with its church to le Val Richer on the D59, where, in the last century, a French ambassador to England chose to retire in the remains of its Cistercian abbey.

A couple of kilometres north along the road you come to Château de la Roque-Baignard and then, bearing left along the D117, continue on to Rumesnil (Druval church is just to the north), and then to Clermont-en-Auge on the D85.

The Streams

Continue travelling for about 12 km (7 miles) eastwards from Dozulé along the D175 and bear left on the D58. It is a couple of kilometres to the village of Beaumont-en-Auge, which is on a hill overlooking the Touques valley and its river as it flows into its final stretch.

The village once had a priory, its church dating from the 11th-century remains. It fell into disuse in the 17th century after its monks rejected Jansenism, an austere but controversial and fashionable branch of Catholicism, and set up a military academy instead. The mathematician and astronomer Marquis de Laplace (1749–1827) was born in the village and an exhibition remembers him through his works. The seaside resort of Villers-sur-Mer is 15 km (9 miles) north-west along the D118; *en route* is the medieval church of Saint Pierre-Azif with its collection of Flemish paintings.

However, to head deeper into lush Calvados countryside, continue along the D58 across minor streams and then the Touques itself. A kilometre or so to the left is the 12th–15th century **Manoir des Evêques** at Canapville. It once served as the home for the Bishops of Lisieux. *Opening times*: 2.00–6.00 p.m. and daily except Tuesdays from mid-June to September; Fridays and weekends only during the rest of the year; tel: 31-65-24-75.

Deauville and the sea (*see* page 177) are 6 km (3½ miles) to the left and Pont l'Evêque 5 km to the right (*see* page 188). However, cross the N177 and cut through the forest along the D279 to Saint Gatien-en-Bois. Then eastwards, picking up the D17 to Saint Benoit-d'Hebertot and the 17th–18th-century château and medieval church at neighbouring Saint André.

South, across the autoroute, the D140 leads into the pretty countryside cut by small rivers, notably the Chaussey, to le Mesnil, with its church, and the canton centre of Blangy-le-Château. Beyond, a minor road bears towards Lisieux (*see* page 188). Just before the city is the village of Rocques with its medieval church. The D262 to the right leads to Quilly-le-Vicomte; the church here is presumed to be one of the oldest in Normandy with parts dating from the 10th century. Downstream the D48 passes through Coquainvilliers, where there is the Calvados distillery of Moulin de la Foulonnerie (visitors welcome, tel: 31-62-29-26); further down the valley is le Breuil-en-Auge where Pont-l'Evêque cheese is made.

Continue on the west bank's D48 and there is Saint Hymer off to the left on the D280. Saint Hymer, a

*F*arm houses are left to rot as youngsters abandon the countryside in favour of the towns.

True Norman Spirit

If a Norman's wine is his cider then his cognac is his calvados. One of the most endearing Norman traditions—and one certainly not trussed up for the tourists—is the itinerant liquorman travelling the back lanes of Normandy with his alambic, a mobile Heath Robinson-like still. He serves the local farmers, who leave him their barrels of fermented apple juice, and from it he creates the strong alcohol in his splendid steam-puffing contraption. It takes 15 litres (26 pints) of cider to make 1 litre (1.7 pints) of calvados.

The quality of home-made calvados is variable, though it is often coarse and powerful enough to burn a hole in the heart. The large factory distilleries manufacture a more refined product under the controls of the *Calvados Appelation Reglementée* and the best calvados is allowed to age for up to 15 years in the barrel.

In true Norman spirit, calvados should be drunk first thing in the morning and last thing at night, and at various times in between: *Café calva*—black coffee and a good measure of calvados—is taken at breakfast; after dinner a glass of calvados should accompany the coffee before going to bed. As for the rest of the day, one important ritual half way through a typical hefty meal is the partaking of the *trou Normand*, a slug of calvados—or sorbet soaked or swimming (depending on your host) in the liquor—which clears a "hole" in the stomach for the next course.

---

flourishing monastery and priory in medieval times, wholeheartedly adopted the doctrines of Jansenism, unlike Beaumont-en-Auge, in the 17th century; the church is 14th century and rich with religious art. The church at nearby Pierrefitte-en-Auge, dating from the 13th century, is also notable. So, too, is the 17th-century church at Manneville-la-Pipard on the other side of Touques *en route* to Pont-l'Evêque.

Pont-l'Evêque

An ancient bridging point , and now at the intersection of the autoroutes and routes nationales, Pont-l'Evêque has long been a crossroads. But its more appealing fame comes from the locally made cheese which bears its name. "Pont-l'Evêque" has been produced here for over 700 years. Strategically placed, the town received its share of destruction in 1944. The old quarter, around rue Saint Michel and rue de

Vaucelles, does retain some of its character. Indeed, the flamboyant church of Saint Michel is of note; opposite is the Louis XIII-style Hôtel Montpensier. The former convent of les Dames Dominicaines de l'Ile is in place du Tribunal and nearby is the town hall–tourist office, the 18th-century Hôtel de Brilly, where writer Robert de Flers was born in 1872.

Lisieux

As capital, important commercial and market town and crossroads of the lush and prosperous Pays d'Auge, Lisieux was a significant headquarters for the Germans during the War. The city was destined to suffer during the Normandy invasion and so it did, with much of the town being flattened. Today, the post-war reconstruction looks unremarkable, but at least an air of provincial prosperity fills its streets. However, all in Lisieux is overshadowed by the extraordinary cult and basilica of Saint Theresa.

Theresa Martin was born in Alençon on 2 January 1873 into a pious bourgeois family. After her mother had died when she was four, her father sold up and moved with his five daughters to Lisieux. No doubt influenced by the religious commitment of her elder sisters, Theresa vowed at the age of nine to forfeit the comforts of home and become a Carmelite nun. At 15 she asked her father's permission to allow her to fulfil this aim; this he reluctantly gave, but she was then refused by a committee of nuns because of her age. Resolved in her objective, Theresa travelled to Rome where she gained papal consent to become a Carmelite.

She entered this, the most deprivative order, in April 1888 and was fully dedicated to her physically demanding life as a nun, attaining satisfaction in her solitude through prayer and in the writing of an autobiography, *History of a Soul,* a simple tale of an innocent girl devoted to Jesus.

Theresa died after a protracted illness in 1897 and was buried in her convent. Those who remembered her were few. Her book was published posthumously and as it circulated it began to touch the hearts of a growing audience. Theresa won fame, the faithful prayed to her and claimed she cured them of ailments. During the First World War, French soldiers held an image of her as a talisman; she was, indeed, a contrast to Saint Joan of Arc, their traditional protectress.

Such was the holy popularity of Theresa, Sister Theresa of the Child Jesus, as she was known, that she was beatified in 1923 and canonized two years later.

The immense **Saint Theresa Basilica,** white and ornate like the Sacré Coeur in Paris, was built high over Lisieux, on a hill, with a commanding view over the city. Its vastness and ostentation has gained it many critics, and presumably Theresa herself would have been alarmed by the creation of such a sepulchre. So, too, would she have been by the hundreds of thousands of pilgrims, which included Pope John Paul II in 1980, who make the journey from all over the world to her tomb each year. A place this large is required to accommodate this flow of devotees.

Work on this basilica commenced in 1923 and was completed in 1954, though it has yet to be adorned with its finishing touches. Complete or not, it is a splendid monument, whatever its detractors say. It covers an area of 4,500 m^2 (5,382 yd^2); the dome rises to 93 m (305 ft) and inside it is covered with gold mosaics and images of saints and angels; slabs of marble decorate the walls and floor; the spectacular design is Byzantine and has more in common with Santa Sophia in Istanbul than with traditional places of worship in Normandy. The surprise of finding such a monument in an ordinary market town is part of its attraction and it is a refreshing change from the usual Romanesque, Gothic, flamboyant, Renaissance churches of the region. The solemn echo of whispers and footsteps and the flickering of numerous candles add a reverent air to the interior. However the laser show which takes place periodically, beaming images of Saint Theresa down the aisle, is rather excessive.

Normandy's "Sacre Coeur" dominates Liseux. It is an ornate and opulent mausoleum for Saint Theresa, the little girl who was canonized for her very simplicity and purity.

When they came to Lisieux, Monsieur Martin and his daughters moved to **Les Buissonnets** in the northeast quarter of the city, and this is where Theresa spent her childhood before entering the monastery. The house has become a museum, her room can be visited and her toys and clothes are on display; a statue in the garden commemorates the moment she asked for her father's consent to become a nun. *Opening times*: daily from February to mid-December.

After she had been accepted into the Carmelite order, Theresa made her home in the Carmel which stands at the foot of the hill now surmounted by her mausoleum. This is where she spent the rest of her life, from the age of 15 to 24. A section of the old Carmel is open to the public and some of Theresa's effects from this era are on view. Nearby is the **Diorama of Saint Theresa** where wax figures of Theresa recount stages in her short life.

Holy Commerce

Saint Theresa is big business. Her pilgrims are the city's customers and local souvenir shops tempt them with a treasury of tacky Theresa mementoes stamped with the famous sepia image of the wan face of the girl saint. Thanks to Saint Theresa, Lisieux is second only to Lourdes as a place of pilgrimage in France. It is ironic that this young girl, who had to obtain the pope's permission before being shut off from the world, is now the focus of such full-blown public attention.

Opening times: daily except Sundays; tel: 31-62-06-55.

Lisieux, an important town during the Gallo-Roman period, has long been a religious centre, having been a bishopric since the 6th century. Down in the centre of town, in place Thiers, is the cathedral of Saint Pierre which, like the basilica, escaped the assault of 1944 relatively unscathed (plans by the British to bomb Saint Theresa's were aborted at the last minute). Constructed between 1170 and 1250, the fine, sombre Saint Pierre is the oldest Gothic church in Normandy and contrasts starkly with the modern pile on the hill. Additions were made in the 15th century, including the Lady Chapel by Bishop Pierre Cauchon, the man who sent Joan of Arc to her pyre; he is buried here in the church.

The former Bishop's Palace is next to Saint Pierre and is now the **Palais de Justice**. The Gold Room, Salle Dorée, the bishop's reception hall, remains intact and can be visited. *Opening times*: afternoons except Tuesdays. In front of the building are the formal lawns which are now public gardens.

A link with the past of Lisieux and Pays d'Auge lies in the **Musuem of Old Lisieux**, on boulevard Louis Pasteur, across the River Touques from the centre, which gives us an insight of the city and region before the War. Displays also include local art, traditional crafts and an assortment of local treasures dating from various periods. *Opening times*: afternoons except Tuesdays; tel: 31-62-07-70. A few of Lisieux's old timber-framed houses still stand; the tourist office can provide details.

East of Lisieux

East of Lisieux the busy N13 cuts a straight path into Eure department while to the west it passes through interesting countryside on the way to Caen.

South-eastwards the D519 runs alongside the River Orbiquet for the 19 km (12 miles) to Orbec. It passes the 17th-century château of le Mesnil-Guillaume which is on the right approximately 7 km (4 miles) from Lisieux. From here the D519 continues into the Eure department.

Debussy lived in Orbec for a while and composed here at the 17th-century Hôtel de Croissy. Indeed, the town retains a fair number of old Normandy houses, most striking of which is the 16th-century **Vieux Manoir**; it now contains the Municipal Museum with its exhibitions and accounts of local arts, crafts and history. *Opening times*: in the afternoons at Easter and in July and August except Tuesdays and weekend afternoons from April to June and September and October; tel: 31-32-82-02. Most conspicuous, though, is the huge tower of the 15th-century church of Notre Dame. It is an attractive few kilometres south from Orbec along the D130a to the source of the Orbiquet.

South of Lisieux

The rich, dairy pastures of the southern Pays d'Auge are the heartland of the soft, full creamy cheeses for which Normandy is so famous. Livarot, 18 km (11 miles) south of Lisieux along the D579, is the "Cheese Capital" of the region. However, 5 km (3 miles) out of Lisieux, bear left off the D579 for the picturesque 15th–16th-century

191

H eavy udders must be milked after a long day at the cud.

château of Saint **Germain-de-Livet**. The turreted gatehouse and main stretch of wall are chequered in design, while on the right the wing is half-timbered. Within, there is also a variety of decors, most notably in Louis XV and Louis XVI styles. *Opening times*: 9.30 a.m. to 12.00 p.m. and 2.00–6.00 p.m. daily except Tuesdays from February to mid-October and mid-October to mid-December; tel: 31-31-00-03.

Moving southwards and along the western bank of the Touques, there are manors, châteaux and churches of local note at Caudemone, Auquainville, Fervaques, Cheffreville-Tonnencourt,

Notre Dame-de-Courson (there is a stud at la Cauvinière manor off the Orbec road), Chiffretot and at Bellou along the D110 from Chiffretot. From Bellou head for Lisores on the D268. The Normandy artist and pioneering cubist Fernand Léger (1881–1955) used to come here and a museum in an old barn now houses some of his works and mementoes. *Opening times*: except Wednesdays from April to November and weekends during the rest of the year; tel: 31-62-53-13. Beyond Lisores, bear right along the D274 for Sainte Foy-de-Montgomery where there is a cider-making factory (visitors welcome).

A few kilometres to the south, in the department of Orne, is the market town of Vimoutiers and the nearby cheese village of Camembert, while to the north is Livarot. *En route*, or rather left off the main road, is the church at la Chapelle-haut-Grue and, on the D155, the twin manor houses and church of Saint Bazile at Heurtevent and the chapel of Val Boutry at le Mesnil-Baclay just outside Livarot.

Livarot gives its name to a very characteristic sharp-smelling, reddened, crusted cheese. The "Livarot" is made only here in this small corner of Pays d'Auge, and the fact that manufacturers use 5.5 litres (10 pints) of milk to produce a 600 g (1¼ lb) cheese reflects the very lushness of the countryside. Furthermore, the quality is guaranteed: The "Livarot" reached perfection in its evolution 700 years ago. While modern machinery can facilitate labour, nothing is done to hasten the process of the cheese's maturing and, as always, it takes 100 days to make a "Livarot". The old methods of cheese-making are exhibited at the **Conservatoire des Techniques Fromagères Traditionelles** on rue l'Evêque. *Opening times*: tours through the day, daily from April to late October and Wednesdays to Saturdays during the rest of the year; tel: 31-63-45-96. Also "traditional" are some of the houses, notably the 16th-century Manoir de la Pipardière, the Château de Neuville and Manoir d'Ouilly. A display of turn-of-the-century steam-operated machinery can also be seen here; visit the tourist office for details.

West of Livarot, the D4 leads past le Mesnil-Baclay with the chapel of Val Boutry, through Sainte Marguerite-de-Viette and the old cheese village of Boissey. Here a minor road bends and heads southwards to Saint Georges-en-Auge and then west again to Ecouts, with the nearby châteaux of Houlbec

and le Robillard, before turning north via Berville to Saint Pierre-sur-Dives.

Saint Pierre-sur-Dives' contribution to the world of cheese is the cheese box: most of the Camembert, Livarot and Pont l'Evêque wooden containers are manufactured here. The town's Romanesque church was destroyed by fire in the early 12th century as William the Conqueror's sons fought over their differences. Its fine replacement, the present abbey church, was built over the following 200 years. Light entering one of the windows hits the "Meridian", a copper gnomon on the floor of the nave. The chapter house to the south displays its medieval, glazed tiles.

Also a victim of fire was the 12th-century market hall which had been built by the abbey's monks. It burnt down during the fighting in 1944. In its place now stands an exact replica in which nearly 300,000 wooden pegs, and not a single nail, were used in construction. Monday is market day.

Here in Saint Pierre-sur-Dives there is also a museum, **Musée des Techniques Fromagères** along the rue Saint Benoit from the chapter house, which recounts the traditional cheese-making methods. *Opening times*: Easter to November except Tuesdays; tel: 31-20-97-90.

Just south of Saint Pierre-sur-Dives is the manor at Carel, though more significant is the château at **Vendeuvre**, a few kilometres further up the Dives.

Jacques Blondel built the Vendeuvre château for the exuberantly named Alexandre le Forestier d'Osseville, Comte de Vendeuvre, in the mid-18th century. The château remains the property of the count's descendants.

The gardens and some of the rooms are open to the public. Amongst the more typical château ornaments there are some unexpected exhibits: a display of games, a collection of smoking pipes and most curious of all, a museum of miniature furniture in the orangery. *Opening times*: 2.00–7.00 p.m. daily from June to mid-September and weekends and holidays from Easter to June and from mid-September to November; tel: 31-40-93-83.

Another 18th-century château within reasonable striking distance of Saint Pierre-sur-Dives is **Canon** at Mézidon; it is almost 10 km (6 miles) to the north-west and is a slight detour on the way to Caen. The main feature is the splendid gardens. French and English in design, they are adorned by Italian statues and a Chinese kiosk. A curiosity is the *chatreuses*, small walled gardens, though stranger is the legend of the *Bonnes Gens*, the indulgent celebration in honour of the Good People which used to be held in the outhouses in the 18th century. *Opening times*: afternoons from July to October except Tuesdays and from Easter to July at weekends; tel: 31-20-05-07.

From Saint Pierre-sur-Dives head north-east along the D511 past the château at Harmonville to le Godet. The pretty route to the left leads towards Sainte Marie-aux-Anglais and Mont de la Vigne, and to Saint Julien-le-Faucon. A couple of kilometres to the north is the church and 17th-century château at Grandchamp, while just to the south is the 16th-century farmhouse at Coupesarte. Roads continue southwards through villages such as Saint Martin-du-Mesnil-Oury, Castillon-en-Auge, Saint Michel de Livet to Livarot. Continuing on the D511 it is 14 km (9 miles) from Saint Julien-le-Faucon back to Lisieux.

Caen to Falaise

Rue Saint Jean leads south from Caen's downtown to the Orne from where there are signs for the D158 and Falaise, 34 km (21 miles) to the south.

Approximately three-quarters of the way along the route, on the left, is Soumont-Saint Quentin with its museum of traditional farm tools, the nearby 18th-century château of Assy and the Laison's gorge of the Breche au Diable, the "Devil's Breach".

There are two other châteaux just north of Falaise: the 16th-century château at Aubigny, on the right of the D158, and the 18th-century château at Versainville, left of the D158 a few kilometres north-east of the town.

Falaise

The romance leading to the Conqueror's conception is popular Normandy folklore. Seventeen-year-old Robert, son of Duke Richard II of Normandy, was returning to Falaise after hunting when he encountered Arlette (sometimes known as Herleva), the daughter of a local tanner, as she washed her clothes at a spring in the valley. The more tantalizing tales claim that Arlette was singing a lovers' ballard, her skirt hitched halfway up her thighs, her bodice only loosely fastened and her full, slightly ruffled locks tumbling on to her shoulders. What is relevant, though, is that a passionate affair ensued between Robert and Arlette, which resulted in the birth of William the Bastard in a chamber of Falaise castle.

Arlette, mother of one of the greatest men of the time, and of a dynasty of English kings, made her own entry into the nobility after she was married off to Herluin, Viscount of Conteville, subsequently bearing a legitimate line of aristocrats. Her humble origins are remembered here in Falaise and the Fontaine d'Arlette at the foot of the castle is said to be the place where, in 1027, Robert first espied his future mistress.

It is as a centre of action at the climax of the battle for Normandy in 1944, however, that Falaise is most famous. The British–Canadian divisions pushing southwards from Caen, crossed the Laison and finally won Falaise, having destroyed over 60 per cent of the place on 17 August. Meanwhile, coming from the south, the Americans and their support had captured Argentan. Thus, the Allies, in control of the north, west and south sides were closing in on the German 7th Army.

The only escape route open to the Germans was eastwards, through what became known as the Falaise Gap, the 22 km (14 mile) corridor between Falaise and Argentan; seizing their opportunity the Germans fled this way, but in retreat they suffered badly under the aerial bombardment. On the 19th, the Allies, arriving from the north and south, closed the Gap when they met at Chambois, a village 13 km (8 miles) north-east of Argentan, and two days later they received the capitulation from the remaining enemy forces at the nearby village of Tournai-sur-Dives. Thus the battle for Normandy was concluded.

Falaise castle is on the east bank of the Ante facing the limestone spur of Mount Myrrha across the river. *Falaise*, meaning "cliff", was so-called because of the Myrrha. It was one of the main citadels of medieval Normandy and was favoured by the dukes as a stronghold and prison. Amongst those interned here was Arthur of Brittany, King John's young nephew, arguably the rightful monarch of the English throne. He was later put to death in Rouen.

It is likely that the castle was of wood, rather than stone, during Duke Robert's time in the early 11th century but William may have partly reinforced it in stone in the 1060s. The origins of the present fortifications, however, date back to the 12th century and to Henry Beauclerk, who built the solid keep.

Inside there is a small chapel housing a list of some 300 knights who accompanied William on to the battlefield of Hastings, giving British visitors the chance to trace their Norman colonial roots. Other quarters open to the public, subject to restoration works, are the dining hall and the dungeon where Arthur, amongst others, was detained at the turn of the 13th century. Here, too, legend pervades: "The window from which Robert watched the lovely Arlette", "The room where Robert and Arlette frolicked", "The chamber in which William was born". Such assertions should probably be treated with a deal of salt, given that the castle was actually built long after William's birth.

The massive round tower, the Talbot Tower, with its 4 m (13 ft) thick walls was constructed in the early 1200s by Philippe-Auguste; 700 years later it served as a watch-post for the Germans and, in trying to dislodge the enemy, the Allies damaged the tower. *Opening times*: 8.00 a.m. to 12.00 p.m.. and 2.00–7.00 p.m. daily from 16 May to 15 September; 9.00 a.m. to 12.00 p.m.. and 2.00–6.00 p.m. daily except Tuesdays and Fridays from 16 September to 15 May; closed from 10–25 January; tel: 31-90-17-26.

Housed in a former cheese factory on chemin des Roches, not far from the castle, is Falaise's war museum, **Musée Août** 1944, which recounts the story of the Falaise Gap. *Opening times*: 10.00 a.m. to 12.00 p.m. and 2.00–6.00 p.m. daily from June to September, closed Mondays and Tuesdays from September to June and closed from December to March; tel: 31-90-37-19. Beyond, a kilometre out of Falaise, is Noron-l'Abbaye with its church's Romanesque belfry.

Heading back into town from the castle, you pass through place Guillaume-le-Conquerant with its dramatic 19th-century bronze equestrian statue of a highly charged William, presumably leading his men into battle; at the base are the figures of the first six dukes of Normandy. On one side is the Gothic–Renaissance church of la Trinité, on the other the 18th-century Hôtel de Ville. Beyond, in the post-1944 downtown, is the place Belle Croix where the Sunday market is held, and by the lake to the left off rue Camp de Ferme is the 14th–15th-century Porte de Cordeliers. On the far side of the main Caen road is Falaise's other church of note, the 11th–16th-century Saint Gervais. The Romanesque church of Saint Laurent is about 500 m (547 yd) north of Saint Gervais along rue Gambetta.

Following the Caen road in the Argentan direction, there is the tourist office on the right, and parks which include the 17th–18th-century Château Fresnaye (local exhibitions are held here in summer), on the left. The

*W*illiam the *Conqueror at Falaise, his birthplace, leading the Normans to another victory.*

196

Guibray quarter is at this end of Falaise and, from the time of William until the last century, it held one of the largest annual market fairs in Europe. Today Guibray, literally the "village of mud", remembers this past in its street names: Leather Merchants' Street, Drapers' Pit, Grocers' Street, in the surrounds of the 11th-century church of Notre Dame.

Suisse Normande

Long rue Saint Jean cuts through southern Caen and crosses the Orne. Its continuation becomes rue Falaise on the other side of the railway bridge. For Suisse Normande, follow directions for the D562 and Thury-Harcourt which is 26 km (16 miles) to the south. Prettier, less busy roads run closer to the Orne and these can be joined at many places. For example, 12 km (7½ miles) out of Caen, bear right at Laize-la-Ville for Clinchamps-sur-Orne. Cross the river and continue upstream, picking up the D212 all the way to Thury-Harcourt.

Just before entering Thury-Harcourt, the D212a branches to the right to follow Boucle-du-Hom, the dramatic meander with only a pinch of land preventing creation of an ox-bow lake. Thury-Harcourt is the northern gateway to Suisse Normande, Normandy's "Little Switzerland". The town was badly destroyed during the fighting of 1944, and amongst the casualties was the Harcourt family **château**. The building was ruined, but the gardens remain lovely and well-cared for. *Opening times*: 2.30–6.30 p.m. Sundays and holidays from April

to July. Besides the famous Harcourts, whose name frequently crops up elsewhere in Normandy, Thury-Harcourt can claim a more exclusive fame through Jean Legardeur, the first mayor of Quebec in 1602, who was born here. One of the town's few relics from ancient times is its 13th-century church façade.

West of Thury-Harcourt the D6 is a pretty route to Aunay-sur-Odon (*see* page 201). However, turn left along the D166 and then right to Saint Martin-de-Sallen, passing by the chapels of Saint Benin and Saint Joseph from where there is a panorama over the surrounding countryside. Return to the D166 at le Mesnil Roger and continue to Caumettes, the D211 to the right also leads to a pretty path towards Aunay-sur-Odon, and on to Saint Lambert, Saint Pierre-la-Vieille and Pontécoulant. The **château of Pontécoulant**, a couple of kilometres north of the village of Pontécoulant, was built by the le Douclet family at different stages between the 16th and 18th centuries and it remained their property until it was bequeathed to the department in 1908. It is unusual and unpretentious in style; the English gardens and part of the house, with period furniture and heirlooms, can be visited. *Opening times*: 10.00 a.m. to 12.00 p.m. and 2.30–6.00 p.m. daily except Tuesdays from mid-April to October; closed during October; 4.30 p.m. closing time in the first two weeks of November; and 2.00–4.30 p.m. daily except Mondays and Tuesdays from mid-November to mid-April; tel: 31-69-62-54. Beyond Pontécoulant is Condé-sur-Noireau, the southern gateway to Suisse Normande.

fame of Jules Dumont d'Urville, one of the great pioneering Antarctic explorers, who was born here in 1790. His statue stands in the square opposite the *mairie*, and, at its base, there are three stones brought back from La Terre Adelie by a later explorer. Indeed, Adelie, d'Urville's wife, probably has greater universal fame, as it was after her that the explorer named the chunk of the southern continent as well as the Adelie species of penguin.

Some 26 km (16 miles) west of Condé-sur-Noireau is Vire and immediately to the south is the department of Orne, with Flers 12 km (7½ miles) along the D962. Thury-Harcourt is only 15 km (12 miles) to the north along the main D562 which cuts through Suisse Normande, passing the Bellevue gliding club, the Cantelou golf club, Clécy (*see* below) and hugging a fair stretch of the Orne over the last few kilometres. Also attractive is the 12 km (7½ mile) route to the east of Condé-sur-Noireau which follows the Noireau and department border to Pont d'Ouilly.

In a land most famed for its artists and writers there was born in 1790 one of the great Antarctic explorers. Dumont d'Urville, from Conde-sur-Noireau, was discoverer of territories and a waddling penguin which he named Adelie after his wife.

The pretty village of Pont d'Ouilly, at the confluence of the rivers Orne and Noireau, is the eastern gateway to Suisse Normande and is in the heart of scenic countryside. The road east, the D511 which leads to Falaise, soon loses its charm. However, there is spectacular geography to the south. Take the D167 upstream along the Orne and bear right at the D43 to follow the meander of the Rouvrou, a tributary of the Orne. Beyond the village of Rouvrou is the 120 m (393 ft) high Roche d'Oëtre, probably Suisse Normande's most dramatic rock. This is in Orne department. Minor roads

Like Thury-Harcourt, Condé-sur-Noireau was damaged severely during the battle for Normandy. There is a medieval choir in the church of Saint Martin, but not much else of note remains from the past, except for the

*S*uisse Normande—
Normandy's little Switzerland—
is hardly alpine territory,
however, there are pleasant
hill walks with pretty views over
lush pastures.

continue an attractive route for the few kilometres south-east to the River Orne's Gorges of Saint Aubin which, for part of their length, serve as the border between Orne and Calvados.

The D1 west out of Pont d'Ouilly bisects the confluence of the Orne and Noireau and runs via the 16th-century pilgrimage chapel of Saint Roch (le pardon de Saint Roch is held here on the first Sunday after 15 August) and the Rendezvous-des-Chasseurs to le Fresne on the D562.

The other option is to follow the Orne downstream, turning left for the villages of Cossesseville and Le Bô, finally leaving the valley floor at Pont du Vey, which bridges the Orne, to climb to Clécy on the left.

Quaint Clécy is, by virtue of its picturesqueness and location in the centre of Suisse Normande, the "capital" of this Little Switzerland, and serves as the hub in the heart of the region, offering hotels, restaurants, and a tourist office which can provide information about the various activities taking place around here. Also in Clécy is a **Miniature Railway Museum**, a fanciful train set with locomotives shunting and whistling through a model France. *Opening times*: 9.00 a.m. to 12.30 p.m. and 2.00–6.00 p.m. daily from Easter to October and afternoons for the rest of the year; tel: 31-69-07-13. A short walk away down at the 16th-century manor of **Placy**, there is a museum of traditional crafts and work utensils. *Opening times*: 9.00 a.m. to 12.00 p.m. and 2.00–6.00 p.m. daily from mid-June to October; Sundays only during the rest of the year; tel: 31-69-75-06.

One of the main activities in Suisse Normande is the walking. Two *Grandes Randonnées* pass through the region: the GR36 "Vallée de l'Orne" from Ouistreham to Ecouche and the GR221 "Sentier de la Suisse Normande" from Pont d'Ouilly to Pont Farcy and beyond. From Clécy itself, there are three short and pleasant walks: west to l'Eminence, a hill on the other side of the D562 and Grand

*S*port in the air, on land and on water, Suisse Normande is the centre for all. Group activities are organized, such as canoeing along the quiet back reaches of the River Orne.

Camp; south to Croix de la Faverie from where there are views over the Orne; and east across the Orne to le Pain de Sucre, Little Switzerland's Sugar Loaf Mountain. Details about these and other walks can be obtained from the tourist office, which can also

provide information about hang-gliding, gliding, flying, rock-climbing, cycling, horse riding, canoeing, fishing and golf, all of which take place in Suisse Normande. Contact the tourist office at place de l'Eglise or telephone 31-69-79-95.

From Clécy, take the D33c for la Serverie on the other side of the Orne. Continue towards the old iron-mining village of Saint Rémy, with its Romanesque church, but turn right and ascend the Route des Cretes in the direction of Saint Omer. Up here, there is a magnificent view over the Orne and Suisse Normande; it is from here that the Deltaplane aviators launch themselves into flight. After Saint Omer, the drama of the scenery lessens. The shortest route to Thury-Harcourt is the road which twists northwards passing through la Courrière and Esson with the nearby church of Bonne Nouvelle.

South-west of Caen

The River Odon approaches Caen from the south-west. Fighting during the summer of 1944 was particularly intense along the stretch of the river just upstream of the city, as the Allies—the British and Canadians— battled to secure the valley. Boulevard

A bird's-eye view of the River Orne flowing through Suisse Normande. Up here, on the Route des Cretes, is the launch pad for Deltaplane aviators and hang-gliders.

Yves Guillou leads south-west out of Caen and at Verson, on the outskirts, the D214 branches to the left over the Odon to Fontaine Etoupefour. The château of **Fontaine**, down a road to the left, with its 15th-century gateway, moat and fanciful styles of architecture, seems suited to the taste of its earlier owner Nicholas d'Escoville, the creator of Hôtel d'Escoville in Caen. *Opening times*: afternoons from Saturdays to Tuesdays in July and August and weekends in September; tel: 31-26-73-20.

The D214 continues and another turning to the left leads to Hill 112, one of the main objectives during the fighting of 1944. There are memorials to those who lost their lives. The D214 follows the Odon through Baron-sur-Odon and a succession of villages. At **Parfouru-sur-Odon** there is an exhibition of the traditional farming techniques of the region. *Opening times*: afternoons during the summer; tel: 31-77-01-13. At Epène, just to the south, a collection of traditional Normandy costumes can be viewed on request; tel: 31-77-22-89. Domestics, employees of the local gentry, used to hold an annual fair by the 13th-century chapel at Banneville-sur-Ajon, in the neighbouring valley to the east. From here, one can pick up the D8 and pass le Mesnil-au-Grain, with its 15th-century church, on the way to Aunay-sur-Odon.

Aunay was badly damaged in 1944 and was rapidly rebuilt in the shadows of its large church after the War. The old times, however, are documented in an exhibition, "Aunay Autrefois", at the *mairie* (open during working hours).

There is pretty countryside around Aunay. The most scenic region is to the east and south leading to Thury-Harcourt and Suisse Normande (*see* page 197). Alternatively, the D7 to the north covers an attractive route to Villers-Bocage.

You could extend the journey to Villers-Bocage. From Aunay, take the D26 to the south-west, bearing right along the D291a to l'Abbaye. The 12th-century abbey was damaged during the Revolution, but was restored and was initially converted into a spinning mill before becoming the present Camembert processing factory. Beyond are la Fresnée and Ondefontaine on the D290, and stretching to the west of them is the pretty Bois de Buron. Just north of la Fresnée is the D54. Follow it west bearing right after a few kilometres for Saint Georges d'Aunay, home of the 19th-century poet Charles Lemaitre; the nearby medieval mill, le Moulin de Raville, was in operation until recently and is open to the public on Saturday and Sunday afternoons. Villers-Bocage can then be reached via Maisoncelles-Pelvey.

The traditional bocage lifestyle of the region is recorded in Villers' exhibition of "Le pre-Bocage au XIX Siecle", which is open during the summer; tel: 31-77-16-14. For a taste of the real thing, visit the cattle market—the town is a centre for the beef industry—which starts at 6.30 on Wednesday mornings.

Roads west lead through *bocage* country to the department of Manche. To the south-west the busy Caen road, the N175, continues; after 5 km (3 miles) the D577 branches to the left. **La Cabosse Zoo**, with wild cats, exotic sheep, deers, reptiles and birds in a 10 hectare (25 acre) park near Jurques, is about 6 km (3½ miles) on the right. *Opening times*: 9.00 a.m. to 7.00 p.m. daily; tel: 31-77-80-58. The road continues as an attractive route to Vire, a total of 34 km (21 miles) from Villers-Bocage.

Alternatively, continue on the N175 passing through Bois du Homme and the village of Saint Martin-des-Besaces, with its local war museum, open on Sunday afternoons and in the holidays during the summer, to la Croix Vengée on the border with Manche. The D186 to the right goes to Torigni-sur-Vire and Saint Lô, while, to the left, the D56 leads to the Gorges de la Vire and the Bocage Virois. A pretty circuit to the west of the D56 can be strung through Mont Bertrand, Campeaux, Bures-les-Monts, Pleines Oeuvres, Pont Farcy, Saint Marie Outre l'Eau, Pont Bellanger, Malloué and Saint Martin Don along the minor roads such as the D185, the D306, the D309 and the D293. The scenery, the villages and a 17th–18th-century château at Pont Bellanger are the main sights. Le Beny-Bocage, canton centre and important market (held on Thursdays) is a few kilometres east along the D56 which links with the D577 10 km (6 miles) north of Vire.

Vire

Pigs' intestines and vauderville have assured Vire of fame even in modern times. The former, chitterlings known as *andouilles*, are thoroughly cleaned, marinated and then smoked on a fire of beech wood for 6 to 8 weeks; the same preparation was used 200 years ago when the Vire chitterlings first gained popularity in Paris. The latter is derived from Vaux de Vire, the name given to the site of the confluence of the rivers Vire and Virene and the title used for a collection of light-hearted, earthy songs composed in the 1400s by Oliver Basselin, a Vire fuller. His compositions won him national recognition in the 17th century, while Vaux de Vire, corrupted to *vauderville*, became a genre of songs.

*F*unctional rather than pretty, the remains of the old granite ramparts are Vire's proud centrepiece.

In its more ancient history, Vire was a fortified town before the colonization of Normandy by the Vikings. In the 12th century, Henry Beauclerk, a prolific builder of defences, constructed the keep in Vire. Today, its broken ruins are all that is left of it. However, you can appreciate the value of the site in the tight meander of the Vire, overlooking the famous Vaux de Vire. The best view of the valleys, though, is from the Rocher des Rames further downstream.

Vire was a much-mutilated casualty of the 1944 Normandy invasion. But, in the heart of the town, the 15th-century clock tower, surmounted on a solid stubby granite gateway dating from the 13th century, survived. There are fine views over Vire from the top.

Along the road from the clock tower are two other 13th-century defence towers, Vire's coat of arms comprises two towers, which were part of the former citadel walls. Like those of the clock tower, they are made from the locally quarried granite, and give an indication of the strength the ramparts must have originally had. The nearby church of Notre Dame was founded around the same time as the keep, though the present structure is predominantly 13th–16th century.

The old **Hôtel Dieu**, the renovated 13th-century hospital situated in rue A Gaston, is now the Vire Museum. Here, the history and the old ways of life in town and surrounding *bocage* countryside are recounted with the aid of reconstructed craft workshops and traditional artefacts; the works of local artists are also exhibited, including drawings by Charles Léandre, a Normandy man, who provided illustrations for Flaubert. *Opening times*: 10.00 a.m. to 12.00 p.m.. and 2.00–6.00 p.m. daily except Tuesdays from May to October; 2.00–6.00 p.m. daily except Tuesdays from October to May; tel: 31-68-10-49.

The makers of chitterlings, as well as of *rillettes* and tripe, are the town's artisans. Monsieur Ruault of Vire, the world champion tripe maker in 1966, is something of a local hero; and the tourist office can arrange visits to these craftsmen's premises.

West of Vire

About 26 km (16 miles) directly west of Vire along the pretty D524 is Villedieu-les-Poêles. The town of Saint Sever, on the northern edge of the 1,528 hectare (3,774 acre) forest of the same name, is halfway.

This is granite country, and the local rust-coloured stone is used in construction, in forts, churches, manors, thatched cottages and walls throughout the region. The local tourist office has devised "La Route du Granit". From Saint Sever, with its 12th–14th-century abbey church, head south through the forest, where there are the granite quarries, to le Gast; just west of here is the old mill of Boisbenatre. The Granite Museum is at Saint Michel-de-Montjoie, to the south in Manche (*see* page 221) while to the east of le Gast, just off the D302, is a dolmen locals call "La Pierre Coupée". L'Ermitage, the site of a now ruined 17th-century Camaldulian hermitage, is in the forest to the left; here, too, is the chapel of Notre Dame des Agnes. The D302 continues to Champ-du-Boult, and then the D150 leads northeast from here in the direction of Saint

Manvieu-Bocage. Just east of this road is the 43 hectare (106 acre) Dathée reservoir which has been converted into a leisure centre with 9-hole golf course, boating and a bird reserve. From Saint Manvieu-Bocage, it is approximately 5 km (3 miles) back to Saint Sever.

Between Caen and Bayeux

British and Canadian soldiers had pushed inland from the beach heads of Gold, Juno and Sword. Within days of D-Day they had liberated the countryside up to the northern fringes of Caen. The shore is dotted with monuments commemorating the events. Inland, between the coast and Caen, the châteaux, churches and mills are the main sights.

The D515 is the main avenue out of downtown Caen for Ouistreham, at the mouth of the Orne, 14 km (9 miles) to the north-east. The road follows the course of canal and river which are, at Bénouville, spanned by the Pegasus Bridge. The bridging point between Bénouville and Ranville, the village on the far bank, was of vital strategic importance and was captured by the British 5th Parachute Brigade in the prelude to the D-Day landings. The regiment's emblem was a Pegasus and hence the name of the bridge. Those who died are amongst the 2,566 buried at the British cemetery at Ranville. An account of the mission against the bridge is related at the **Pegasus Bridge D-Day Museum**. *Opening times*: guided tours every day during the summer and weekends only in the low season;

tel: 31-44-62-54. From Bénouville, which has an 18th-century château, it is a further 4 km (2½ miles) to Ouistreham.

Cross-channel ferries from Portsmouth berth at Caen's port of Ouistreham. Again memories of D-Day are displayed, notably at the Landing Museum in Riva-Bella, Ouistreham's conurbation and seaside resort. The French Commandos were in action along this stretch of the coast and, understandably, their victory is especially cherished; their museum is on boulevard 6 Juin, opposite the casino, and nearby, on the beach, is a memorial commemorating the 40th anniversary of D-Day. The church, Saint Samson, a monument to medieval craftsmanship, is at the southern end of Ouistreham; it has a splendid west front and doorway, and was extremely fortunate to survive the War.

From Saint Samson, the rue de Colleville leads the 3 km (2 miles) to Colleville-Montgomery (grateful citizens attached "Montgomery" to the name of their village), and, as the D35, it proceeds to Hermanville-sur-Mer, with its British cemetery, and on to la Délivrande, a total of 10 km (6 miles) from Ouistreham. The soaring spired neo-Gothic 19th-century basilica of la Délivrande stands on a site of one of Normandy's oldest places of Christian worship and pilgrimage. Even prior to Christianity, pagans were praising their effigies here. The church's 16th-century statue of the Virgin is the present object of veneration.

From la Délivrande, the D83 runs 9 km (6 miles) south-west to Thaon (see below). Alternatively, continue on the D35 the 7 km (4 miles) to Reviers with its Canadian cemetery at the entrance of the village.

*S*word, a wide windswept sandy beach, where thousands of British and Canadians came ashore on D-Day, the start of the offensive to liberate France.

The D514 corniche runs alongside the Allied landing beaches of Sword, Juno and Gold for the 31 km (19 miles) from Riva-Bella to Arro-manches. Lining the way are a string of minor resorts, all modest in size and style compared to the chic Deauville and its neighbours further up the Calvados coast. Immediately west of Riva-Bella is Colleville-Montgomery-Plage, followed by la Breche d'Hermanville and the larger Lion-sur-Mer, which has a 16th-century château and medieval church. Neighbouring Luc-sur-Mer, 3 km (2 miles) beyond, is a spa resort with attractive gardens and the bones of a whale which lost its way and ran aground here in 1885.

Langrune-sur-Mer, the next resort along the line, has Viking ancestry which is revealed in its name if nothing more: "Langrune" has become "Grönland" in present Scandinavian languages which translates as "Greenland"; why "Greenland" remains is, however, a mystery.

A further 2 km (1 mile) on is Saint Aubin-sur-Mer followed by the old fishing port of Bernières-sur-Mer, on "media" beach, the first landing place for journalists covering D-Day, with its splendid bell tower and spire rising from its church. Neighbouring Courselles-sur-Mer and Graye-sur-mer, on "celebrity" beach, where Churchill, de Gaulle and George VI came ashore, served as the Allies port until the Mulberries at Arromanches had been erected. Courselles's 16th-century château was damaged during the War and has undergone restoration. A few kilometres inland is Reviers.

There is less congestion beyond Courselles as the resorts thin out. Small Ver-sur-Mer, 4 km (2½ miles) on and a kilometre or two inland, has an impressive Romanesque church tower and a more modern lighthouse with a range of 49 km (28 miles). Finally, there is the even smaller resort of Asnelles. It is only a few kilometres from here to Arromanches. By the shore, you can see the remains of Mulberries; by road you ascend and pass the Romanesque church of Saint Côme and then look down over the town and harbour of Arromanches before making the descent.

Other remains and a full account of Mulberries are at the Invasion Museum. Opening times: 9.00 a.m. to 7.00 p.m. from mid-June to mid-September;

The Mulberries

Arromanches, no more than a seaside village, was transformed virtually overnight by the Allies into their all-important continental port. On the day after D-Day they started towing the prefabricated pieces across the Channel. Then, on site, the breakwaters, the piers and the floating roads were assembled to create the "Mulberries". Or, more, correctly, Mulberry B, as the similar Mulberry A was built by the Americans further along the coast at Omaha beach. The creation of the Mulberries was a key to the liberation of Normandy: 2.5 million men, half a million vehicles and millions of tonnes of other provisions were landed at Arromanches during the first 15 weeks after D-Day. From here, they were pushed forward to feed the Allied war effort. After the capture and rebuilding of Cherbourg harbour, the Allies shifted their hub there. The Mulberries were never meant to be more than temporary "stop-gap" ports. They had served their purpose admirably. Today, relics of this makeshift harbour can be seen out at sea.

closed for lunch during the low season; tel: 31-22-34-31. Bayeux is 10 km (6 miles) south-west of Arromanches along the D516.

Leaving Caen for Bayeux on the N413 you pass, on the right, the now restored 12th–13th-century Premonstratensian Gothic Abbey d'Ardenne. Continue for Bayeux, but turn off at Rots, with its medieval church, and head north, via Lasson, with its Renaissance château, to Cairon. Thaon, with its Romanesque church and mill, la Mine a Poivre, is a couple of kilometres to the north along the D170. The prettiest route to Fontaine-Henry, just beyond, is by way of the D83 which follows the course of the River Mue.

Ernault de Tilly, a lieutenant serving William the Conqueror, built his castle here, above the Mue, in the 11th century. Several generations later, the home and hamlet gained its name from Henry de Tilly. The prominent Harcourt family took over the premises and constructed on the ruins, the castle had been damaged during the Hundred Years War, erecting the present **château** in the 15th–16th centuries. The spiky, spiring roofs dominate the Renaissance building; the nearby 13th-century church survived the destruction. *Opening times*: 2.30–6.30 p.m. Wednesdays, Saturdays, Sundays and holidays from Easter to June and from mid-September to November; afternoons daily from June to mid-September except Tuesdays and Fridays; tel: 31-80-00-42.

Nearby is Moulineaux which has a mill and a chapel, and from here the D170 continues along the Mue to Reviers. There is another old mill at

*B*eside the expected château, manor and mill there is the extraordinary tree house hidden in the hinterland of the Côte de Nacre.

Amblie, a couple of kilometres south-west of Reviers. Beyond this is Pierrepont, with its church, and then Lantheuil.

Jacques Turgot, who was an eminent accountant–bureaucrat during the time of Louis XIII, built the château at Lantheuil. It remains neat and houses grandiose heirlooms belonging to Turgot and his family. *Opening times*: 2.30–6.30 p.m. Wednesdays, Saturdays, Sundays and holidays from

Easter to June and from mid-September to mid-October; afternoons daily except Tuesdays and Fridays from June to mid-September; afternoons on Sundays and holidays from mid-October to Easter; tel: 31-80-11-12. It is 3 km (2 miles) northwards from Lantheuil to the canton centre of Cruelly with its mill and château.

Henry Beauclerk bequeathed the 12th-century castle to his illegitimate son Robert of Gloucester. Additional buildings were added over the centuries, including the 17th-century stables. During the Normandy invasion, the Allies commandeered a section of the château, converting it into a **radio room**. A display of wartime broadcasting is on view. *Opening times*: 9.00 a.m. to 12.00 p.m. and 2.00–6.00 p.m. daily.

Creullet château is nearby, and here, in the grounds, Montgomery had a caravan converted into his HQ. Churchill, George VI and Smuts rendezvoused on 12 June 1944 in the 17th-century château.

There is a mill and priory at Saint Gabriel-Brécy just to the west of Cruelly. The priory was built by monks from Fécamp in the 11th century; however, there were later additions, such as the 15th-century Justice Tower and the 17th-century priors' quarters; the medieval church has a notable 12th-century choir. Since 1929, the **priory** has been a horticultural centre and, as one would expect, the gardens are attractive. *Opening times*: 10.00 a.m. to 12.00 p.m. and 2.00–4.00 p.m. daily; tel: 31-80-10-20.

The terraced gardens are the main feature at the 17th-century château of **Brécy**, to the south of Saint Gabriel-

Brécy; Britain's Queen Mother planted a tree here in 1967. Entrance is through a fine 17th-century gateway, and also of note is the 13th century chapel. *Opening times*: 9.00 a.m. to 12.00 p.m. and 2.00–6.00 p.m. daily except Wednesdays from March to November; tel: 31-80-11-48. To the west of Saint Gabriel-Brécy, some 4 km (2½ miles) along the D35, is the grander 18th-century château of

Bayeux cathedral, which is a jigsaw of architectural styles spanning several centuries, may displease the purists; however, it reflects an eventful history which has absorbed much love, sweat, money and antagonism.

Vassieux, which is also in a park (closed to the public). It is about 6 km (3½ miles) along the D126 from here to Bayeux.

Bayeux

Bayeux, ancient capital of the Bessin region, is one of the most historically relevant places in Normandy. Here,

important history was made. It was the Gallo-Roman town of Baiocassium Augustodurum in the 1st century AD and it became a bishopric in the late 3rd century AD. In 905, Rollo, chief of the Northmen, married Popa, the daughter of the Governor of Bayeux, which leads to speculation that this liaison influenced his decision to settle down, accept the Treaty of Saint Clair-sur-Epte six years later and adopt these lands as his new home. The couple's eldest boy, William Longsword, the first native Duke of Normandy, was a son of Bayeux and thus the city suckled the Norman line.

Rouen was then, as always, the main city in Normandy and there, and elsewhere, the Northmen blended in with the existing culture. But, in Bayeux the old Nordic heritage survived, indeed, William Longsword despatched his son, Richard, to Bayeux to learn the ancestral tongue because it was no longer spoken in Rouen.

Three generations later, Duke William the Bastard, later the Conqueror, received Harold, England's Earl of Wessex, in Bayeux in 1064. The Normans claimed that Harold pledged to William the crown of England on the death of Edward the Confessor. Harold violated this, the Oath of Bayeux, by succeeding Edward in January 1066, an action which motivated William to invade England.

Christianity, once so violently rejected by the Northmen, was passionately embraced by the descendants of Rollo who injected new life and money into creating numerous holy buildings. Work on the great **Bayeux Cathedral** began in the mid-11th century and was

dedicated to Notre Dame on a summer's day in 1077 in the presence of William the Conqueror, senior nobles, Lanfranc, by now Archbishop of Canterbury, and other prominent prelates.

Bayeux suffered its share of damage over the centuries, but it survived unscathed the Battle of Normandy which wreaked so much destruction throughout Normandy in the summer of 1944. Only 10 km (6 miles) from the D-Day beaches, Bayeux, on the 7 June, was the first main town in France to be liberated from the Germans. Happily, it avoided being turned into a bomb site.

The **Bayeux Tapestry** recounts the Norman version of the events of 1066. The "Tapestry" is really a coloured wool embroidery sewn on linen and measures 70 m (230 ft) in length by ½ m (1½ ft) in width. It vividly relates the sequences in the build-up to

> **The Odo Method Does Not Stain**
> Already consecrated as bishop was Odo, William's half-brother through his mother, who had been married off to Heluin, the Viscount of Conteville, after her affair with William's father. Odo's ambitions were more secular than holy. He had fought alongside William at Hastings, wielding a mace, as can be seen in the Bayeux tapestry, rather than a sword. He reasoned that it was acceptable for someone of his high religious post to bludgeon his enemy, while the blatant drawing of blood through blade was reprehensible. His loyalty on the battlefield earned him the earldom of Kent, but his desire for more later turned him against William, and then William Rufus and Lanfranc, and he spent his last years waging messy rebellions against them.

William's conquest of England: Harold in Normandy in 1064; his oath to William; Harold returning to England; the death of Edward the Confessor; Halley's Comet, interpreted as an unlucky portent for Harold; Harold's coronation; William's preparations for invasion; his crossing to England with an army; feasting after landing; the eve of the Battle of Hastings and the battle itself, with scenes depicting all the action and violence leading up to the death of Harold with an arrow in his eye.

The tapestry has survived nine centuries in remarkably good condition. Aside from its artistic appeal, it is a valuable historical document from a time when records are scarce. But it should be appreciated that this is the Norman interpretation of events: Harold is the villain who has stolen the English crown; William, with papal approval, is in pursuit of justice. It was propaganda to besmirch the English; indeed, in the same way as the English have used Shakespeare's Henry V to rouse the hearts of patriots in times of war, Napoleon took the tapestry to Paris to stir the passions of the French against the old foe across the Channel.

Today, the tapestry, an extraordinary medieval account of one of history's most important events, hangs in an 18th-century seminary in **rue de Nesmond** near the cathedral. *Opening times*: 9.00 a.m. to 12.30 p.m. and 2.00– 6.30 p.m. daily from 16 March to 12 May and 18 September to 15 October; 9.30 a.m to 12.30 p.m. and 2.00–6.00 p.m. daily from 16 October– 15 March; 9.00 a.m. to 7.00 p.m. daily from 13 May to 17 September; tel: 31-92-05-48. The museum advises visitors

La Tapisserie d'Anglais
The old story that the Bayeux tapestry was embroidered painstakingly by William's queen Matilda, hence "La tapisserie de la reine Mathilde", has been repudiated by the British. It is more likely that Odo had it commissioned and executed in England by local artisans in the late 11th century, and then brought it home to Bayeux to decorate his cathedral.

to arrive an hour before closing time; guidebooks and cassette guides are available.

A fire swept through **Odo's cathedral** early in the 12th century, leaving only the 75 m (246 ft) high towers and crypt of the original monument intact. Restoration began later that century and continued into the next. The result is a blend of Romanesque and Gothic architecture with a magnificently tall nave, high windows and graciously carved stonework. The tympanum depicts the Henry II–Thomas à Becket story. Some histories recount that it was at nearby Arromanches, others say that it was at Avranches, that the four knights overheard Henry's exasperated off-the-cuff cry, "Are there none of the cowards eating my bread who will rid me of this turbulent priest?", before hastening to Canterbury to butcher the archbishop. There were further additions to the church, the most curious being the 19th-century copper top to the 15th-century Renaissance central tower, which, even amongst the cathedral's melange of styles, looks incongruous. *Opening times*: 8.00 a.m. to 12.00 p.m.. and 2.00–7.00 p.m. daily, except Sundays: 8.00 a.m. to 12.30 p.m. and 2.30–7.00 p.m.. The cathedral is floodlit in the

The cool, lofty, elegant, Romanesque–Gothic nave of Bayeux's cathedral of Notre Dame.

evenings from July to October, and on some special occasions during the rest of the year.

Just south of the cathedral, the **Museum of Religious Art** displays a valuable collection of manuscripts, paintings and ecclesiastical paraphernalia gathered from the cathedral. Here, too, is the room where St Theresa of Lisieux asked permission from the bishop to enter the Carmelite Convent. *Opening times*: 10.30 a.m. to 12.30 p.m. and 2.00–6.00 p.m. daily except Sundays; from July to October the museum closes at 7.00 p.m. and from July to 15 September it is open on Sundays.

The north side of the cathedral faces the place des Tribunaux which is sheltered by the boughs of the grand *arbre de la liberté*, a plane tree planted 200 years ago. Also overlooking the small square is the bishop's former residence, now the **Baron Gérard Museum**, housing displays of old Bayeux lace and porcelain (both are traditional local crafts) antique furniture, 16th-century Italian and Flemish paintings and more recent French works of art from the Baron Gérard collection. *Opening times*: 9.30 a.m. to 12.30 p.m. and 2.00–6.30 p.m. daily from 16 March to 31 May and from 1 September to 15 October; 10.00 a.m. to 12.30 p.m. and 2.00–6.00 p.m. daily from 16 October to 15 March; 9.00 a.m. to 7.00 p.m. daily from June to September; tel: 31-92-14-21.

A combined ticket can be bought for Bayeux's four main museums: the

---

Backstreet Bayeux

The timber-framed houses and narrow lanes of old Bayeux which escaped the destruction of 1944 are a heritage lost in many other Normandy towns and cities. In Bayeux, they have been preserved and coddled, and the tourist office provides a list of noteworthy buildings:

1, rue des Cuisiniers: tourist office (14th century).

4, rue Saint Malo: Grand Hôtel d'Argouges (15th, 16th centuries), note the façade and figurines and the courtyard.

5, rue Franche: Hôtel de Rubercy (15th century), turreted dwelling house.

7, rue Franche: Hôtel La Crespellière (18th century).

13, rue Franche: Manoir de Saint Manvieu (16th century).

18, rue Franche: Manoir Gilles Buhot (15th century).

10, rue Bourbesneur: Governor's House (15th–17th centuries).

Corner of Rue des Chanoines: The "lanterne des morts", 13th-century hollowed pillar, a chimney, indicating burial place for those who died of plague.

10, rue Général-de-Dais: Hôtel de Castilly (18th century).

39–41, rue Larcher: Manoir de "La Comtesse du Barry", after the famous countess who once stayed here.

6, rue de Bienvenu: Adam and Eve's House (15th century) decorated with wood carvings.

51, rue Saint Jean: Hôtel du Croissant.

45, rue des Teinturiers (across the River Aure): the smallest house in Bayeux. Continuing north-east you reach the 19th-century church of Saint Vigor-le-Grand built on the site of a 6th- and then 11th-century monastery.

Bayeux Tapestry, the Baron Gérard Museum, the Museum of Religious Art and the Memorial Museum of the Battle of Normandy 1944 (see below), giving an overall discount per visit.

The lace workshop, **Atelier de la Dentelle**, south of the cathedral endeavours to preserve the old Bayeux tradition of lacemaking. Visitors are welcome and courses are available for those wanting to learn the craft. Open daily at approximately the normal working hours; closed on Sundays during the low season. Address: Hôtel du Doyen, 6, rue Lambert-Leforestier; tel: 31-92-73-80.

The tapestry and embroidery workshop (**Artisanat d'Art et Ateliers de la Reine Mathilde**) holds exhibitions and runs courses on embroidery, weaving and lace-making. *Opening times*: daily, except Sundays and holidays, during approximate working hours. Address: 2, rue Poissonnerie; tel: 31-92-70-76.

West of the centre is place Saint Patrice, follow rue Saint Malo, where the main market is held on Saturdays and cattle are sold on Tuesdays. To its south is the pleasant place Charles de Gaulle where the general made his first speech on free French soil on 14 June 1944. Further south, on the outskirts of town, is Bayeux's war museum.

The modern war museum, the **Memorial Museum of the Battle of Normandy 1944**, is on boulevard Fabian-Ware on the south-western perimeter of town. It recounts the events and consequences of the War, the savage impact of which Bayeux itself was mercifully spared. Exhibits include weapons, uniforms, photos and documents. *Opening times*: 9.30 a.m. to 12.30 p.m. and 2.00–6.30 p.m. daily from 16 March to 31 May and 1 September to 15 October; 10.00 a.m. to 12.30 p.m. and 2.00–6.00 p.m. daily from 16 October to 15 March; 9.00 a.m. to 7.00 p.m. daily from June to September; tel: 31-92-93-41.

Along the road from the war museum is the British War Cemetery with the graves of over 4,500 of those who fell in the region; the Memorial to the Missing is dedicated to their brothers in arms who are remembered only in name.

Along boulevard du 6 Juin is Rond Point de Vauceles and the pink granite Monument de la Liberation. Beyond this is the Jardin Botanique, Bayeux's botanical gardens.

The Western Coast of Calvados

A kilometre down the Bayeux road, the D514 bears to the right to Longues-sur-Mer, site of the ruined 12th-century Benedictine abbey of Sainte Marie. No longer "sur-Mer" Longues is, however, linked to the coast by a 1½ km (1 mile) road to the north. Here the German artillery lay prepared for a possible Allied naval attack. When, though, Operation Overlord did swing into action this, the Longues Battery, was, in fact, an early victim of the very ships it was set to destroy; the shells of the gun casements remain. To the left, the cliff face, comprising clay and chalk, has crumbled, tumbled and fallen into a jumble. Thus it is called le Chaos.

Back on the D514 and 5 km (3 miles) on, just beyond Commes

manor, is the pleasant Port-en-Bessin. Often referred to merely as "Port" this is still very much a fishing port. The serious fishermen travel for days in their vessels and search off the shores of the English West Country for their catch. The less earnest do not stray from home and just dangle a line from the quay. Aside from further

*L*est we forget: a monument to the 80 American soldiers of the 299th Combat Engineers who died for liberation in France in World War II.

remnants of the destroyed German defences, there is, as Port's historic site, a 17th-century tower.

Continue westward along the D514 through Sainte Honorine-des-Pertes the 7 km (4 miles) to Colleville-sur-Mer. The division between Gold and Omaha Beaches has now been crossed. The Allied cemeteries are no longer predominantly British and Canadian, but American. Monuments above the beach, next to the ruined German gun houses, commemorate the American divisions which participated in the Normandy landings. Those who fell are buried in the nearby American Military Cemetery of Saint Laurent-sur-Mer: 9,385 white crosses, neatly lined on the manicured lawns, mark the graves, while a list of the soldiers whose bodies were never retrieved is inscribed by the gateway.

Another decisive battle was fought at Formigny, a few kilometres inland: this time the date was 1450 and the contestants were the old foes, England and France. The French won and, as a consequence, the English abandoned their fight for Normandy. This, however, is just a brief dip into deeper history, for this stretch of coast is dominated by the events of the summer of 1944.

After Saint Laurent-sur-Mer comes les Moulins and Vierville-sur-Mer. The Americans suffered heavy casualties here when they landed. Monuments commemorate the dead, and a museum records the events.

Pushing on, the D514 passes the châteaux of Englesqueville and Saint Pierre-du-Mont before rounding Pointe du Hoc, where the Americans had to scale the cliffs on rope ladders before

Simple white crosses at the Saint Laurent cemetery at Colleville-sur-Mer commemorate the Americans who lost their lives in the fight for the liberation of France.

they were able to dig into their offensive to the small fishing town resort of Grandcamp-Maisy. Some 6 km (3½ miles) to the south is la Cambe and its military cemetery: 21,500 German dead lie buried here.

The D514 swings south and away from the coast to Isigny-sur-Mer, the

butter town famed through France. On the Aure, and near the mouth of the Vire, is Isigny's "passage" which leads out through the shallow, and dramatically tidal, Bay of Vey into the deeper waters of the Channel. The bay's waters seep into the soils of the low-lying fields with their salt and give rise to the présalé, the salt meadow sheep, for which Isigny is also duly famous. The town itself was damaged during the Normandy landings, though the 13th-century church and the 18th-century château, now the Hôtel de Ville, were notable survivors. Beyond the Vire lies the department of Manche and the town of Carentan, 11 km (7 miles) from Isigny-sur-Mer.

South-west of Bayeux

The D572 branches southwards from the peripheral road, from near the Memorial Museum, and leads to the Forêt de Cerisy. During medieval times, the forest was known as La Forêt du Bur, or Burg meaning village, and subsequently La Forêt de Bur-le-Roy. The Marquieses of Balleroy gained their name from the forest. It was their forefather, the 17th-century Comte de Choisy, who called the forest the Buisson des Bairds, the Woods of the Bairds, and it is this more

> **Popularity of the Poor Man's Pottery**
> Noron-le-Poteries' salt glaze ware—*gres au sel*—is Normandy's coarser rustic pottery compared to the more elegant faience ceramics from Rouen. The vitreous quality of the clay was achieved traditionally by firing the pottery for up to four days at temperatures of 1,200°C. Now the old beechwood fuelled kilns have been replaced and the same process is done in less than a day. The final result, though, is much the same and, glazed with the distinctive *gres au sel* sheen, the pottery is on sale at craft shops in Noron-le-Poteries.

lyrical title which is creeping into popular usage today.

About 8 km (5 miles) out of Bayeux is Noron-la-Poterie where they make the unique Normandy *grès au sel*, salt glaze pottery. The tradition of making pottery with this characteristic local clay dates back over 1,000 years. Just beyond is la Tuilerie and, to the right, along the D178, is le Tronquay, another old pottery centre, and le Molay-Littry.

In 1741, the Marquis de Balleroy, who was already involved in the iron business, was fortunate to discover the much required coal at le Molay-Littry. A mine was opened soon after and coal continued to be collected, off and on, until the closure of the pit in 1950. The local **museum** here documents the history of the mine. *Opening times*: 10.00 a.m. to 12.00 p.m.. and 2.00–6.00 p.m. daily except Wednesdays from April to October; afternoons from November to April on Tuesdays and Saturdays and all day Sundays; tel: 31-22-95-14. The D5 runs north via the 14th-century château of Colombières; exterior visits during most summer afternoons, through *bocage* countryside to Isigny-sur-Mer, a total of 21 km (13 miles).

The D15 continues westward from le Molay-Littry. Bear left off it, taking the D160 for Cerisy-la-Forêt via Moulin de Marcy, where the 19th-century mill is now a museum (same times as the museum of mines above). Vigor and his monks built the original abbey at Cerisy in the 6th century. It was destroyed by the pagan Vikings, only to be resurrected by their descendants, the Dukes of Normandy, who had by then embraced Christianity. Duke Robert made amends, when he built the abbey in the 1030s, by naming it in honour of Vigor. The trend of destruction continued over the centuries, however, the abbey church we see today, though not as extensive as it once was, is one of the finest examples of Romanesque church architecture in Normandy. The Abbot's chapel is 13th century and

---

"Building in the Blood"

François Mansart's fate seemed inevitable. Born in 1598 the son of a master carpenter, grandson of a master mason and nephew of sculptors and architects, the young Mansart learnt the trade of building under the guidance of his brother-in-law, himself an architect. The arrival of Henry IV in Paris in 1594 heralded a building boom in châteaux, manors and mansions, and the budding François Mansart quickly blossomed as the rising star in architecture. His career took off in 1623, and the splendid three-blocked château Balleroy, built in 1626 for Jean de Choisy chancellor to duc d'Orleans, is one of the few examples of his early works still standing. These were days when those who commissioned had real money and those who were commissioned were outrageously extravagant. Mansart cared little about budgets, costing one client, it was noted, "more money than the Great Turk possesses". But times changed and the trend in châteaux building waned. Mansart remained in demand, but he was unreliable and his plans too lavish. Indeed, he had his enemies who in 1651 issued a pamphlet entitled "La Mansarade" attacking his extravagance. By this time Louis XIV—"The Sun King" around whom France revolved—was on the throne. It seems that Mansart was out of step in the world, but none the less, on his death in 1666, his work and reputation survived as testimony to his talent.

shows the progression to Gothic design. Pieces salvaged from the ruins of the abbey are displayed in the **archaeological museum**. *Opening times*: 10.00 a.m. to 6.00 p.m. daily from April to mid-October; tel: 33-56-10-01.

The D8 rue Dorée runs eastwards through the heart of the Forêt de Cerisy to the crossroads of l'Embranchement where there is an arboretum. One road, the D13, continues the few kilometres to **Balleroy and its château**. Alternatively, take the D122. Pass through la Platière; then double back along the D209 via the old slate working village of la Bazoque before turning left on the D28 for Balleroy and its château.

The drive, a continuation of the village high street, leads through neat formal gardens to the château. In the 17th century, Comte de Choisy commissioned young François Mansart, then an aspiring château architect, to build him his residence here by the forest. A line of Marquises of Balleroy lived in the château for generations. More recently, the stately home was owned by Malcolm Forbes, the American publisher. A **Museum of Hot Air Balloons** is housed in the old stable block and recounts the history of ballooning. *Opening times*: 9.00 a.m. to 12.00 p.m. and 2.00–6.00 p.m. daily except Wednesdays; closed from November to April; tel: 31-21-60-61.

Every year, the *Forbes Magazine*-sponsored International Balloon Meet is held over the back lawns. The interior of the château, and the *salon d'honneur* in particular, is richly adorned in Louis XIII and Louis XIV decor.

Some 4 km (2½ miles) east of Balleroy on the D73 is Castillon. Continue eastwards on the minor D99a through Saint Paul-du-Vernay to the junction with the D178 and bear right across the D67 for the few kilometres to Juaye and Abbey de Mondaye. The Premonstratensian abbey was built in the 18th century by dedicated local architect–prelate Eustache Restout on the site of a ruined 13th-century abbey. It was virtually a one-man show and with, one hopes, great labour of love it took Restout 37 years to complete. Monks of the order still live, work and pray at Mondaye. Visitors are invited by *l'Association des Amis de Mondaye* to join prayers and retreats (contact: Abbaye de Mondaye, Père Hotelier, 14250 Tilly-sur-Seulles; tel: 31-92-58-11). *Opening times* for sightseeing: 2.30–5.30 p.m. on Sundays and holidays through the year. The château at Juaye is also 18th century.

The D67 returns northwards to Bayeux. Southwards, cross-country roads lead to Tilly-sur-Seulles. And beyond, to the east, is Caen and, to the south, is Villers-Bocage (*see* pages 161 and 202 respectively).

Rugged Headlands and Vast Beaches, Bocage Countryside and Mont-Saint-Michel

Manche, or more particularly the Cotentin peninsula, is Normandy's remote quarter. An extremity jutting into the Atlantic, this is a savage coast when the ocean unleashes its fury. Inland, the soil is more stony and less fertile than elsewhere and *bocage* country consists of small fields divided by hedgerows. The wildness is Manche's appeal and its—indeed Normandy's—crowning beauty is the extraordinary rock and church of Mont-Saint-Michel rising starkly from mudflats in its south-western corner.

Eastern Cotentin Peninsula

The lower reach of the River Vire serves as the border between Calvados and Manche. The N13 crosses the river after Isigny and enters the marshlands which characterize Manche's easternmost coastlands. The road runs across the Penesme, the wedge of flatlands between the Vire and Taute, and the 7 km (4 miles) to Carentan, which is the first main town on this side of the departement.

Wild flowers add the smell and colour of spring long into the summer months.

Carentan

Although an unspectacular entrance to Manche, Carentan is a pleasant town, well known beyond these parts as a centre for cattle and dairy produce. Of local fame is its fine, flamboyant 12th–15th-century church of Notre Dame, with its octagonal spire being a particularly prominent landmark in this low-lying countryside. The quarter around the church is something of an "old town" and by the main square, place de la République, the arches from the 14th-century covered market, now lining the pavement, are a further historic legacy. These relics may well have tumbled had not the town been liberated by the Americans

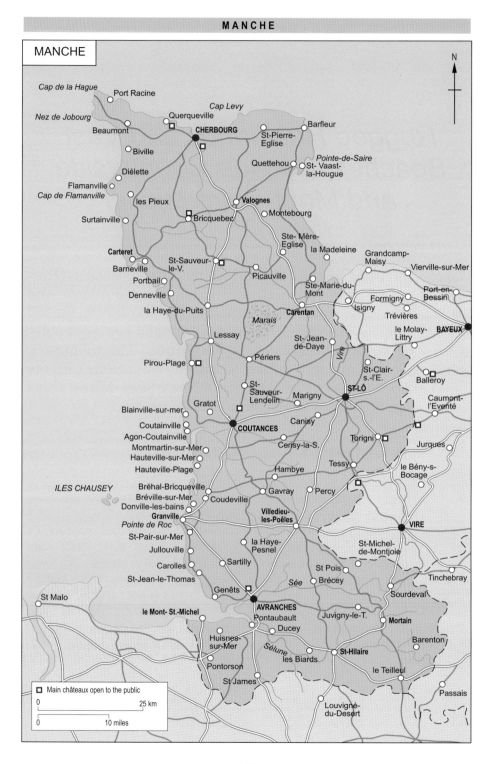

MANCHE

N

Cap de la Hague
Port Racine
Cap Levy
Nez de Jobourg
Querqueville
Beaumont
CHERBOURG
St-Pierre-Eglise
Barfleur
Biville
Quettehou
Pointe-de-Saire
St- Vaast-la-Hougue
Diélette
Flamanville
Cap de Flamanville
les Pieux
Valognes
Montebourg
Surtainville
Bricquebec
Ste- Mère-Eglise
la Madeleine
Grandcamp-Maisy
Vierville-sur-Mer
Carteret
St-Sauveur-le-V.
Picauville
Ste-Marie-du-Mont
Port-en-Bessin
Barneville
Portbail
Formigny
Isigny
Trévières
Denneville
la Haye-du-Puits
Carentan
le Molay-Littry
BAYEUX
Marais
St- Jean-de-Daye
Lessay
Vire
Pirou-Plage
Périers
St-Clair-s.-l'E.
St-Sauveur-Lendelin
ST-LÔ
Balleroy
Blainville-sur-mer
Gratot
Marigny
Canisy
Caumont-l'Eventé
Coutainville
COUTANCES
Cerisy-la-S.
Torigni
Jurques
Agon-Coutainville
Montmartin-sur-Mer
Hauteville-sur-Mer
Tessy
le Bény-s-Bocage
Hauteville-Plage
Hambye
ILES CHAUSEY
Bréhal-Bricqueville
Bréville-sur-Mer
Donville-les-bains
Coudeville
Gavray
Percy
Granville
Pointe de Roc
Villedieu-les-Poêles
VIRE
St-Pair-sur-Mer
Jullouville
la Haye-Pesnel
St-Michel-de-Montjoie
Carolles
Sartilly
St Pois
Brécey
Tinchebray
St-Jean-le-Thomas
Sée
Sourdeval
St Malo
Genêts
AVRANCHES
Mortain
le Mont- St.-Michel
Pontaubault
Juvigny-le-T.
Barenton
Ducey
Huisnes-sur-Mer
Sélune
les Biards
St-Hilaire
Pontorson
le Teilleul
St James
Passais
Louvigné-du-Desert

☐ Main châteaux open to the public

0 _____ 25 km
0 _____ 10 miles

Map of the Manche region.

within the first week of the D-Day landings. Carentan was lucky, the 17th–18th-century convent, now the Hôtel de Ville, and the 18th-century Lavoir des Fontaines were also re-prieved from the bombardments of Normandy's most cataclysmic summer.

Beyond the church is the small and modern yacht marina. Its channel to the open seas is long and straight, cut-ting through the often mist-shrouded marshlands before entering the inlet, an outlet for both the Vire and Taute, which is an intermediatory zone of wa-ter and mudflats before the Channel it-self.

La Madeleine

The N13, the main avenue through the Cotentin peninsula and to Cherbourg, heads northwards from Carentan. After 4 km (2½ miles) just before Saint Côme-due-Mont with its 11th-century church, the D913 bears to the right. It is 13 km (8 miles) along this way, via the villages of Vierville and the "hill-top" Saint Marie-du-Mont, both of which have medieval churches, to la Madeleine.

The 4 km (2½ miles) stretch of shore between la Madeleine and les Dunes-de-Varreville is the Utah Beach, where the American 4th Division landed on 6 June 1944. From here, they pushed inland under the fire of the German defence in their bid to link with their colleagues who had parachuted into the hinterland. The whole area was a battlefield during those first days of the Normandy invasion. Legacies, such as the German blockhouse and memori-als to the Americans and others who served and died are reminders of the invasion; the Leclerc monument at Varreville marks the spot where the general and his French contingent landed on 1 August. Also at Utah is the **Musée du Débarquement**, which re-counts the events and displays relevant War relics.

The D421, the *route des Allies*, runs alongside the coast to Quinéville, a total of 15 km (9 miles) from la Madeleine, and from here there are views across the bay to Saint Vaast-la-Hougue. At Quinéville the road turns inland for a few kilometres, to avoid marshes, before bearing right and coastwards once again for the 10 km (6 miles) to Quettehou.

Alternatively, there is the inland route: a road at Ravenoville-Plage, 9 km (5½ miles) from la Madeleine on the *routes des Allies*, turns left for the 10 km (6 miles) to Sainte Mère-Eglise on the N13.

Bocage

Bocage—the small fields parcelled by rows of hedges and trees and country lands—is the landscape of Manche's Cotentin peninsula and also of the west-ern parts of Calvados and Orne. Progress into the interior of the Cotentin peninsula by the American Allies land-ing at Utah in 1944 was somewhat hin-dered by the "bocaged" nature of the terrain. Their tanks were often unable to pass down the lanes, and the hedges proved tiresome obstacles. And so tanks became bulldozers—lanes were widened and hedges flattened. Thus the path to victory was cleared.

Sainte Mère-Eglise

Sainte Mère-Eglise, 04.30 hours 6 June 1944: Lt Col Krause, of the 3rd Battalion of the 505th Parachute Infantry Regiment of the 82nd Airborne Division, hoisted the Stars and Stripes outside the town hall. In doing so, he declared Sainte Mère-Eglise the first town to be liberated from the Germans. At this spot, stands Milestone Zero, "Km 0", to commemorate the start of the road to freedom.

Amongst those to make the drop on Sainte Mère-Eglise was John Steele, whose parachute got caught on the tower of the church, leaving him dangling helplessly and a sitting target for the enemy snipers. He was wounded, but survived, and he subsequently became a local celebrity and symbol of the day's historic events. A hotel was named after him and there is a model of a uniformed John Steele hanging from the church tower, his misfortune thus ensuring his continued fame. The 82nd Airborne Division are remembered further by a stained-glass window in the church.

Across the place de l'Eglise is the **Airborne Museum**, shaped like a billowing parachute. Amongst the mementoes it displays in celebration of Sainte Mère-Eglise's liberation is a Douglas C 147. *Opening times*: 10.00 a.m.–12.00 p.m.. and 2.00–5.00 p.m. daily from February to mid-November and weekends from mid-November to mid-December and from mid-January to February; tel: 33-41-41-35.

Traditional rural life is portrayed in the Sainte Mère-Eglise **Cotentin Farm Museum**, which is housed in a restored 17th-century manor farmhouse. Four rooms provide accommodation. *Opening times*: 10.00 a.m.–12.00 p.m.. and 2.00–7.00 p.m. daily in July and August and daily except Tuesdays from Easter to July and in September; weekend afternoons in October; tel: 33-41-30-25.

It is a further 10 km (6 miles) along the N13 to Valognes. West of this road

*J*ohn Steel's contribution to liberating France got off to a shaky start as he entangled himself in the church tower at Sainte Mère-Eglise.

is the heart of Cotentin's *bocage* countryside. From Sainte Mère-Eglise, the D67, and its continuations, leads westwards, bypassing the Château at Crosville-sur-Douve for the 19 km (12 miles) to Saint Sauveur-le-Vicomte; from here it is 15 km (9 miles) along the D2 to Valognes. Within the Sainte Mère-Eglise–Sainte Sauveur-le-Vicomte–Valognes triangle is the German military cemetery at Orglandes and the site of a medieval abbey at le Ham. And just outside, to the east of the N13, is Montebourg which was a focal point of heavy German–Allied fighting and as, a result, was almost completely razed to the ground.

Valognes

Valognes, too, was severely scarred in 1944. However, the past is remembered. The 18th-century gentry took a liking to the town and Valognes, proud to be known as the "Versailles of Normandy", became home to smart schools and seminaries. Author and aristocrat Barbey d'Aurevilly (1809–99) spent part of his youth in Valognes. He wrote about the place, and his accounts provide an insight into the fashionable lifestyle long after high society had been sacrificed to socialism.

Amongst the survivors of Valognes' elegant era are a number of "Hôtels" and mansions, notably those to the south of the central place Vicq d'Azir. Hôtel de Thieuville, dating from the 17th century, houses two museums. The important art of distilling calvados is described at the **Museum of Eau-de-Vie**, while in the leather galleriesthe

Local Dandy

Born in 1808 in Cotentin, the outspoken flamboyant Barbey d'Aurevilly studied law in Caen before becoming a journalist in Paris and later a novelist. He wrote about the traditions and atmosphere of his home countryside in works such as *L'Ensorcelée* and *Le Chevalier des Touches*—the latter based on the Chouannerie royalist insurgency into Normandy. He was acquainted with Beau Brummell, the British consul in Caen, and wrote *Du Dandysme et G Brummell*—one dandy to another—in 1845. He died in 1899.

various stages of the traditional leather industry are portrayed . *Opening times*: 10.00 a.m.–12.00 p.m.. and 2.00–6.00 p.m. daily except Wednesdays and Sunday mornings from mid-June to late September and some school holidays during the rest of the year; tel: 33-40-26-25.

Down the rue des Religieuses is the 17th–18th century **Hôtel de Grandval-Caligny**, where d'Aurevilly lived for a while. *Opening times*: morning and afternoon tours Wednesdays–Saturdays from July to October. Alongside the River Merderet is the **Maison du Grand Quartier**, a 15th-century house and the present Museum of Cider exhibiting ancient and modern presses and other tools used in the making of Normandy's most famous brew. *Opening times*: same as Hôtel de Thieuville; tel: 33-40-22-73. Across the rue Petit Versailles is the 18th-century **Hôtel de Beaumont,** the finest of Valognes mansions, with its long gracious façade and formal terraced gardens. *Opening times*: afternoon tours daily except Tuesdays from July to mid-September.

Old schools and seminars around town have been patched up and modernized. So too has the church of Saint Malo in place Vicq d'Azir, comprising a collection of styles spanning seven centuries to the present, all pieced together like a jigsaw to reveal a picture of an unsettled history.

North-east Tip of the Cotentin Peninsula

The N13 continues north-westwards from Valognes for 20 km (12 miles) to Cherbourg where it concludes. On the left, just short of halfway, a minor road leads the kilometre or so up to the village of Brix. The castle here, long destroyed, was home of the de Bruis family who accompanied William the Conqueror to England. Their descendants achieved greater fame as the Bruce contingent in Scotland, with King Robert the Bruce being their crowning glory.

Alternatively, the D902 leads from Valognes for 15 km (9 miles) eastwards to Quettehou and the stubby peninsula which constitutes this extreme corner of Manche. From Quettehou, which had a medieval church and a fine seaward panorama, it is a further 3 km (2 miles) to Saint Vaast-la-Hougue.

Picturesque Saint Vaast-la-Hougue, reduced in the local parlance to the pretty sounding Saint Va, is where England's Edward III landed before heading to his historic victory at Crécy in 1346. Saint Va itself was host to a famous battle 346 years later: this time

*S*aint Vaast-la-Hougue: nowadays as famed for its import of yachtsmen as it is for its export of oysters.

the French were to embark from the port and cross the Channel to England where they were to lend support to James II and his cause; however, the alert Anglo-Dutch navy decisively snuffed out their fleet in these off-shore waters before they had gathered the wind in their sails.

Smarting from this tragic encounter, the French admiralty initiated the construction of defences. These included the Fort de la Hougue, at the tip of Saint Va's narrow peninsula, and the tower on the nearby Ile de Tatihou. Some 13 km (8 miles) to the south-east are the two small fortified islands of Saint Marcouf, which the British secured as a base to monitor these waters at the turn of the 19th century. In summer, there are boat trips to the islands from Saint Va.

Today, Saint Va is a favourite port of call for yachtsmen. However, its

*T*he view from Parnelle *across flat bocage countryside in the direction of Barfleur, on the north-eastern point of the Cotentin peninsula.*

fame is more universal thanks to the excellent "Saint Vaast-de-Hougue oysters", which are bred in these waters, and are a special feature on menus and at fishmongers throughout France.

A minor road northwards follows the curve of the coast the 6 km (3½ miles) to Pointe de Saire, the most easterly promontory north of Utah Beach; it is a further 11 km (7 miles) via la Froide-Rue and the Château of la Crasvillerie to Barfleur. An alternative country route requires a return to Quettehou and, having taken the D902, bear left along the D26 to incorporate a scenic "triangle". Take the D26 to le Vast on the River Saire; from here one cross-country road follows the river upstream for a while before branching off for Cherbourg. However, follow the Saire downstream, on the D25, to Valcanville; then right, on the D125, via la Pernelle, where the view from the churchyard is over the flatlands which form the end of the peninsula, and back down the D902 from where it is 9 km (5½ miles) to Barfleur. The church at Montfarville, just short of Barfleur, dates back to the 13th century, and its interior was painted by local artist Guillaume Fouace.

With a population of about 750, Barfleur can boast a high quota of history per capita. The small port provided William with the boat and navigator which took him across the Channel to win at Hastings in 1066. A descendant of the Conqueror's pilot was at the helm of the splendid White Ship which 54 years later was to carry William Atheling, son and heir to Henry I, to England. The navigator got drunk during the pre-sailing party, and smashed his vessel on the rocks as he left Barfleur harbour. He, along with the young Atheling and many of the new blue-bloods from the fast-evolving Anglo-Norman upper class, were drowned. Indeed, all but the cook lost their lives.

Barfleur became the royal route to Westminster as both Henry II and Richard the Lion Heart, undaunted by the omen of the ill-fated White Ship, sailed from here to their coronations in 1154 and 1194 respectively. At the time of the French Revolution, a local woman, Julie Postel (who later became

The 13th-century church at Omoville-la-Hougue, stone buildings set in bocage.

Sister Mary-Magdalen), used to hide priests at her home in the neighbouring hamlet of la Bretonne until she could secure them safe passage to England. Her house can be visited and she is commemorated by a stained-glass window in Barfleur's church.

Today, this medieval cross-Channel ferry port is a small, pretty fishing village, quainter and quieter than Saint Va, though the treachery of these waters, which have claimed many a life since the White Ship tragedy, is all too evident when the winds blow and the waves gather their strength. The Conqueror is remembered by a plaque down on the waterfront, near the lifeboat ramp.

Gatteville-le-Phare is a couple of kilometres north of Barfleur; the original 12th-century belfry is still in the village church, and in the square there is the sailors' chapel. Beyond there is the low, bleak, windswept Raz de Barfleur, a crooked finger of land jutting out into the Channel, a peninsula upon a peninsula upon a peninsula. At its end, the Pointe de Barfleur, is a 71 m (233 ft) tall lighthouse, flashing an essential beacon to sailors as far as 56 km (35 miles) out at sea, and providing a spectacular panorama for those who climb its 365-stepped spiral stairway.

It is about 20 km (12 miles) westwards by road, the D116 from Gatteville-le-Phare, from Pointe de Barfleur around the flat headland to Cap Levy, another small peninsula with a lighthouse. Here the road meets the sea and it is an attractive 10 km (6 mile) stretch, with viewpoints at Pointe du Brulay and Anse du Brick, and from up at Belvedere which is a

---

Fame Through Democracy
Born in 1805, the historian Count Alexis de Tocqueville—Charles Henri Maurice Cherel—gained fame for his works on "democracy". Most significant were his *Democracy in America* and an unfinished history of the French Revolution, *The Old Regime and the Revolution.* He served in the government—as deputy and a minister to Louis Napoleon—before retiring after the coup of 2 December 1851. He died in 1859.

---

short distance inland, before finally approaching Cherbourg through suburbs.

The alternative and main route from Barfleur to Cherbourg is the more direct 27 km (17 mile) course along the D901. It passes through Tocqueville, home of 19th-century historian Alexis de Tocqueville, and Saint Pierre-Eglise, home of the 17th-century writer Abbé de Saint Pierre; both men lived in their families' respective châteaux, that of the abbé's though has been replaced by the present 18th-century building. Just beyond the aerodrome is a turning to Belvedere (*see* above) and, further on, D320 to the right leads to a burial chamber, *allée couverte*, dating back to 2000 BC. On the outskirts of Cherbourg is the Renaissance château of **Tourlaville** set in a beautiful park which is open to the public, the gardens, not the house, in the afternoons; tel: 33-22-29-22.

Cherbourg

For centuries great hype has surrounded Cherbourg's potential as a port, but only for brief spells has its ambition been realized. Predicted to be "Tomorrow's Channel Inn" in the 17th

*T*all *ships moor alongside quai Alexandre III, a poignant reminder of Cherbourg's heyday as a port.*

century, it was developed belatedly into a military harbour in the late 1770s, when large cones loaded with ballast were submerged 20 m (65 ft) on to the seabed to form the foundations of the moles. One hundred or so such building blocks were laid, a feat of engineering which drew publicity and a visit by Louis XVI, amidst flurry and fanfare, to witness the placing of one such cone: a symbol of defence against the outside on, paradoxically, the eve of the revolution from within. Nature then took over the construction. Its tides and currents shifted cones and sands to create an island and the backbone of the breakwater to which man added his final touches in time for presentation to Napoleon III in 1858.

Cherbourg's debut in the international limelight was not as a naval base but a trans-Atlantic passenger port. In 1869, a Hamburg Amerik Line vessel crossed the ocean and berthed in its harbour. Cherbourg's role grew in stature reaching a climax during the heyday of liner travel in 1930s. The maritime world, however, is fickle and Cherbourg's livelihood collapsed when cruise voyaging slumped. A few years later the old port was revived and contributed its most masterful and significant performance as the Allies' terminal for PLUTO in 1944. The War over and an exhausted Cherbourg once again sank into the doldrums. Nowadays, it gets by with its summer season as a cross-Channel ferry port, as a submarine base for the French navy and as a calling point for yachtsmen. Meanwhile le Havre further up the coast holds centre stage, basking in its importance at being star billed as Normandy's major port.

M arket day in Cherbourg and flowers are spread across the square in front of the old theatre.

There is more than just being a port and Cherbourg turned inwards and, stuck out here on this extremity of France, it, the largest town in Manche, is an important market centre. The main shopping district is inland at the top (bridge) end of quai Alexandre III; follow rue Maréchal Foch, the tourist office is on the corner, into the square where open-air markets are frequently held in front of the theatre; then head north beyond the main pedestrian precincts into the narrow streets, such as rue Tour-Carrée and rue de la Paix and their offshoots; here, in the old sailors' quarter, there are popular and intimate restaurants and bistros. In one direction, across the main avenue Cessart, is a yacht marina, various port authorities and the military harbour (only French nationals can visit). A short walk the other way, to the west and off rue de l'Abbaye, is the **Emmanuel Liais botanical garden**, dedicated to the 19th-century astronomer. Here, there are hothouses and also galleries exhibiting items pertaining to a range of natural and cultural science disciplines from anthropology to zoology. *Opening times*: 10.00 a.m.–12.00 p.m.. and 2.00–6.00 p.m. daily except Tuesdays and holidays from May to mid-September and afternoons only during the rest of the year; tel: 33-53-51-61.

The **Thomas Henry Museum**, named after the prominent 19th-century art collector who was a native of Cherbourg, is behind the theatre and just off quai Alexandre III. Amongst the paintings are collections with a Cherbourg theme as well as work by local artists such as 19th-century Jean-François Millet, who was born in the nearby village of Gruchy. *Opening times*: 10.00 a.m.–12.00 p.m.. and 2.00–6.00 p.m. daily except Tuesdays and holidays; tel: 33-44-40-22.

The docks accommodating the cross-Channel ferries to Weymouth, Portsmouth and Poole and to Ireland, Guernsey and Jersey are on the other side of town, alongside the Gare Maritime. The straight avenue A Briand eventually leads into avenue de Paris from where there is a turning up the hill to Fort du Roule. The fort was built in the mid-19th century and adapted by the Germans during their occupation in the Second World War. This formidable HQ, with an all-important panoramic vista, was the strategic defence for the Germans during their fight against the Allies in 1944. Inside is the **War and Liberation Museum** which recounts the local battles, highlighting the efforts of the French Resistance movement, within the context of the War as a whole as well as Cherbourg's older history. *Opening times*: 10.00 a.m.–12.00 p.m.. and 2.00–6.00 p.m. daily except Tuesdays in the low season and holidays; tel: 33-20-14-12.

West of Cherbourg

The D901 is the main road west of Cherbourg and it runs 28 km (17 miles) to a crossroads just short of the tip of the Cap de la Hague. A preferable route to this dramatic extremity of France is the D45, a road which sometimes hugs the pretty coastline and other times cuts a path through attractive countryside, and its even smaller offshoots.

Cherbourg's western exit through its outskirts is along the rue de l'Abbaye. On the right is the part restored Abbaye du Voeu which was founded by Matilda, the daughter of England's Henry I. Beyond, the D45 bears to the right. A couple of kilometres on, at Querqueville with its panoramas over the sea, another turning to the right leads to the small church of Saint-Germain; it dates from the 10th century and is believed to be one of the oldest churches in Normandy.

Continue, and at la Rivière there is a turning to the left: a steep lane leads up from the hill past villas with their

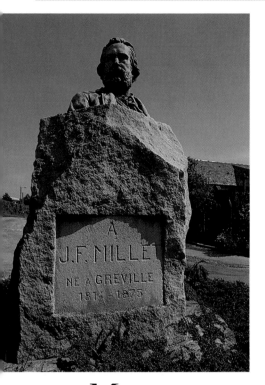

*M*illet, the country
boy who made good as an artist,
was a link in a chain of Norman
painters. He inspired Eugene
Boudin who in turn influenced
Claude Monet.

views of the sea in the mid-distance, while, at the start of the ascent, a driveway constitutes the entrance to the château of **Nacqueville**.

The approach to the building is through rhododendron gardens, across a stream and under an ivy-covered twin-towered gateway. The 16th–18th-century manorial château stands dwarfed by the dense forest which forms its backdrop. As for the interior, visitors are admitted to the main hall

which is noted for its Renaissance fireplace. *Opening times*: tours every hour from 2.00–5.00 p.m. daily except Tuesdays and Fridays, unless they are holidays, from Easter to late September; tel: 33-03-27-89.

A couple of kilometres along the D45 from la Rivière is the village of Urville-Nacqueville, with its stretch of sandy beach, and the restored, fortified, early medieval manor of Dur Ecu. Landemer also has a beach and, from a point above and beyond, there is a splendid vantage from where Cap Levy to the east and Pointe Jardeheu, to the west, can be seen.

The D45 cuts inland to Greville-Hague, with an offshoot bearing right to Gruchy, birthplace of Jean-François Millet (1814–75), whose inspiration to become an artist was nurtured in these fields. The road peters out after Gruchy at a cliff-top point high above the sea and on the ramblers' GR 223 shore walk; to the right is the Rocher Du Castel-Vendon, a

---

Romanticizing the Workers

A son of the land, Millet worked in the fields until the age of 19, when he embarked on his vocation as an artist. He studied at Cherbourg, but recognition was slow in coming, his first real success being "The Milkmaid" which he painted in 1844 when he was 30. These were tense times, the republicans were on the rise again—France would be a republic from 1848–1852—and Millet's romantic depictions of peasant life were seen by the conservatives in power as liberal and socialist imagery. More correctly, Millet's style essentially was classical in approach, but it was not until the 1860s that his works gained the wide acclaim they deserved. Millet died in 1875.

---

well-known landmark amongst locals, seafarers and walkers.

Millet's artistic talent can be seen in the paintings in the medieval church at Greville-Hague and his likeness in the bust by Marcel Jacques which stands in the village. Many minor roads splay out from Greville-Hague, tracing their crooked paths across the countryside. It is 6 km (3½ miles) along the increasingly scenic D45, beyond the 120 m (394 ft) high Mont Pali, to Omonville-la-Rogue. Road meets sea further on at Pointe Jardeheu and then turns sharply westwards, following the curve of the bay to Port Racine, which, the locals claim, is the smallest port in France.

The final approach to Cap de la Hague, one of the more credible contenders for France's official "Land's End" title, is through the village of Saint Germain-des-Vaux to Goury, the last inhabited settlement on this bleak and windswept peninsula. Opposite,

out at sea, the Gros du Raz lighthouse guides ships around the cape; beyond the island of Alderney is visible. Many a vessel has come to grief in violent waters off this headland. On numerous occasions, the lifeboat men of Goury have braved the tempest to rescue sailors from drowning or from being dashed to death against the rocks.

One of the most spectacular views of this rugged corner is from the D401 which runs from Auderville, 1 km (½ mile) or so inland from Goury, along the Baie d'Ecalgrain the 5 km (3 miles) to Dannery. From the road,

T he notoriously hazardous waters around the northern shores of the Cotentin peninsula have claimed countless victims. The Goury lighthouse offers a guiding light through the sailors' nightmare.

The wild coastline of the north-western tip of the Cotentin peninsula is not dissimilar to Cornwall in England. And like there the waves often thrash the exposed beaches.

you look down, along the sandy bay, to the headland of Nez de Voidries. Out across the waters is Alderney, and Sark and Guernsey are also visible to those who pass this way on a clear day. The D202 from Dannery leads part of the way to the Nez de Voidries and its "sister" promontory, Nez de Jobourg. The two "nez" are worth wandering along, for they, with waves thrashing on their jagged cliffs, epitomise the wildest character of Cotentin.

Continuing in a southerly direction, you pass by the La Hague atomic plant where they produce plutonium; visits to some zones of the centre are possible. But, instead of continuing the

3 km (2 miles) directly to Beaumont, there is a more interesting route. The steep 6 km (3½ mile) road leads via Herqueville to the sea and on to Herquemoulin before turning up towards the old smugglers' refuge of Beaumont.

It is 18 km (11 miles) from Beaumont east along the D901 back to Cherbourg. Alternatively it is 4 km (2½ miles) south on the D318 to Vauville. Before reaching the village, there is a path off the road up to Pierre Pouquelee, an ancient gallery grave; ascend further and, on a clear day, there is a magnificent 360-degree panorama over sea and countryside.

Vauville itself has its views, and a medieval church and 16th-century château, as do Petit Thot and Camp Maneyrol beyond. Around here, in this quarter of Cotentin, is gliding and hang-gliding territory. Biville, 3 or 4 km (2–2½ miles) from Vauville depending on the road taken, is an old pilgrim centre; devotees have come

here for centuries to pay homage at the medieval church where the Blessed Thomas Heyle (1187–1257), a venerated local, lies buried. Again, there are the views, especially spectacular from the Calvaire des Dunes which lie between Biville and the sea.

The most direct southward path from Biville is the D37, 2 km (1 mile) inland from the village. The first point

*M*anche's stone cottages are as pretty as the half timbered houses elsewhere in Normandy.

along the coast which warrants a detour, for beach and cliff-top views, is Cap de Flamanville. The D4 at Helleville bears right and it is 6 km (3½ miles) to the small resort of Siouville-Hague, with its wide, sandy beach exposed at low tide, and the iron mines of Dielette at the foot of the cliffs. Beyond Dielette, and overlooking the sea, is the Flamanville nuclear power station (visits are possible). Up on the top of the headland, a small restaurant has capitalized on the views by securing a cliff-edge vantage. Just inland is the 17th-century Flamanville château with its park open to the public.

The D517 follows the coast through Sciotot, with a view down over the bay, and le Rozel to Pointe du Rozel. The high contours of the cliffs now give way to the less dramatic dune and *mielles* (this is the local name for the grassy dips between the sand mounds) and beach, which characterize the shoreline to the Cap de Carteret.

The D904, the main road running parallel to the coast, though a few kilometres inland, passes by Barneville-Carteret, a town whose fame is in its name, the fusion of Barneville and

*T*he beach near Dielette, a vast expanse of sand just down the coast from Normandy's most rugged rocks.

Carteret, the two seaside resorts it serves.

The first turning for Carteret is down the D201, via Hatainville. The significance of the small fishing port here on the northern side of the Gerfleur estuary has been overshadowed by Carteret's role as a holiday resort for a long time. Indeed, the harbour, a safe haven for colourfully painted boats, with fisherwomen selling their catch and their weatherbeaten men mending their nets and lobster pots on the quayside, is a quaint focal point. However, it is the tourists which provide Carteret with its life and revenue.

Access to the first beach is along the rue de la Corniche, the other side of the headland from the harbour. At the far end is the Cap de Carteret, a substantial rocky promontory. From here, there are footpaths: the *Sentier des Douaniers* which follows the outline of the headland and the rue des Deux-Plages which leads to the summit. The main approach by car is from the town centre along the rue du Cap—there is a panoramic view from Roche Biard to the left of Carrefour de France—which joins the avenue du Phare leading to the lighthouse. There are splendid views from here: Carteret is the nearest port to Jersey and the island can be seen on a clear day. To the north stretches the resort's second beach, the Plage de la Vieille Eglise, a long, sandy expanse, underused in comparison to the cluttered smaller beach between the headlands. It was over 300 years ago that locals turned their backs on the headland's old church, after which the beach is named, and its surrounding settlement.

Their descendants today claim it was the exposure and inaccessibility which persuaded them to move to the more tolerable present location of Carteret.

Barneville, across the Gerfleur estuary, is seemingly less raucous and brazen than its twin, though its streets and beach attracts its full complement of clientele in the summer time. Barneville, too, has its *vieille église*, which dates from the 11th century and has been restored rather than abandoned.

A further attraction of the Barneville-Carteret resort is its proximity to Jersey. In summer, between May and September, there are ferries from Carteret's port to the Channel Islands; the duration of the trip is approximately 1 hour.

*M*arket day at Bricquebec and the brown and white Normandais—bespectacled with brown patches—are up for sale.

On the road out of Barneville is a monument to celebrate the severing of the Cotentin peninsula by the Allies on 18 June 1944 from the rest of occupied France. Efforts were then concentrated on the thrust to capture Cherbourg.

A cross-country road, the D902, cuts a path inland from Barneville-Cartetet to Valognes, a total of 28 km (17 miles). Just over halfway, and amidst attractive *bocage* countryside, is Bricquebec.

Visit Bricquebec and you are back in Normandy's other world, where your nostrils are filled with the smells of the pasture rather than the spray of the sea, and where beef features more prominently than fish both at market and on menu. Bricquebec's boast is its 14th-century castle, a significant fortification for the dukes of Normandy which was won by Henry V after Agincourt in 1415. Henry bequeathed it to the Earl of Suffolk, who then returned it to the French as part of a ransom payment. The lawns within the walls are an attractive meeting place,

and refuge, here in the centre of town. The Vieux Château Hotel, a hostelry used by Queen Victoria in 1857, survives in this inner sanctum. Dominating all is the original 23 m (75 ft) keep; an exhibition of local history is displayed in the clock tower.

To the north, 2 km (1 mile) along the D121, is the early 19th-century Trappist monastery of **Abbaye Notre-Dame-de-Grace** which is now home of Cistercian monks; both men and women can attend services at the abbey church (8.15 a.m. and 6.20 p.m. during the week and 11.00 a.m., 3.30 p.m. and 8.00 p.m. on Sundays and feast days). To the south, 13 km (8 miles) along the D900, is Saint Sauveur-le-Vicomte.

Valognes seems to have bagged Barbey d'Aurevilly, the stylish 19th century novelist, as its celebrity. However, the sharp-penned d'Aurevilly was a son of Saint Saveur-le-Vicomte and was born here in 1808 and buried here 91 years later. His bust by Rodin is by the château; his life and works are displayed by the locals (gallery opening times from the tourist office).

The 12th-century fortified château, with large 14th-century keep, was the final refuge during the town's frequent sieges. Then, in 1691, Louis XIV converted the stonghold into a hospice and, today, the château is an old people's home. Elsewhere in town is the 13th-century church—with its 15th-century statue of Saint Jacques de Compostelle and 16th-century Ecce Homo—and the often-destroyed medieval abbey, which was given a new lease of life after its reconstruction by the Sisters of Saint Mary Magdalen Postel in the early 19th century.

Back on the coast, the next place of interest is Portbail, 8 km (5 miles) from Barneville-Carteret. From the centre of town at the mouth of the Ollon, it is 2 km (1 mile) across the causeway to the seafront. The port has an ancient heritage and certainly existed during the Viking era. The church of Notre Dame dates back to the 11th century and remains of a 6th-century abbey were also discovered here; relics of the early baptistry can be seen in town. Today, Portbail is another of Cotentin's popular small seaside resorts and, during the season, another place to board the Jersey ferry.

Just inland from Portbail, two roads continue in a southerly direction: the D903 to la Haye-du-Puits, 13 km (8 miles) from Portbail (and only 24 km (15 miles) west of Carentan) and then a further 8 km (5 miles) along the D900 to Lessay; or the D650, a more coastal route, which, at some 28 km (17 miles) from Portbail, passes a few kilometres west of Lessay.

Turstin Haldup, influential Norman baron from la Haye-du-Puits, founded the Benedictine abbey church of Lessay in 1056. For nearly 900 years it survived wars—except some battering during the Hundred Years War—revolutions, nature and time surprisingly well. Then calamity befell during the fighting of 1944 and the complex was severely damaged. Today, a visit here is as much to admire the meticulous reconstruction work as it is to appreciate a significant Romanesque church. The team of restorers, obsessive purists it would seem, devoted the 12 years after the War to replacing the tumbled cream stones and so re-creating the buildings in their original form.

Strong and simple is the initial impression on entering. The arched bays along the nave were, though, of pioneering design in their day and the recent stained-glass windows add colour to the chilly, austere interior.

Lessay's other attraction is the annual fair of Sainte-Croix which is almost as old as the abbey and is held in the second week of September. The event is large, and horses are the main article for bargaining, though other animals are also presented for bids.

From Lessay, the D900 now turns south-eastwards and cuts a straight route across bocage countryside through Périers the 36 km (22 miles) to Saint Lô. The D2 is the southbound road from Lessay which passes through the Lande de Lessay, an arid quarter of squat shrubs, the 21 km (13 miles) to Coutances. At 4 km (2½ miles) before the cathedral city is the turning to the right to Gratot and the 14th–18th-century château of Argouges which can be visited in July and August; tel: 31-85-25-93. Or there is the D650 from Lessay, which continues its path near the coast. Early owners of the splendid 11th–12th-century moated castle of **Pirou**, left of the main road, about 6 km (4 miles) south of Lessay, were Norman knights who won prominence during campaigns in Sicily. *Opening times*: daily except most Tuesdays, *son et lumière* performed in late July–early August; tel: 33-46-34-71. After Lessay, 15 km (9 miles) on the D650, a turning to the right becomes a short stretch of seaside corniche along the Blainville beach to Coutainville.

Coutainville has developed on the seaward side of the upper lip of the mouth of the Sienne. Unlike Carteret and Portbail further up the coast, it has no harbour or old town snugly sheltered in the estuary. Quite the contrary, Coutainville, developed long ago as a resort, has spread along the seafront. Its modest holiday flats, villas and tourist shops are now several blocks deep inland, attaching Coutainville to the village of Agon. The beach is long and very wide at low tide. At the town's northern entrance are golf and race courses. To the south, a road leads several kilometres to Pointe d'Agon, the tip of the lip, with the small resort, harbour and ruined 13th-century château of Regneville-sur-Mer across the estuary.

It is only 13 km (8 miles) directly inland from Coutainville, via Tourville-sur-Sienne from where there are views over the estuary, to Coutances. Indeed, the former is the latter's beach resort.

Coutances

"Cosedic" to the Celts, "Constantia" to the Romans, probably other names to the Vikings and early Normans and, finally, Coutances to us. The city used to be of greater significance than it is today, and it was capital of the region until the honour was transferred to Saint Lô in 1796.

The **cathedral**, its silhouette can be seen from afar as it rises high above the city's rooftops, is regarded as one of the finest in Normandy. As great as any in France for its "balance of proportions and purity of lines" according to a proud, unabashedly partial local brochure, it reflects Coutance's former importance. Indeed, the prominence of

240

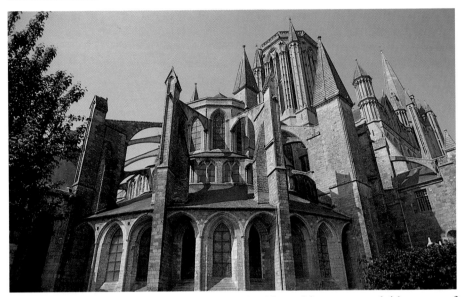

The eastern end of the Coutances cathedral, with its double flying buttresses, reveals why this is one of Normandy's great examples of medieval construction.

the cathedral's patrons gives the place further pedigree. The nave was built by Geoffrey de Montbray, the warrior-bishop who accompanied Duke William to Hastings, while much of the rest of the construction was under-written by the Hauteville boys, who had achieved remarkable conquests in southern Italy and Sicily and had sent home Mediterranean plunder to finance the completion of a splendid cathedral.

Their sponsorship, however, went up in smoke after fire swept through Coutances in 1218. The subsequent restoration introduced new designs, as Gothic architecture was laid on top of the ruined Romanesque foundations; the result is a mixture of the two styles. Fortunately, the cathedral survived relatively well during the later ravages, notably the Second World War which severely damaged Coutances.

Aside from "proportions and lines", it is the lantern tower which is exceptional and justly can be compared with any. From up here, they say, you can see Jersey on a clear day; gaining access to this vantage, it seems, is more the problem than being blessed with suitable weather. The locals come here to venerate the gracious 14th-century statue of the Lady of Coutances.

Just to the south, and forever destined to be in the shadows of the neighbouring cathedral, is the 15th–16th-century church of Saint Pierre, which was built on the ruins of older places of worship. Currently, its doors are locked while restoration is under way; here, too, the lantern is the most noteworthy feature.

Countance's other attractions are its neat, terraced public gardens which overlook the main Carentan–Granville road and the River Bulsard beyond; amongst the flower-beds and exotic trees are the statues and commemoratives in honour of worthy locals. At the entrance is the Quesnel-Morinière Museum, named after a past mayor, with displays of traditional crafts and works by regional artists, as well as a few paintings by masters from further afield which by quirks of history have ended up here in Coutances.

It is 27 km (17 miles) east along the D972 to Saint Lô.

Saint Lô

Capital of Manche, "Capital of Ruins", Saint Lô was flattened by the Allies like no other town, in the prelude to its liberation. Its fate, however, seemed inevitable: Saint Lô was a German stronghold against the advancing Americans, as Caen, to the east, was against the British and Canadians, and was therefore a prime target for Allied attrition. The city suffered 80 per cent destruction and, now, covering the deep wound of July 1944 is a modern concrete city, itself a memorial to that devastating summer, with the 1950s tower in place du Gènèral de Gaulle a symbol of the new Saint Lô.

What remains of the old is, most notably, parts of the 13th–17th-century Notre Dame cathedral. Since 1944, it has been patched up like a war wounded and reveals such contrasts as a fine Gothic pulpit and a splendid 20th-century Max Ingrand stained-glass window. The medieval ramparts which contain the "old town", including Notre Dame, still stand on their rocky crag, a reminder of a long history of belligerence, and there are

Town plan of Saint Lô.

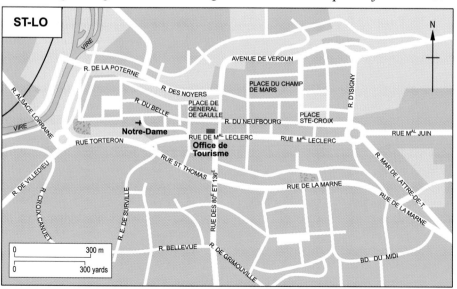

242

views over the River Vire from their western section.

The **Museum of Fine Arts**, a short walk east of Notre Dame, houses works by Millet, Boudin, Corot, Rousseau and other French artists of the period as well as tapestries, a display of snuff boxes and collections of other locally acquired crafts. *Opening times*: 10.00 a.m.–12.00 p.m. and 2.00–6.00 p.m. daily except Tuesdays during the summer and afternoons only in winter; tel: 33-57-57-01. Unfortunately, art was lost in 1944 along with the buildings; on show are the survivors. Fernand Léger's contribution to Saint Lô's art are the mosaics decorating the wall of the French–American hospital.

Heading in the direction of Bayeux along rue Maréchal Leclerc, there is, at the roundabout, the memorial to Major Thomas Howie, who was leading a contingent of fellow Americans during the drive towards Saint Lô in 1944. He had told them that his ambition was to be the first to enter the liberated city. Sadly, he was killed the day Saint Lô was freed. His colleagues, though, fulfilled his wish by carrying his coffin at the front of their column as they entered the ruined city.

Continue on the Bayeux road and on the left is the **Haras of Saint Lô**, one of the most important studs in the country. Here, thoroughbreds, English and French, Pecherons and other local breeds of horses are paired. Sections of the stables are open to the public and there are various dressage routines with smartly turned-out horses trotting around. *Opening times*: 10.00–11.30 a.m. and 2.00–4.00 p.m. (½ hour tours every ½ hour) daily from

mid-July to mid-February; carriage displays at 10.00 a.m. every Thursday from late July to early September; tel: 33-57-14-13. The D972 continues into Calvados.

It is a pretty route south of Saint Lô following the course of the Vire upstream via the Roches de Ham, with its dramatic views down over the river, to the ancient pilgrim centre of la Chapelle at Troisgots. Nearby, is the Renaissance château of l'Angotière with its lovely setting. *Opening times*: tel: 33-56-32-91 for details. Beyond is the canton centre of Tessy and the border with Calvados.

Alternatively, the main south-eastern road, the N174, passes through Torigni, with its **château des Matignon**. *Opening times*: daily from April to October, before entering Calvados.

From Coutainville on to Granville

The coastside route continues: the D650 runs along the northern shore of the Sienne estuary, before crossing the river itself and, as the D20, heading south. There are turnings to Regneville-sur-Mer and to the beach at Hauteville. However, the next main resort is Granville, 30 km (18½ miles) from Coutainville, which is larger, grander and more chic than the other resorts along Manche's coast and, as a port, second only to Cherbourg.

Granville's feature, and the reason for its growth, is its long, narrow, high rocky promontory. Upon this sturdy foundation, the English built their fortifications in 1439 from where they could attack Mont-Saint-Michel across the bay. Their stay was short: after only a few years they were ousted by those they were assailing. The battlements were dismantled in the 17th century. Granville remained a pitch for Anglo-French skirmishes, however, and in 1695 the English bombarded the port, to teach a lesson to the notorious Granville pirates, who were quasi-mercenaries fighting alongside the French navy.

The essential Norman fisherman with his yellow Gaulloise and basket of crab.

The trend for piracy gave way to fishing in the 18th century and Granville prospered on cod. Then, in the 19th century, sea bathing became fashionable and the townsfolk switched their attention from port to resort.

Fort, port, resort, Granville has been, and still is, all. The town is divided into upper, the rocky promontory, and lower Granville. Access up to the former is through the latter and the main entrance in the defence walls is by the drawbridge of the Grand Porte. A plaque here recalls the locals' defiant stand against Marquis de la Rochejaquelein's siege of 1793. For the most part, this old quarter of town dates from the 18th century, though a number of houses have undergone restoration. The streets are narrow, some allow access to vehicles, and they, and the grey stone buildings, retain their historic air. The church of Notre Dame at the western end dates between the 15th and 18th centuries, though the statue of the sacred Lady of Cape Lihou, the adored local patron, is from the 14th century.

The Museum of Old Granville in the gatehouse of the Grand Porte recounts the town's eventful past, right up to the Germans' occupation during the War, and also displays local traditional crafts and ways of life. At the eastern end of the upper town is the **Richard Anacreon Museum**, which exhibits works of modern artists. *Opening times*: 10.00 a.m.–12.00 p.m.. and 1.00–5.00 p.m. daily during the Easter holidays and from June to mid-September; Thursdays and Sundays during the rest of the year; tel: 33-50-44-10. Just beyond, on the far side of place de l'Isthme, is a view which, on

*T*he austere church of *Notre Dame overlooks the port at Granville. It houses the 14th-century statue of* Our Lady of Cape Lithou, *a greatly vener-ated idol and protectress of sea-farers.*

a clear day, stretches north along the coast to Carteret. Directly below is the Granville casino. To gain a fuller feel of this dramatic vantage, follow the rue du Nord alongside the ramparts; directly below is the rockface, lashed by waves on stormy days.

The promontory extends beyond the walls. Upon its plateau summit are various military buildings, an aquarium, with model ships and live fish displaying Granville's maritime history and its aquatic present, and a lighthouse at Pointe de Roc, the northern extent of the Bay of Mont-Saint-Michel. The Promenade du Roc runs from the lighthouse, along the southern rockface, down to the port.

Along with the sea-life at the aquarium, Granville has its shell sculptures and mineral mosaics displayed at the Feerie du coquillage and Palais mineral respectively; all exhibitions are open from late March to mid-November. Granville's history is presented in wax at the waxwork museum, in the lower town on rue Couraye; open from mid-June to mid-September.

The port lies well sheltered beneath the promontory. Though the heydays when it used to harbour pirates and long distance trawlermen are long over, it is still an active port. Today there are ferries from here to Jersey and the Chausey Islands (*see* below).

The resort is on the other side of town. From the casino, sandwiched between sea and the upper town, the beach stretches to the Jardin Public Christian Dior, a garden with views, once owned by the family of the couturier. A couple of kilometres beyond is the smaller resort of Donville-les-Bains. The 10 km (6 miles) of shore immediately to the south is dotted with a succession of resorts: Saint Pair-sur-Mer, Kairon-Plage, Jullouville, Carolles-Plage, which many people find preferable to the busier Granville.

It is 12 km (7½ miles), 55 minutes by the seasonal ferry service, to la

Grande Ile, the main island of the Chausey archipelago. Most of the other "islands" are small barren rocks, some of which are submerged during the high tides. Old folklore relates how this cluster of rocks was part of the Scissy Forest which was inundated in AD 709. More certain is the fact that stone was quarried here and used to build Granville and Mont-Saint-Michel. La Grande Ile, measuring 2 km (1 mile) by some 700 m (766 yd) at its widest, is, with a small lobster fishing community of a few score (it fluctuates according to the season), the only inhabited island. The mid-19th-century castle on the east side was constructed in preparation for a British attack which never came. As well as plage de Port Homard there is the old castle, le Vieux Fort, which dates from the mid-16th century, though it was rebuilt in the 1920s. There is also a church and lighthouse and various facilities catering for tourists.

Villedieu-les-Poêles

28 km (17 miles) directly east of Granville, along the D924, is Villedieu-les-Poêles; *en route* is Champrepus, a zoo where a substantial variety of animals from all over the world enjoy quasi-freedom here in the French countryside. South of the road in the Thar valley, 12 km (7½ miles) southeast of Granville, is the 12th-century **Premonstratensian abbey of La Lucerne**, which was left to ignorance and decay after the Revolution. The ruins were salvaged some 30 years ago; the rot came to a stop and some restoration is under way. The remains

God's Town of Frying Pans

While certainly one of the great frying pan manufacturing centres in France, the origins of the town's name is not as straightforward as it may initially seem. In the 12th century, Henry I of England founded at the village of Siennetre a commandery of the Knights' Hospitaller of Saint John of Jerusalem. In the 16th century the guild of knights altered their title to the Knights of Malta and also changed the name of the village to Villa dei, hence Villedieu.

A further legacy from this past is the Grand Sacre procession, which has been held here every 4 years since 1655 to commemorate the creation of the order of knights: the festival will take place next in 1995.

Villedieu prospered under the patronage of the knights. Craft workshops were established and it was the metal smiths, in particular, who excelled; thus "les Poêles" was added to Villedieu in appreciation of their talents.

of the abbey church, cloisters, lavatorium, chapter house and refectory constitute the early complex; the aqueduct is from the turn of the 19th century and is used to bring water to a spinning factory which had been established in the grounds. *Opening times*: daily except Tuesdays; tel: 33-48-83-56. Ruins of an 11th century château are nearby at La Haye-Pesnel.

Villedieu-les-Poêles, God's Town of Frying Pans, as the name translates, does more than justice to its epithet. It produces not only pots and pans, but also bells, mugs, plates and anything else the artisans care to shape. Tourists are today's main market, and souvenir shops are packed with copper, brass and pewter ware, which are destined for sitting rooms around the globe.

*V*illedieu-les-Poêles, "God's Town of Frying Pans", has extended its choice of copper utensils to beyond its kitchenware range.

The 15th-century church of Notre Dame replaced the original 12th-century place of worship built by the knights; their heraldic emblems still adorn the church. Just across the river, on rue du Pont Chignon, is the old bell foundry, also founded by the knights, which is still in operation and is still fashioning bells for churches all over the world; visitors are welcome from June to October, closed Sundays and Mondays; tel: 33-61-00-56. The copper workshop, and copper and lace museum, are at the other end of town in rue General Huard. *Opening times*: early June to mid-September; tel: 33-61-00-16. Market day, held on Tuesday, is especially lively and attracts a wide variety of vendors besides the artisans.

12 km (7½ miles) north of Villedieu-les-Poêles, along the D9, then bear right on the D51 is **Hambye Abbey**, one of the great ruins of Normandy. Built here in the lovely Sienne valley in 1145 by the illustrious Paynel family, the abbey was home to an active community of Benedictine monks until the English disrupted the peace after Agincourt in 1415. In the 19th century, in the wake of the Revolution, Hambye, like Jumièrges and other monasteries, was sold. Walls were dismantled and the stone blocks carted off to construction sites elsewhere. Despite its ruinous state, the abbey is still spectacular. Indeed, the eye can appreciate aspects of architecture which would probably go unnoticed if the building was in full repair. Two tombs are of note: that of Jeanne Paynel and her husband Louis d'Estouteville, who had stoutly defended Mont-Saint-Michel from the English in the 15th century. Besides the broken skeleton of the abbey church, there are other monastic buildings including the 13th-century chapter house, the Hall of the Dead, the library, the kitchen, the 17th-century refectory and dormitory and out houses including the stables. *Opening times*: daily from early February to mid-December; closed Tuesday and Wednesday mornings during the low season; tel: 33-61-76-92.

From Carolles, 11 km (7 miles) south of Granville, the build-up to "Le Mont-Saint-Michel" intensifies: signs along the road indicate the best viewpoints signs along the road indicate the best viewpoints, such as Cabane Vauban, of the Mont across the bay. It is an attractive patch of countryside between this stretch of coast and Sartilly, on the main D973 Granville–Avranches road. However, staying by the bay, the D911 passes through the pretty village of Saint Jean-le-Thomas. Just beyond Dragey is a turning to the Manoir de Brion, which, part 11th century, part 16th century, is where Jacques Cartier was given authorization to embark on the venture which led to the discovery of Canada in 1535.

The road continues to Genets, the D35e to the right leads to dunes at Bec d'Andaine and another view of the Mont. As the tide draws out, it reveals an expanse of glittering mudflats cut by channels, making it possible to walk across to the Mont. However, the aid of a local guide is essential, for the flats are treacherous and the tide returns at a galloping pace.

It is a further 10 km (6 miles) from Genêts to Avranches continuing

248

along the D911, longer by the minor roads which hug the coastline.

Avranches

"Avranches" is derived from Abricanti, the name of a long-extinct Gaulish clan of these parts. A central boulevard bears their name, and other peoples of historical significance are also remembered around town. But it is the Americans who have the most brazen commemorative plaque.

"Making the Avranches breakthrough in the roar of its tanks while marching towards victory and the liberation of France, the glorious American Army of General Patton passed over this crossroads." Such is the translation of the inscription at the Patton Monument besides the road to Pontorson in the outskirts of Avranches: richly melodramatic lines for the Americans' remarkable multipronged assault from Avranches into France which commenced here on 1 August 1944. The Americans' breakthrough and surrounding events are remembered at the Second World War Museum, 5 km (3 miles) south of Avranches on the N175.

In the old town, at place Daniel Huet at the other end of town, is *la plate-forme* and a paving stone with the inscription: "After the murder of Thomas à Becket, Archbishop of Canterbury, Henry II, King of England and Duke of Normandy, received on his knees from the Papal legates the apostolic absolution, 21 May, MCLXXII". A cathedral stood here in Henry's time (it tumbled in 1794) and the king, barefoot and wearing a

*H*ere *stayed General Patton before his crucial offensive, known as the Avranches breakthrough, in July 1944. This spot, in the southern outskirts of Avranches, has been laid with American turf and is deemed US territory.*

simple white gown, knelt at the altar while the Abbot of Mont-Saint-Michel conducted the ritual of accepting him back into the Christian fold. Here, too, is one of the viewpoints from where to see the Mont across the bay.

On the way back to the town centre is the museum,which is housed in the

15th-century **Bishop's Palace**. The most outstanding exhibits are the unique, priceless manuscripts; many were brought from the abbey at Mont-Saint-Michel, and date from the 8th to 15th centuries. *Opening times*: 9.00 a.m.–12.00 p.m.. and 2.00–6.00 p.m. daily from Easter to October; tel: 33-58-25-15.

Another notable moment in history occurred in Avranches: Jean Quetil, commonly known as John Barefoot, led a revolt against the introduction of the Salt Tax in 1639. He rallied great support in the surrounding country-side; the movement was brutally suppressed by the national troops.

There are many botanical gardens in the Cotentin peninsula and the one at Avranches is much celebrated, not least because of the view of Mont-Saint-Michel from the terraces. The Mont is a small silhouette in the distance. It seems a rather overrated spectacle, though they say this is one of "the views" of France when the moon is full and the night is clear. During the summer, there are excursion flights over the Mont-Saint-Michel; tel: 33-58-02-91 for details.

Today Avranches is a solid, busy, mid-sized administrative town over-shadowed by the romance and reputation of Mont-Saint-Michel across the bay. Indeed, this has probably always been the case.

The main N175 heads south from Avranches and continues 22 km (14 miles) to Pontorson, a thoroughfare for traffic on the border with

*A*cross the flats and through the haze, the pyramidal shape of Mont-Saint-Michel is unmistakable. Normandy is blessed with a "wonder" as great as any in France.

Brittany, which suffers, and no doubt thrives, as the "Last Stop" before Mont-Saint-Michel. From here it is 11 km (7 miles) directly north to the Mont.

But the circuitous journey via Pontorson can be avoided. Some 8 km (5 miles) out of Avranches, on the N175, just beyond Pontaubault, the D43 bears right along the flat marshlands for some 13 km (8 miles) to Mont-Saint-Michel.

Mont-Saint-Michel

A divine request for a house of God was relayed by Archangel Michael to Aubert, Bishop of Avranches, in a vision in the 8th century. It proved to be the inspiration from which one of the world's most spectacular churches evolved.

The Mont was once a hillock in a vast forest which stretched from the present shores of western Manche to, and beyond, the Channel Islands. Then the water levels rose and flooded the low-lying lands, leaving the Mont, the Chausey Islands and the Channel Islands as the sole survivors of the lost forest. Today, the daily tides recedes dramatically, but all they reveal is mile after mile of grey mudflat.

The Mont lies a kilometre off the coast. It is a part-time island: at low tides it can be reached by walking across the muds, though the quicksands and astonishing speed (sometimes 30 kph/18 mph) with which the waters return make such a venture extremely hazardous; when the sea has risen, it is transformed into its island state.

Aubert, in response to his vision, built an oratory. The Mont, then known as Mont Tombe, had been selected for centuries as a site for veneration, and Druids and Romans had both worshipped here. With Aubert, there commenced a new era: the seed of his faith was sown on the Mont, and from it grew one of Christianity's most glorious creations.

Mont-Saint-Michel soon became a significant place of pilgrimage. Furthermore, it also served as a refuge from the marauding Vikings. But then the Vikings settled and became God-loving Normans and in the 10th century Duke Richard built a Benedictine abbey on the Mont.

Since then the Mont's patronage and fame has been assured. It was England's Edward the Confessor who gave the monks the "sister" mount of Saint Michel's Mount off the coast of Cornwall and his successor, William the Conqueror, was also a great benefactor. Philippe-Auguste damaged much of the Romanesque abbey when he attacked the Mont in 1203. But he replaced his destruction with a Gothic abbey, the Merveille, the Marvel, the core of the present complex which has been frequently modified over the succeeding centuries. A village grew on the gentler, lower slopes on the south and east side of the Mont; locals enclosed themselves within a fortified wall, which proved to be a sound defence when the flak began to fly during the Hundred Years War.

A commendatory system, whereby non-resident abbots were in charge, was introduced in the 16th century. The rot set in as appointees, favourites of the king, cared more for their personal interests than those of the abbey and its community. Morale amongst the monks dwindled. Then came the Revolution and the remaining monks were forced to flee; in the aftermath the abbey served as a gaol. Finally, good sense prevailed and in 1874 Mont-Saint-Michel gained protection as a classified national monument. A restoration programme was inaugurated, and amongst the new additions was the bell tower with its statue of Saint Michel. However, it was not until 1966, the 1,000th anniversary of the

An endless quantity of souvenirs are on offer; there is little sacrosanct along the path up to the holy goal.

Take your pick, a remembrance of Mont-Saint-Michel at its best.

founding of Duke Richard's abbey, that the Benedictine monks returned to the abbey.

A causeway, built in the 19th century, is now the Mont's permanent link with the shore. Entry on to the "island" is by the King's Tower. To the right is the King's Gate and the Grande Rue, the path leading to the summit. Restaurants, cafés and souvenir shops line this steep, narrow lane and cater for the thousands of daily tourists (the Mont is France's biggest attraction outside Paris and Versailles). The scene is merely a modern version of that experienced by the more traditional pilgrims over the past centuries, who doubtless had food and religious paraphernalia thrust upon them by eager vendors.

At the lower end of the Grande Rue is the Maritime Museum, which tells of the relationship between the Mont and the sea. Further up is a waxworks, which recounts a more general history of the Mont. Opposite, is the parish church of Saint Pierre which dates from the 11th century though most of it, and its contents, date from later times. The architects and warrior-defenders of the abbey are amongst those buried here. The 14th-century Tiphaine House stands close by the side of the church.

The paths behind the church offer a quieter stroll to the top than the

Grande Rue thoroughfare can provide. Also, just above Saint Pierre is the Grevin Museum which relates the Mont's folklore, history and anecdotes through a S*on et Lumière* display. The Sentry Walk curls from here around the southern base of the summit, and from here there are views down over the village.

The ascent along the Grande Rue steepens and twists for the final climb up the Grand Degré, the stairway to the abbey defences, the link between the ordinary folk below and the monks above.

More steps lead to Gautier's leap, the landing from where a prisoner called Gautier is said to have thrown himself to his death, and to the entrance to the abbey church.From the nearby West Platform there is an excellent view across the bay. There are guided tours, lasting about 45 minutes, of the abbey complex.

The tour proceeds through the magnificent abbey church and various buildings of la Merveille, including the cloisters, the refectory, the guests' hall, the knights' hall, also the crypts, the old Romanesque abbey, the pre-Carolingian—now subterranean—church of Notre Dame-Sous-Terre, dungeons, cellars and the almonry. The guide gives an account of all these and more.The abbey gardens on the northern slopes of the Mont can also be visited and, perched on a lower rock, is the small chapel of Saint Aubert.

An alternative descent to the Grande Rue is via the ramparts. There is a path upon the sturdy defensive wall along the east and south sides of the Mont.

East of Mont-Saint-Michel and Avranches

Travel east from Mont-Saint-Michel and Avranches and you are back in the heart of the Normandy interior. Patton's forces won glory in these fields in August 1944. It is 15 km (9 miles) from Pontorson to Saint James, where there are the ruins of a castle built by Duke William, and nearby are the graves of 4,400 American soldiers who did not survive to enjoy the victory. Continuing eastwards past the château and la Paluelle, it is a further 20 km (12 miles) to Saint Hilaire-du-Harcouët and another 14 km (9 miles) from there to Mortain.

Alternatively, follow the Sélune valley, south of the N176 between Pontaubault and Saint Hiliare-du-Harcouët, which has been dammed to create a long meandering reservoir. However, the most scenic countryside is further north around small towns such as Mortain, Brécey, Saint Pois and Sourdeval. The D5 and the D911 lead from Avranches. The first of these roads runs almost the full 36 km (22 miles) distance to Mortain; the latter path follows alongside the river Sée via Brécey, from where you can make a detour to Saint Pois, and Sourdeval before entering into the department of Orne.

It is pretty around Saint Pois. Just to the north is Calvados and the Forêt de Saint Sever, and 4 km (2½ miles) to the east is Saint Michel-de-Montjoie with its Granite Museum. South of Saint Pois the D33 crosses the Sée and the G911 at Clarence-le-Roussel. It continues past **Bellefontaine** and its children's centre with model villages, miniature railway and playground. *Opening times*: daily from mid-April to October; tel: 33-59-01-93. Beyond, is Saint Barthelemy, then the curiously named junction of Tête-à-la-Femme followed by Mortain, a total of 18 km (11 miles) from Saint Pois.

Mortain is built on a craggy hillside, surrounded by forests and waterfalls. The setting seems theatrically medieval; in fact, the town was of greater importance then, as home of Count Robert de Mortain, William the Conqueror's half-brother, than it is now. Much of Mortain was rebuilt, in the usual local granite, after its destruction in 1944. This was where, on the night of 6–7 August, the Germans chose to counter Patton's offensive. Their objective was to sever the links between the American base at Avranches and the advancing 3rd Army. However, the Allies bombed the Germans, as well as Mortain, forcing them to retreat through the Falaise Gap after a week of heavy fighting. A memorial, on the way to la Petite Chapelle just to the south-east of the town, is dedicated to the Americans who died during this encounter. Near the chapel is a viewpoint overlooking the Forêt de Mortain and in the other direction is the sea; in the past, pilgrims would come here to gain their first sight of Mont-Saint-Michel which is visible on a clear day.

The 13th-century Gothic church of Saint Evroult survived 1944 and its treasury stores the unique 7th-century chrismale, which was probably pillaged and brought over from England by William the Conqueror. On the way out of town, on the road to Sourdeval, is the **Abbaye Blanche**, a 12th-century monastery built by the de Mortain family and still used as a retreat. Many of today's intake, though, tend to come for short spells of spiritual healing, merely a brief hiatus from the outside world. The abbey, with its church, cloister, chapter house, refectory and out room, can be visited. *Opening times*: daily except Tuesday and Sunday mornings from June to mid-September; tel: 33-59-00-21.

From the abbey you can follow the course of the Cance through the woods to the Grande Cascade, the Great Waterfall, which tumbles over boulders for 25 m (27 yd); continue, and the lower part of the town is up on the left. The Petite Cascade, the Small Waterfall, is along a tributary to the right off the Cance.

Roads east of Mortain lead into the Parc Régional Normandie-Maine and on to Orne. The main one, the D907, leads the 9 km (5½ miles) to Barenton; here **La Maison de la Pomme et de la Poire** documents the activities associated with the region's all-important apples and pears. *Opening times*: daily from mid-June to late September and weekends from mid-April to mid-June; tel: 33-59-56-22. It is 15 km (9 miles) from Barenton to Domfront in Orne.

Rich Countryside, Châteaux and Horses, the Forgotten Corner of Normandy

Landlocked Orne is a department of deep countryside, unexposed to the sea and all that it brings. It is a land of manors and stud farms, of the fairy-tale château and the forgotten cathedral. But it is not a backwater without innovation. From the region of Perche, the rich heartlands of Orne, came the first settlers to Quebec; this is also home of the *Percheron*, the great sturdy dray-horse. Birthplace of the Canadian and the cart-horse is the curious distinction cherished in this quiet corner of Normandy.

Alençon

Alençon administers Orne from the southern frontiers of Normandy. The city almost spills over into the neighbouring department of Sarthe, and its

*H*ome of the Os,
a fairytale-like castle, with its moat and swans, which was built over centuries. The richness of Château d'O reflects the prominence of the family over the years, and in particular Francis d'O the Finance Minister and Master of the Wardrobe to Henry III.

proximity to greater France has diluted its Normandy character. Maybe the people of Alençon even have a certain antipathy for Normandy which dates back to an incident in the mid-11th century. Duke William had laid siege to the town, which was occupied by his enemy, the Count of Anjou. Despite the severity of the situation, the inhabitants chose to taunt the Duke. They hung hides over the city walls and shouted "A la pel", the tanner's market cry, as a poignant reminder of William's mother's family trade and thus his lowly and illegitimate origins. Infuriated, William had the limbs of 30 local prisoners lopped off and lobbed over the walls. The people of Alençon realized the folly of their joke and duly surrendered.

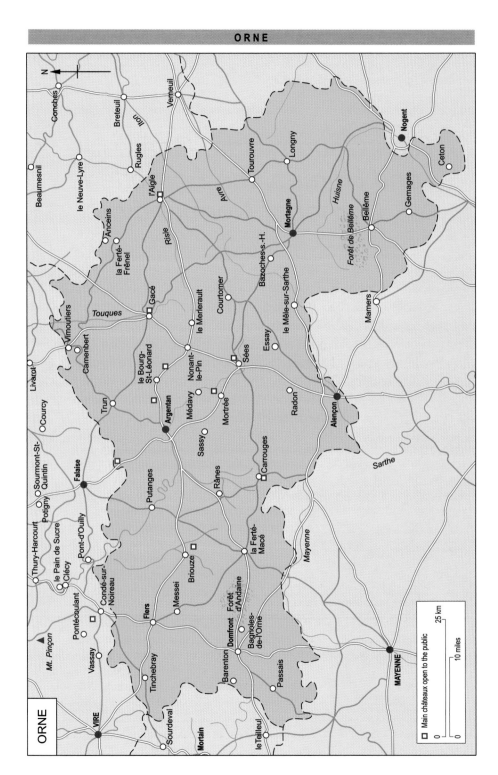

ORNE

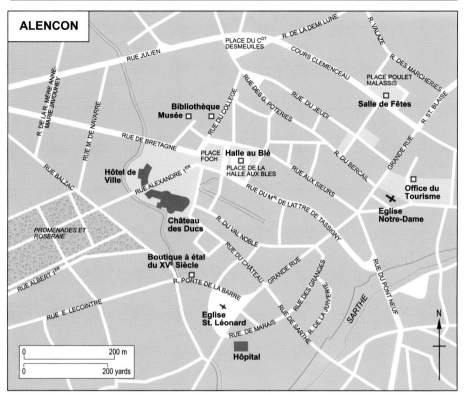

ALENCON

RUE JULIEN
PLACE DU C^DT DESMEUILES
R. DE LA DEMI LUNE
R. VALAZE
COURS CLEMENCEAU
R. DES MARCHERIES
PLACE POULET MALASSIS
RUE DES G. POTERIES
RUE DU JEUDI
Salle de Fêtes
R. ST. BLAISE
R. DE LA R. MÈRE ANNE-MARIE JAVOUHEY
RUE M. DE NAVARRE
RUE DE BRETAGNE
RUE DU COLLEGE
Bibliothèque Musée
GRANDE RUE
R. DU BERCAIL
RUE BALZAC
Hôtel de Ville
RUE ALEXANDRE 1ER
PLACE FOCH
Halle au Blé
PLACE DE LA HALLE AUX BLES
RUE AUX SIEURS
Office du Tourisme
PROMENADES ET ROSERAIE
Château des Ducs
RUE DU M^AL DE LATTRE DE TASSIGNY
R. DU VAL NOBLE
Eglise Notre-Dame
Boutique à étal du XVE Siècle
RUE DU CHÂTEAU
GRANDE RUE
RUE DES GRANGES
RUE DU PONT NEUF
RUE ALBERT 1ER
R. PORTE DE LA BARRE
RUE E. LECOINTRE
Eglise St. Léonard
R. DE LA JUVERIE
RUE DE SARTHE
SARTHE
RUE DE MARAIS
Hôpital

N

0   200 m
0   200 yards

Town plan of Alençon

The centre of the town is dominated by the mid-15th-century church of Notre Dame, most noted for its flamboyant-styled porch and stained glass—that of the clerestory windows dates back to 1530. Part of the church, notably the tower, was rebuilt in the 18th century. In its shadow is place Lamagdelaine and the 15th-century Maison d'Oze which is now occupied by the tourist office. This central old town has been tastefully restored and is a lively shopping precinct.

Going beyond the centre, north along Grande Rue and into rue Saint

Map of the Orne region.

Blaise, you reach the Chapel of Sainte Theresa. Next to it is the house where Theresa Martin, later Saint Theresa of Lisieux (*see* page 98), was born in 1873. On the other side of the road is the 17th-century Prefecture.

Follow Grande Rue in the other direction, and you come to the restored 15th-century church of Saint Léonard. But just before, rue du Château bears right and at the end of the road are the grim towers, the remains of the first Duke of Alençon's 14th–15th-century château, which today serve as the entrance to the prison. Just beyond is

The sensible citizens of Alençon converted their sturdy castle into the city prison.

French Cambodia at the turn of this century.

At the other end of town, on the rue du Pont Neuf, beyond Notre Dame and by the river, is the Lace Museum. Here, it takes 16 hours to make 3 cm^2 (0.5 in^2) of lace and 10 years to

place Foch. A conspicuous landmark to the right on the other side of the road is the round 19th-century grain hall, while, along rue du Collège is the **Museum of Fine Arts and Lace**.

The museum was formerly a Jesuit college, but now houses paintings by 17th–20th-century French and European artists—including Courbet and Boudin—and lace. Also, incongruous though fascinating, is a collection of 500 Cambodian artefacts; they were gathered by Adhemard Leclère, an Alençon man who was governor of

Mode d'Alençon

Alençon's fame was built on lace, the *point d'Alençon*. Its reputation was already secure when, in 1655, Colbert, Louis XIV's minister, founded a "royal" lace workshop. The ever style-conscious courtiers had been purchasing their lace, at increasingly exorbitant prices, from Venice. In introducing quality, chic Alençon lace, Colbert wooed the fashionable to the home market. The museum also relates the rise of the lace centres of Europe. *Opening times*: 10.00 a.m.–12.00 p.m.. and 2.00–6.00 p.m. daily except Mondays; tel: 33-32-40-00.

*A*dding style to the mundane: a spouting gargoyle, an artistic means of channelling water.

complete just "one piece"; the work requires such intense concentration that it damages the eyesight of the needle-women. The dedication necessary for such a labour-intensive craft is as much to be admired as the beauty of the final product itself. Examples of the extraordinarily fine, delicate lace is on display; so, too, are a small group of lacemakers who can be seen patiently continuing the city's tradition. The high price paid for today's hand-made lace reflects an appreciation not only for the craftsmen's skill but also their time.

Travellers from the north will see Alençon as the last stop in Normandy. For those coming from the south the city is the gateway: Normandy spreads beyond.

Beyond Alençon

Excursions can be made into the Forêt de Perseigne and to the Alpes Mancelles, to the south-east and south-west of Alençon respectively. However, neither region is in Normandy. To the north though, is land encompassed by the huge Parc Régional Normandie-Maine and more specifically by the Forêt d'Ecouves, covering 14,000 hectares (37,000 acres).

The main N12 bypasses the northern fringe of Alençon: to the east, it leads to Montagne-au-Perche 36 km (22 miles) away; to the west it runs into the department of Mayenne, though the D909 does branch northward to Carrouges, a total of 30 km (18½ miles). The main road north is the N138 to Sées, 22 km (13½ miles) from downtown Alençon; however, the preferable northbound route is the smaller D26.

Forêt d'Ecouves

The D26 cuts through the heart of the Forêt d'Ecouves, which covers hills rising up to 417 m (456 yd) at Ecouves Signal Station and meets the east–west D908 on the far side, some 20 km (12 miles) from Alençon. To the right is Sées, 12 km (7½ miles), and to the left is Carrouges, while the north-westward continuation of the D26 leads into a circuit of châteaux which lie between Sées and Argentan. On the way to Carrouges there is a turning to the right (D204) to Goult and its Romanesque chapel; here too is a Roman site on the hill by the chapel and there is a viewing point for Saint Michel.

Carrouges

Upon a hill, the old small town of Carrouges, seat of the medieval Counts of Carrouges, has now been designated as "headquarters" of the Parc Régional Normandie-Maine; its office and information centre are housed in the château's Ferme du Chapitre.

Le Château de Carrouges, a replacement for the original hilltop fort, is a couple of minutes' drive to the south of the town. Entrance to the grounds is through the splendid spiky, pepper-pot-towered, mitre-roofed, 16th-century gatehouse; to the left is the large, solid, impressive, red-brick and granite castle–château surrounded by a wide moat. The château is built around a rectangular courtyard and dates back to the 14th–15th century. In 1450 the property passed through marriage to the illustrious Norman family

*S*urrounded by a moat of murky green water, the
Château de Carrouges, once home to the Comtes de Carrouges,
one of Normandy's ancient warrior families, has undergone
extensive restoration.

The inner sanctum of the Château de Carrouges, one of Normandy's finer stately homes, which was rescued from further decay in 1936 by the department of Monuments Historiques, the present owners.

Receiving Jesus' blessing in Ferté Macé. Old and modern stained glass in Normandy is an important aspect of religious art.

of Le Veneur de Tillières and was owned by them until 1936 when it was acquired by the state.

A tour of the interior starts with the Louis XI bedroom, where the king is said to have stayed in 1473, and continues through a succession of chambers: the 15th-century state anteroom and the kitchen from the same period; then the dining room with its great fireplace, the summer drawing room, the portrait room, the state drawing room and the grand staircase—

a masterpiece of brickwork—all dating from the 17th century, with most of the furniture and decorations also from that era. Daily tours; tel: 33-27-20-32.

La Ferté-Macé

About 17 km (10½ miles) west of Carrouges is the attractive, prosperous, busy market town of la Ferté-Macé; a slight detour south of the main road takes in la Motte-Fouquet and Magny-le-Désert, villages known locally for their medieval churches. La Ferté-Macé itself is famed for its tripe, *tripes fertoises en brochettes*, and, to a lesser extent, for its restored 11th-century chapel which William the Conqueror gave to the local Benedictine monks. The town is now something of a hub for the tourists here in the Parc Régional Normandie-Maine, and certainly its proximity to Bagnoles-de-l'Orne, 6 km (3½ miles) to the south-west, has enhanced its prominence.

Bagnoles-de-l'Orne

Bagnoles-de-l'Orne proudly promotes itself as "Capital of the veins, the foremost thermal spa resort for the treatment of venous ailments". The spa's reputation has been known for many centuries, though its unselfconscious boast "Capital of the veins" probably dates to the mid-1800s when Bagnoles was frequented by royalty and aristocrats in search of therapy.

The resort remains elegant and fashionable—though sometimes dull and geriatric depending on who is in town—and is centred around a lake, which is all the more attractive for its manicured banks and the white casino reflected in the waters. The Vée, which feeds the lake, continues southwards. Here, along allée de Dante, you will find the *Etablissement Thermal* and the wooded park spreading beyond. High above the right bank is the Roc au Chien, which can be reached by a path through the woods, from where there is a view down over the town and the surrounding forests. Another approach to the Rock is from Tessé la Madelaine, a village now welded to the southern part of Bagnoles, which can be reached along the avenue du Château. The château is now the Town Hall.

*B*agnoles-de-l'Orne, *still a grand spa town in the midst of the woods.*

Class Waters

Bagnoles' spring has a temperature of 25 °C, unique in western France, and its various properties do ease circulatory problems and prevent disorders such as varicose veins. Anybody can bathe in these curative waters, and when the fad for doing so evolved there was flagrant discrimination amongst the patients. The noble men immersed themselves farthest upstream; next in line were their ladies, and finally the farthest downstream were the plebeian classes of both sexes!

Treatment under the supervision of a thermalist consultant can be had at the *Etablissement Thermal* (tel: 33-30-82-31) and courses last from a few days to 3 weeks; the season is from early May to November and attracts 20,000 patients a year. The main ailments are venous problems, "heaviness of leg", varicose veins, phlebitis, haemorrhoids and menstruation unease.

South of Bagnoles

Apart from hot water, Bagnoles' attraction is that it is also a good base for travels into the surrounding Forêt des Andaines and beyond. The following villages and sights can serve as a basis for an itinerary into the countryside just to the south of Bagnoles: The 17th-century château of Couterne, beside the D335 and River Vée; the church of Notre Dame-de-Lignou with

Window shutters, a feature on old and new houses, provide extra decoration and insulation.

its black virgin; Couterne village itself; Antoigny and its church just to the east—beyond, on the way to Saint Patrice-du-Désert, are the local beauty spots of Vallée de la Cour and Gorges de Villers; Méhoudin, south of Antoigny, on the site of a Gallo-Roman settlement; the villages of Haleine and Tessé-Froulay to the west of Couterne, both with sturdy 19th-century churches but dwindling populations of only a few hundred as potential congregations; the larger la Chapelle-d'Andaine, with its "Corso Fleuri" fête on the third Sunday in July; Juvigny-sous-Andaine, canton centre, with both the extraordinary Phare de Bonvouloir, a 15th-century 27 m (88 ft) lighthouse in the middle of the countryside, and the chapel and viewpoint of Sainte Geneviève just to its north. Domfront is 19 km (12 miles) from Juvigny-sous-Andaine along the N176, alternatively return to Bagnoles via the D235 and on to Ferté-Macé along the D386, through the Forêt des Andaines and the village of Saint Michel-des-Andaines, and the D908.

"Lancelot of the Lake"

In Bagnoles they promote the rather curious "Lancelot of the Lake" circuit. It incorporates places connected with King Arthur's legendary Knights of the Round Table, in particular Lancelot, and the beauty spots and sights in the area. The route starts at Bagnoles, heads north to la Sauvagère, north-west to la Ferrière-aux-Etangs, on to Châtellier, via Banvou and Vieux Banvou, and southwards on to Saint Bômer-les-Forges, Lonlay-l'Abbaye and la Fosse Arthour. From here,

there is an extension via Barenton to Mortain and back; continue south-east to Domfront and then south-west to Passais-la-Conception; on then to Ceaucé and la Gue-de-Lore and on to Lassay and Saint Fraimbault-de-Lassay, both in Mayenne *département*; return north via Couterne and Notre Dame-de-Lignou to Bagnoles. References to some of the above-mentioned places on the circuit are made on the next few pages.

The tourist office at Bagnoles has a brochure which describes the relevance of the places on the itinerary. The *"Festival au Pays de Lancelot du Lac"* comprises different events: drama, dance and music, though they do not have much bearing necessarily on the Arthurian legend; it is held in the area during the summer and the book *Les Romans de la Table Ronde la Normandie et Au-Dela* is also available.

North of Ferté-Macé

Roads splay northwards of Ferté-Macé. Along the D18 to Flers are the villages of: Saint Maurice-du-Désert, with notable 17th-century church, manor and old yew; la Sauvagère, with the nearby chapel of Notre Dame built singlehandedly by Brother Pascal; and la Ferrière-aux-Etangs, an old mining village on the northern edge of the Parc Régional Normandie-Maine with picturesque countryside to its south and west. At some 10 km (6 miles) north of la Ferrière-aux-Etangs is Flers. Alternatively 12 km (7.5 miles) to its east, along the D20, is Briouze, a rail and road junction on the edge of marshlands, whose name is derived from the old Gallic word for sludge; the nearby chapel of Saint Gervais is the site of an 11th-century priory.

Off the D19, the la Ferté-Macé–Fromental road, are le Grais and les Yveteaux, both with châteaux. North of Fromental, the D909 leads to Putanges-Pont-Ecrepin; Crèvecoeur château is off to the right.

The D916 out of la Ferté-Macé by-passes Saint Georges-d'Annebecq, site of a ruined château, on the way to Rânes. Rânes, itself badly damaged during World War II, has the wings of its château attached to an imposing 15th-century brown, stoned keep; the building now serves as headquarters for the local *gendarmes* and stands near to the town's racecourse. From Rânes it is 20 km (12 miles) to Argentan via Ecouché.

Flers

Flers, a town developed through the making of hemp, expanded with the arrival of the cotton industry and destroyed by the aggression of World War II, reveals its history inside its château. The 16th–18th-century building is partly enclosed by a moat and, today, houses the town's *mairie* as well as the **Museum of the Norman Bocage.** There is a fairly eclectic array of collections, but that of local relevance includes a traditional Norman kitchen and a countess's boudoir as well as art, some not so local, and illustrated accounts of Flers' role during the Revolution and World War II. *Opening times*: afternoons from Easter to mid-October; tel: 33-64-01-02. The château overlooks parks and ponds.

West of Flers

About 12 km (7½ miles) north of Flers, and just over the border in Calvados, is Condé-sur-Noireau and 21 km (13 miles) to the south is Domfront. Approximately 10–20 km (6–12 miles) west of this line are Calvados and Manche. There is attractive *bocage* countryside within this westernmost margin of Orne, and

*T*he country squires may have left, but their old mansions, often hidden deep in forests, remain private residences, an increasing number in the hands of the English.

places of interest include: Cerisi-Belle-Etoile, north-west of Flers, with its 13th–15th-century abbey and mount from where there are views over the surrounding *bocage*. The rhododendrons blossom in May and June, and on the last Sunday in May, locals hold the annual Rhododendron Festival. A road leads north to les Vaux and the Roman bridge at Saint Pierre-d'Entremont.

Tinchebray, about halfway along the Flers–Vire road, was the site of a crucial contest, the result of which determined the future of Normandy and England. On 28 September 1106 the sons of William the Conqueror—Robert Curthose, the Duke of Normandy, and the younger Henry Beauclerk, King of England—fought over the principles, and indeed the vast estates, of their disputed inheritance; Henry was victorious and thus the "English" had revenged the Normans' conquest of England at Hastings in 1066. Tinchebray's old prison is now a museum and it gives an insight into traditional Normandy lifestyles as well as the prison life experienced by the different grades of convicts.

It is a pretty route along the D22 south from Tinchebray to Domfront. 15 km (9 miles) along the way is Lonlay-l'Abbaye, with its abbey church dating from the founding of the abbey in 1020, but restored most recently after destruction in 1944; the town is also famous for its shortbread. One alternative to the main route to Domfront is the narrow road which leads south-westwards to la Fosse-Arthour, a scenic river setting on the Sonce; it has associations with the Arthurian legend and is part of the "Lancelot of the Lake" circuit. Lanes continue south to Rouelle on the D907 and the manor of la Saucerie just beyond. Domfront is about 5 km (3 miles) to the east. Another alternative from Lonlay-l'Abbaye is to take the D54 eastwards to Saint Bômer-les-Forges and then to pick up minor roads south to Domfront.

Domfront

Domfront's feudal castle remains strong and impressive despite its state of ruin. William de Bellême, the local noble, founded the fort in 1011, which makes it one of the oldest in Normandy. The townsfolk turned against Robert de Montgomery, their lord, 89 years later, and sided with Henry Beauclerk, King of England, who took the town, made it "English", and developed the castle into one of the most formidable in Normandy. The English interest continued through the reign of Henry II who used to come to Domfront, accompanied by his Eleanor of Aquitaine and an assortment of colourful minstrels and courtiers. It was here, in 1170, that the pope's envoys tried to forge peace between him and Thomas à Becket, the Archbishop of Canterbury. The mission failed and Becket was to be murdered soon after. Domfront passed between the English and French on several occasions over the following centuries, finally to become a French possession for good in 1450.

Remains of the old ramparts poke through among the more recent constructions of the old town, itself restored to its quaint traditional half-

Misfortune of a Scots Guard

The unfortunate Captain Gabriel de Montgomery, once of the Scots Guards, is the most colourful character in Domfront's "Hall of Fame". The captain had given his allegiance to King Henri II of France against the English, but had, in 1559, unintentionally—so it is claimed—killed Henri in a tournament. He converted to Calvinism and took it upon himself, and his band of 150 soldiers, to defend Domfront from the royalist Catholic army. He lost the battle, surrendering after his force had been whittled down to 15, and then his life when Catherine de Medici, Henri's widow, reneged on her promise of clemency and had him executed in 1574.

timbered glory; in the public gardens, across the old moat at the western end of the town, there is the keep, as well as a panoramic view over the Passais *bocage*. The nearby town hall exhibits pictures by local artist Charles Léandre (1862–1934) and just beyond is the place du Panorama, so-called for obvious reasons.

Down by the River Varenne is the 11th-century church of Notre Dame-sur-l'Eau. The church was partly destroyed by the early 19th-century road constructors, philistines who ploughed their progress through this historic place of prayer where Thomas à Becket had celebrated Christmas Mass in 1166, and it was defaced further by soldiers during battle in 1944. The building has now been restored.

Domfront is in the heart of pear-growing country, and in the farms around about they make perry, pear cider. A "Pear Route" has been devised by the local tourist office and includes farms and manor houses within the vicinity of Domfront. A meandering, anticlockwise circuit along minor roads to the south of the town can be threaded through the villages of: Torchamp, Passais-la-Conception, Mantilly, which holds a pear festival at the end of July, Saint Fraimbault, Ceaucé, Avrilly—near Mont Margantin—and back to Domfront via Saint Brice.

Putanges has been linked by a bridge across the Orne to Ecrepin for centuries, hence the twin village of Putanges-Pont-Ecrepin, though the medieval bridge, blown up in 1944, has been replaced by the present structure. At 9 km (6 miles) to the north-east is Habloville with its 13th–15th-century church notably adorned with fine 15th–18th-century furnishings and decor; the church is open in the afternoons from mid-April to mid-September; tel: 33-35-05-24 for other appointments. Putanges, the abbreviated name familiar to most, is a southern gateway to the picturesque Suisse Normande region. Downstream is Lac de Rabodanges, a lake-reservoir used for water sports; the 17th-century Rabodanges château is north of the lake, while Le Moulin de la Jalousie, an old mill, is by the Orne, off the road running west of Rabodanges. Follow the flow of the river to the Gorges de Saint Aubert and Suisse Normande proper.

Alternatively, the D15 leads the 29 km (17 miles), through the *bocage* Athisien, to Condé-sur-Noireau. Along the way there is Taillebois with its manors and Saint Honorine-la-Chardonne with its châteaux. La Carneille, 3 km (2 miles) south of

Taillebois, is one of the prettier old villages in the surrounding countryside; west of Sainte Honorine-la-Chardonne is the picturesque Vère valley.

Sées

The soaring spires of Sées cathedral, silhouettes seen from afar, are welcome landmarks for motorists on the busy and boring N138. A city by title, a town by size, Sées is an interesting stop along this road. Visited at dusk in summer, Sées seems a forgotten backwater, maybe it is always like this, despite the juggernauts thundering past its outskirts.

Sées' heyday was during more religious times. It has been a bishop's see since AD 400 when Saint Latuin based himself here and introduced the Gospels to the folk of the region. The city has had several cathedrals which were destroyed by various natural or man-inspired means. The present one of Notre Dame, dating back to the 13th–14th centuries, also looked destined to tumble, owing to less than solid foundations; it has had to have structural supports added over the centuries to keep it propped up.

None the less, Notre Dame is a magnificent cathedral, one of the most splendid examples of Norman Gothic architecture, and the nave, the transepts, the chancel, and the stained-glass windows of the choir are particularly impressive aspects of the original construction; the hallowed marble Notre Dame of Sées, facing the altar, dates back some 600–700 years.

An ecclesiastic air still pervades in Sées. Just to the north of the cathedral,

*S*ées, an ancient see with its much battered—though very fine—Gothic cathedral, is a rather forgotten city.

and housed in the canon's former quarters, is the **Museum of Religious Art**. *Opening times*: 10.00 a.m.–12.00 p.m.. and 2.00–6.00 p.m. daily except Tuesdays from mid-June to mid-September. East of the cathedral is the fine 18th-century Ancien Evêché, the old bishop's palace, built for Plessis d'Argentre, Bishop of Sées and tutor to Louis XVI; opposite is the 16th-century Maison du Jardinier.

Beyond, on the other side of the Orne, is the Abbaye Saint Martin which is now a children's home. To its south is the church of Notre Dame-de-la-Place with its 16th-century reliefs depicting events from the New Testament. Walking westwards along rue Saint Martin you reach rue de la République. To the right is the old Hôtel Dieu, a hospital originally built in the early 13th century and later run by Augustine nuns for the poor. In 1765, Nicolas-Jacques Conté, a 14-year-old local lad who later became a celebrated chemist and engineer, painted the panels in the hospital chapel. On the opposite side of the road is the Saint Pierre bell tower, the sole standing relic of Sées medieval castle. Continue west, and there is the 19th-century covered market in the place des Halles.

Argentan

Argentan was virtually destroyed as the Allies engulfed the Germans during one of the final clashes of the Battle of Normandy in August 1944. Today, the town has been rebuilt and its neat, pleasant, prosperous centre is virtually surrounded, at a fair distance, by the busy thoroughfares of routes nationales and railways. Survivors of 1944 in the downtown place Mahé–place Saint Germain quarter include: the 14th-century château of the dukes of Alençon, now the Law Courts; the nearby 18th-century chapel of Saint Nicholas, now the tourist office; the flamboyant 15th–17th-century church of Saint Germain, badly damaged but deemed worthy of repair because of its fine lantern tower and northern porch.

Continuing across rue Saint Germain, and down from the main shopping area, you reach the 15th-century Tour Marguerite. Beyond, on the other side of the busy rue de la République, in the shabbier rather forgotten district of Saint Martin, is the Gothic–flamboyant–Renaissance, and much restored, church of Saint Martin.

Like Alençon, Argentan is famous for its lacemaking, *la Point d'Argentan* being its unique style, a craft painstakingly continued by the nuns of the local Benedictine Abbey in rue de l'Abbaye; visits can be made by arrangement at the tourist office.

Incidents pertaining to the troubled Henri II–Thomas à Becket relationship are said to have occurred in several places in Normandy: Argentan housed a conference for papal delegates who tried to provide a peace formula between the two factions.

East of Argentan

Argentan's boast is not so much itself, however, but the cluster of châteaux and stud farms within its catchment area to the east and south.

East of Argentan, 10 km (6 miles) along the N16, is **le Bourg-Saint Léonard**. Its 18th-century **château**, 1 km along the D16, was built on the eve of the Revolution; while elegantly formal in façade, without folly and fairly typical of the Louis XV era, it has a rich interior filled with ornate pieces of its age. *Opening times*: 9.30 a.m.–12.00 p.m.. and 2.00–4.00 p.m. in July and August and afternoons only in September; tel: 33-67-15-73.

*E*ast of Argentan,
the 18th-century château of Le
Bourg-Saint Leonard, with its
English park, is one of several
châteaux here in the heart
of Orne.

A further 5 km (3 miles) along the D16 is Chambois with its medieval keep. Here, at this small town, the Allied flanks, coming from the north and from the south, met on 19 August 1944. The Falaise Gap was closed and, with the fall of Tournai-sur-Dives, a few kilometres to the west, and the beleaguered German 7th Army retreating to the east, the Battle of Normandy was over. There are several war memorials in the area commemorating these historic events and the valiant men who made them possible.

There is a short, pretty circuit east of Bourg-Saint Léonard. Follow the D14 eastwards to Exmes, once capital of the region, and with a Romanesque church, and then north along the D26 (see below for its extension), bearing left after 5 km (3 miles) to Omméel. Return south along the D305, Argentelles Manor is to the left just after Villebadin, and cross the D14, continuing along the minor road for the few kilometres to Haras du Pin. Alphonsine Plessis, "la Dame aux Camélias", worked for an umbrella merchant in Gacé, a market town 11 km (7 miles) east of Exmes, before going to Paris where she became an instant hit with the fashionable men of the capital. She died of tuberculosis in 1847, aged only 23 years, but has been immortalized as *La Dame aux Camélias* the title of the book written by her companion Alexander Dumas junior. This book served as inspiration

for Verdi's *La Traviata*. Gacé was badly damaged in 1944, but its 15th-century château still stands impressive.

The main N138 continues from Gacé into neighbouring Eure. Off to its left at Chaumont a minor road follows the pretty course to Touques northward, while from Exmes the D26 continues its route through rich meadows alongside the River Vie to Vimoutiers on the border of Calvados. Vimoutiers is set amidst lovely countryside, though the town itself, rebuilt after being destroyed during the War, is not of great beauty. It is a busy market and a centre for Calvados and

M useum display: plump cows and smiling farmers, the images of Normandy which commonly decorate the round Camembert cheese box.

cider (there are local distilleries and breweries), and home of Camembert, the most celebrated of Normandy's cheeses. The village of Camembert is a few kilometres to the south, up the River Viette (D426), and it was here, at the farm called Beaumoncel, that

---

"The Creation of Camembert"

Set in rural France during the dark days of the Revolution, "The Creation of Camembert" is the beautiful story of a friendship between a farmer's wife and a fugitive priest which climaxes wonderfully with the birth of a full-fat, delicious cheese.

Marie Harel harboured a priest during the Revolution who repaid her kindness by bequeathing to her a recipe for a cheese. Harel improved on the formula and began selling the cheese in the locality. From this modest beginning, "Camembert"—named after Harel's village—soon became a huge international "hit".

Some, however, dispute the authenticity of the tale. The origins of the "Camembert" are said to pre-date Harel, and a cheese of this type known as an augelot, traditionally a cheese from Pays d'Auge and now a name given to the Pont l'Eveque cheese, was recorded in a 17th-century dictionary. Furthermore, some claim Harel was not from the village of Camembert.

Fact or fiction, what is not contended is the leading role played by Marie Harel, the humble farmer's wife, in "The Creation of Camembert" as a popular modern cheese which is now produced in factories in three-quarters of France's departments generating a multi-million pound industry. Enthusiasts, though, pilgrim to Camembert to pay homage to their star and to sample the genuine article.

---

farmer's wife Marie Harel lived. During the Revolution, she gave safe lodging to a priest, who repaid her kindness by bequeathing to her the recipe for the cheese.

A history of cheese is recounted in the **Camembert Museum** at the Vimoutiers tourist office. *Opening times*: daily except Monday and Saturday afternoons and Sundays between October and May; tel: 33-39-30-29. A statue of Marie Harel stands in Vimoutiers' market square; it was donated in 1956 by American cheesemen to replace an earlier statue damaged during the War.

Haras du Pin, only 4 km (2½ miles) from Bourg-Saint Léonard by way of the N26, is the great and stylish stud so often dubbed the "Versailles of Stallions". At the height of the summer, from mid-July to mid-August, over 100 thoroughbreds are lodged and grazed in the château's splendid stables and pastures. Some of the world's finest horses, from the sturdy local Percheron to English and Arab racers, have been reared and retired here. The stud was founded in 1662 by Colbert, Louis XIV's alert aide and a man always ready to boost home industry, whose intention was to produce quality horses on French soil. The **château**, designed by Mansart, was not built until 1726; it, and the stables and park, can be visited. *Opening times*: 9.00 a.m.–12.00 p.m.. and 2.00–6.00 p.m. daily and at 3.00 p.m. every Thursday from mid-May to mid-September, there is a carriage driving display; other equestrian displays are held on some Sundays in September and October; tel: 33-39-92-01.

Nonant-le-Pin, another stud, is 8 km (5 miles) further on. Alternatively, take the minor road to la Cochère and on to Almeneches, with its Renaissance abbey church, and Médavy, 10 km (6 miles) from Haras du Pin. Two great towers from the 15th-century Médavy castle still stand. They flank the entrance to the present **château**, a grand pile of impressive proportion built for an heroic field marshal in the 18th century, but abandoned as a "white elephant" by his successors. *Opening times*: 10.00 a.m.–12.00 p.m.. and 2.00–6.30 p.m. daily from 14 July to 14 September; tel: 33-35-34-54. There is also a stud at Médavy.

A few kilometres along the D26 is **Château d'O**, the most famous château in the region. Set in lovely parkland, surrounded by a wide moat, across which glide pet swans, and surmounted by the spikiest of mitred roofs, the château is also the most enchanting in Normandy. Entrance across a drawbridge, through the splendid gateway and into the courtyard further enhances the romantic imagery of the place. A distinguished line of d'Os, descendents of a champion crusader, built and occupied the château. Founded in the 15th century by Jean I d'O, the chamberlain to Charles VIII, it was further adorned with new wings and apartments by later d'Os over the next two centuries. The interior was refurbished in the 18th century. *Opening times*: 2.30–6.00 p.m. in summer and 2.30–5.00 p.m. in winter; closed Tuesdays; tel: 33-35-34-69. There is a restaurant in the old stables; alongside is a fine old dovecote.

Just beyond the Château d'O is the village of Mortrée. South-east on the N158, 7 km (4 miles) is the cathedral city of Sées. In the other direction, 15 km (9 miles) away, is Argentan. Just short of 4 km (2½ miles) along the way is a minor road to the left, leading to a junction at le Vieux Montmerrei; bear right and right again after a kilometre or so for Sassy château up on a hill to the left. More

palatial and symmetrical in its grand design than Château d'O, the Château Sassy overlooks a spread of terraced gardens, decorated with neat floral designs of a type so fashionable at the time of the château's construction in the late 18th century. Building continued into the 19th century—and into this century—and it was Etienne-Denis Pasquier, Chancellor of France and occupant in the mid-1800s, who collected the magnificent library; the tapestries, too, are of note and paraphernalia, such as a lock of Louis XVI's hair, gathered by Pasquier, is of interest. *Opening times*: weekends and holidays from April to November; mornings in July and August on request; tel: 33-35-32-66.

There is a monument to Saint Christopher at Saint Christophe-le-Jajolet, a kilometre north of Sassy. This shrine to the one-time patron saint of travellers still attracts large numbers of pilgrims, especially on the last Sunday in July—Saint Christopher's Day is 25 July—and the first Sunday in October when motorists come to have their cars blessed. Argentan is 9 km (5½ miles) to the north.

Eastern Orne

East of the N138, the road linking Alençon, Sées and Gacé, are l'Aigle and Mortagne-au-Perche, the two main towns of eastern Orne. The D13 from Gacé leads the 27 km (17 miles) to l'Aigle. Just short of halfway along the route is Saint Evroult-Notre-Dame-du-Bois, by the forest of Saint Evroult and on the banks of the

Charentonne. Here in the forest, in the 6th century, Saint Evroult lived the life of a hermit, and the abbey, which was built in his memory, became one of the most prominent in Normandy during the 11th and 12th centuries. The ruins of the abbey are now preserved.

L'Aigle

L'Aigle is also linked to the N138 by the N26 and the D3 from Nonant-le-Pin and Sées respectively. At Aube, 7 km (4 miles) before l'Aigle on the N26, a **16th-century forge** is on view. *Opening times*: 2.00–6.00 p.m. Saturdays–Mondays and Wednesdays from June to September. Also on display is the life of Countess Eugène de Ségur who lived in les Nouettes, the château on the outskirts of the village, at the **Ségur-Rostophine Museum**. *Opening times*: 2.30–6.00 p.m. Wednesdays and Mondays from mid-June to October.

L'Aigle, meaning "Eagle", was so named because a local medieval lord, Fulbert de Beina, is said to have found an eagle's nest here. Today, the town is medium-sized and busy, and was once famed for its pins and needles industry (the similarly spelt *aiguille*, meaning "needle", is a coincidence).

The prize boast, though, is the Tuesday morning market: the third largest weekly market in France after Bourg-en-Bresse (Ain) and Partenay (Deux Sèvres). Over 1,000 farm animals are up for sale and, in addition, the streets are packed with stalls selling other farm produce from the surrounding Pays d'Ouche and a mass of manufactured merchandise for domestic and agricultural use.

L'Aigle's oldest church, the 12th-century Saint Barthelemy, is now deconsecrated. The main place of worship, and of historical and artistic interest, is the church of Saint Martin. It is a mixture of styles spanning centuries, predominantly 14th–16th century, though its most recent addition is the 20th-century Max Ingrand stained glass. "La Porcienne", the church's 1.820 kg (4,000 lb) bell was cast in 1498.

The 17th-century château, the other side of place Saint Martin, is now the town hall and also houses an exhibition of musical instruments donated by Marcel Angot, a local bandmaster. Nearby is the "June 1944 Museum" which recounts l'Aigle's wartime role within the greater context of the Battle of Normandy. Other exhibits are of archaeological finds and a model of Lourdes made by Louis Verrière, a local farmer.

It is 6 km (4 miles) north-east of l'Aigle to the border with Eure; *en route* is Saint Sulpice-sur-Risle with its old priory church housing religious art of note.

L'Aigle to Mortagne-au-Perche

South of l'Aigle is the Perche region and, 31 km (19 miles) along the D930, the town of Mortagne-au-Perche. Halfway along the route, the road clips the western part of the Forêt du Perche, and there is a turning to the right, the D251, to Abbaye de la Trappe. The abbey, founded in the 12th century, evolved into the strict Cistercian Order—the term Trappist, from la

Trappe, originates from here—in the 17th century under Abbot de Rance. There are no visits into the abbey, though a 20-minute slide show documenting the monks' life and "la Trappe's" history is projected throughout the day; tel: 33-34-50-44. There is a shop on the premises selling monk-made products and abbey souvenirs.

The village of Soligny-la-Trappe is 4 km (2½ miles) away, on a hill with a Romanesque church and a panorama over the surrounding countryside. Beyond to the west, and reached by a circuitous route along minor roads, is the church of Saint Ouen-de-Sècherouvre, its nave decorated with a collection of ceramics known as the "Quinze Mystères du Rosaire". Southwards, narrow roads lead past the manor at Poix. East of here is the church of Saint Evroult at

---

In Search of Solitude

The seed of Trappism, the extreme branch of the Cistercian Order of monks, was sewn by Armand Jean De Rance in the abbey of La Trappe in the mid 17th century. It was a period when morale was low and corruption high. When de Rance, a commedatory abbot, visited La Trappe with a view to cleanse the ill within, he was threatened with death. However, with the help of Louis XIV, he pensioned off the wayward monks and introduced a new lot willing to accept his discipline which was more penitential than in any other order, requiring, for example, abstinence from meat and talk. De Rance died in 1700, however, Trappism gained wider appeal in the early 19th century, after the Revolution, under the guidance of Augustine de Lestrange. Today there are Trappist communities throughout the world.

Champs and the **Musée d'Epicerie** (grocer) at Lignerolles. *Opening times*: Sunday afternoons from April to October; tel: 33-25-32-75. South of Poix is Fontaine de l'Orion, its waters able to cure eye ailments. The D205 continues through Sainte Céronne-les-Mortagnes, with its 12th-century church and history— though no remains—of a 5th-century monastery, and on to Mortagne-au-Perche on the far side of the N12.

Mortagne-au-Perche

"Mortagne-au-Perche, the most beautiful town in France", "Home of the best *boudin-noir* (black pudding) in the country" are the two common Mortagnais boasts, and ones not so readily ridiculed by the less partial visitor. The medium-sized, brown-grey stoned, busy market town—once capital of Perche—is attractive. Its *boudin-noir* is a famous local delicacy. A competition organized by the Brotherhood of Black Pudding Tasters (founded in 1966) is held on a Sunday in March and draws the pudding's makers and experts from around Europe; Perche calvados and local cider are the accompanying drinks.

The Flamboyant–Renaissance turn of the 16th-century church of Notre Dame stands in the town centre. Its most celebrated feature is the 18th-century woodwork, at the eastern end of the church, which was brought from the Val Dieu monastery in the nearby Forest of Réno. Of note, too, is the stained-glass window which commemorates the migration of locals to Canada in the 17th century (the Musée

*M*ortagne-au-Perche, *the attractive former capital of the prosperous and lovely Perche countryside.*

de l'Histoire de l'Emigration Percheronne au Canada is at Tourouvre; descendants of the first 250 settlers from this region now number 1½ million. Just east of the church is the Porte Saint Denis, part of the city's 12th-century fortifications, though 16th-century construction upon it has more or less disguised its origins; the archaeological, local folklore museum is here; tel: 33-25-25-87. Nearby is the 17th-century former **Maison des Comtes du Perche** and the **Musée Alain** which commemorates philosopher Emile Chartier, alias Alain, who was born in Mortagne-au-Perche in 1868. *Opening times*: 3.00–6.00 p.m. Tuesdays to Saturdays; tel: 33-25-25-87. On the other side of the place du Tribunal is the Tribunal and the 13th-century crypt of Saint André. Continuing, one reaches the old hospice, once a convent, with its 16th-century cloister. A short walk away, on the southwestern side of town, is the Hôtel de Ville and the public gardens with views over the countryside.

The interesting and sometimes lovely surrounding countryside deserves as much acclaim as "beautiful Mortagne-au-Perche"

There evolved in Perche in the latter part of the 15th century, during the aftermath of the Hundred Years War, a trend in building manors. These substantial constructions, frequently built in grey-white stone, often had towers, dovecotes, gardens and a variety of farm outhouses.

South of Mortagne-au-Perche

A circuit into the countryside south of Mortagne-au-Perche incorporates old villages, manors and various other sites of historic interest: Mauves-sur-Huisne, 11 km (7 miles) along the D9, is famous for the great stallion "Jean le Blanc", who was born here in 1825 of a local mare and Arab stallion and is, according to one legend, the ancestor of the solid Percheron carthorse. Nearby is Corbon, an important local centre during the reign of Charlemagne, but barely a village today. Continue on the D256, alongside the railway, passing the manor of la Vove—on the left—after a few kilometres. Join the D10 and the 17th-century château of Maison-Maugis is on the left. The manor of Moussetière is on the other side of the Jambée and the D111 and, further on, in the woods of Saint Laurent, is an ancient Druid stone. However, Maison-Maugis' nearest village is Boissy-Maugis, just to its south, and beyond are the manors of Mehery and Perrignes.

Continue to Rémalard, with its church of Saint Germain d'Auxerre, and Bellou-sur-Huisne where William the Conqueror built strongholds while besieging Rémalard in 1077. North along the D920, the 17th-century Château de Voré is on the right and beyond is Moutiers-au-Perche, site of a medieval priory. Longny-au-Perche is 10 km (6 miles) north along the D918 via the 18th-century château of Feillet, halfway on the right, and the village of le Mage with its 18th-century presbytery. However, along the D918 in the other direction is Bretoncelles, with its church of Saint Germain, and Condé-sur-Huisne, with its chapel of Saint Jean Baptiste being the remains of a castle destroyed by the English in 1428. Almost "next door" are Condeau and Villeray and its 16th-

*R*etire in an ivy and rose covered cottage in the heart of Normandy.

century château. Either return to Rémalard along the River Huisne, 7 km (4 miles) by the D10 passing through Saint Germain and Dorceau, both with medieval churches and manors, or head south-west to the village of Dance, with the church of Saint Jouin. Beyond is Nocé, with the manors of Saint Quentin and Lormarin along the way. A kilometre or so north of Nocé, on the D9, is the manor of Courboyer, on the right, and a few kilometres further on is Colonard-Corubert, a village on the border of four old parishes; the Romanesque Courthioust chapel is off the D283 to the west (continue for Saint Quen-de-la-Cour, the manor of Chene, off on the right, and the D938 Mortagne-au-Perche–Bellême road)

From Colonard-Corubert take the D920 for Bellême. Bear left, though at la Mariette, following the D295 south through Saint Jean-de-la-Forêt—with

the manor of Daguerie on the way to Bellême—to the main D955. Head eastwards, bearing right on to the D9 after a few kilometres and follow the River Erre to Préaux-du-Perche, with its 12th–17th century church of Saint Germain and the la Lubinière manor just beyond. Travel west, once again, along the D277. The manor-farm "Les Chaponnières" is on the right, followed by the medieval priory of Saint Denis at Sainte Gauburge and the village of Saint Cyr-la-Rosière; the **Musée des Arts et Traditions Populaires du Perche** is housed in the deconsecrated church; tel: 33-73-48-06. Here, too, is Clemance with its pilgrims' chapel; south is the manor of Angenardière and beyond lies the village of Gémages with its church of Saint Martin and "Stone of the Procuress". A few kilometres further south is Saint Germain-de-la-Coudre with its church containing a 12th-century crypt to Saint Blaise.

The D7 leads northwards, via La Chapelle-Souëf and les Feugerets, a château frequented by le Grand Dauphin, the son of Louis XIV—for the 12 km (7½ miles) to Bellême.

Bellême, the capital of the Perche region, is smaller (population 2,000), less celebrated, but as historic as its rival Mortagne-au-Perche. Once a substantial medieval centre, it fell, in 1229, to Blanche de Castille; the site of her camp is marked by the Croix-Feue-Reine (this particular cross was erected in 1885). Bellême's original, and subsequent, fortifications have tumbled or been incorporated into later constructions. Now the most eye-catching buildings are from the 17th–18th centuries, notably some of those in rue Ville-Close and, in particular, Bansard

des Bois at number 26; also from this period is the church of Saint Saveur. The church in the neighbouring village of Saint Martin-du-Vieux-Bellême dates back to the 14th–15th centuries. Bellême has further fame: Roger Martin du Gard, the Nobel Laureate for Literature in 1938 and author of *Les Thibault*, lived nearby at "le Tertre". Furthermore, since 1953, the town has been a meeting place for mycologists who, at the end of September, organize excursions into the nearby forest to study fungi. Indeed, Bellême, with its views over the forest and fields

---

The Fat One

Martin du Gard was a withdrawn man, not wishing to be interviewed or photographed. An aquaintance, the critic André Rousseaux, said he bore a resemblance to one of his characters: "The Fat One was ugly with an ugliness which was ridiculous and yet sympathetic. He was tall, with great shoulders and a large stomach. The most permanent feature of his face were his nostrils. He had an overwhelming nose protruding from the middle of his comedian's white and fatty face. His hair was brown and combed back. Two thin lines of a meagre moustache emphasized the outline of the upper lip [du Gard, however, had no moustache], while the lower one hung limp and fleshy. The chin deepened into two fatty furrows. The rather heavy impertinence of the nose and the subtle irony of the eyes gave to his whole physiognomy a mocking expression which offended at first, but softened by the general good nature expressed in his features, particularly by the mouth, and a certain fleeting quality of gentleness in the eyes". It is a fine description, irrespective of how closely "The Fat One" resembles his author.

from its high vantage, is an alternative hub from Mortagne-au-Perche for ventures into the Perche countryside.

At Gué-de-la-Chaîne, 3 km (2 miles) west of Bellême on the D955, a road bears to the right to la Perrière—a name originating from *petraria* meaning "stone quarry" in Latin—village built from the local red ferruginous sandstone known as *grison*. The **House of Threads** is the locals' museum about the craft of embroidery. *Opening times*: 2.30–6.00 p.m. daily in July and August; tel: 33-25-45-74. There are panoramas from la Perrière over the plain of Saosnois. Outside the town, on the north side, is the château of Montimer. And to the east of la Perrière spreads the Forêt de Bellême, covering 2,047 hectares (5,058 acres), mainly oak (66 per cent) and beech (22 per cent). A track road leads from the village into the forest and to the Chêne de l'Ecole, a 300-year-old oak with a height of 40 m (130 ft); the way continues to the main D938 just north of Bellême.

Heading north along the D938 you soon pass, on the right, the pleasant Pool of Herse, consecrated, so they say, to Aphrodite. Even deeper in the forest is the Stone of the Druids at the Crossroads of Seven Arms. The D938 continues its northward route another 15 km (9 miles) to Mortagne-au-Perche and on the right, just before Eperrais, are the remains of Château de la Vallée.

East of Mortagne-au-Perche

The N12 runs north-east of the neighbouring department of Eure and to the town Verneuil-sur-Avre. Some 10 km (6 miles) from Mortagne-au-Perche a

turning left off the N12 leads to Tourouvre, a village on the southern edge of the Forêt du Perche. Robert Giffard, a chemist–doctor from Tourouvre, was one of the pioneering settlers in Nouvelle-France (Canada) in the early 17th century. He saw a great future in this new land and, after five years, he returned to his corner of Normandy and persuaded fellow Percherons to follow him back across the Atlantic to Quebec where he had made his base. The **Musée de l'Histoire de l'Emigration Percheronne au Canada** in Tourouvre recounts the story of this early wave of migrants to Canada. *Opening times*: 10.00 a.m..–12.00 p.m. and 2.00–6.00 p.m. daily from late May to November; tel: 33-25-74-55. Stained glass in the church of Saint Aubin features the historic move from Perche to Quebec; also of note in the church is the 15th-century painting of the *Adoration of the Magi*.

The predominantly oak and beech Forêt du Perche, once the property of the French kings and the Perche counts, though owned by the state since the Revolution, spreads to the north of Tourouvre. The D290 to the south of the village crosses the N12, the early 18th-century manor of Bellegarde is on the left, to Autheuil with its 11th-century church of Notre Dame. Continuing, it is a couple of kilometres to Malétable with, in contrast, its 19th-century church of Notre Dame de la Salette topped by a curious neo-baroque clock tower. The D291 follows along the west bank of the River Commeauche the 3 km (2 miles) to Brochard, a hamlet with thermal waters, at the "Source de

Graft before glory: a would-be champion puts in the miles, cycling the country lanes in minor competitions to gain experience for the major league.

Madame Jean", which might have received greater attention had not Bagnoles been developed into a major spa.

Brochard is on the eastern edge of the 1,600 hectare (3,954 acre) Forêt de Réno Valdieu with its ancient and tall oaks and beeches; the abbey of Valdieu once stood in the forest and, today, many of its relics furnish and decorate churches in the region. Scenic routes lead in all directions. South, between forest and river, the D291 continues to Saint-Victor-de-Rene and passes by Monceaux, 7 km (4 miles) from Brochard, to Maison-Maugis.

The manors of le Gué and le Pontgirard are in the proximity of Monceaux. There is, from here, a pleasant extension to the circuit to the east. Take the D111 from Monceaux and follow it alongside the Jambée, a trout river, the 6 km (4 miles) to Longny-au-Perche.

Though attractive in its valley setting, Longny-au-Perche has been nicknamed the "Chamber Pot of Perche" on account of the humidity of its very locale. The town's historic sights include the hôtel de ville, the hôtel dieu and the old market, but most noteworthy are the Renaissance chapel of Notre Dame-de-Pitié and 15th–16th century church of Saint Martin. There are relatively few settlements beyond Longny-au-Perche. However, of local

interest, there is, to the north: Moulicent, with church of Saint Denis, the château of Persay and château de la Grande Noe on the way to les Epasses; l'Hôme-Chamondot with noteworthy religious art in the church of Saint Martin and, within a few kilometres to the east, the château of Brotz and ruins of a medieval castle, destroyed by the English in 1428, at Gannes.

From Longny-au-Perche routes cut eastwards through the Forêt de Longny to the department of Eure. The most attractive of these is the D11 via the lakeside Marchainville with its priory of Saint Evroult now re-established as the church of Notre Dame. In the other direction, westwards, the pretty course taken by the D8 leads westwards over the Commeauche and through the Forêt de Réno Valdieu. It continues past the château of la Goyère, on the right, and through the village of Loisé, with its 16th-century church of Saint Germain which has woodwork from the abbey of Valdieu, before reaching Mortagne-au-Perche.

Westwards from Monceaux minor roads lead to la Chapelle-Montligeon. This village of less than 1,000 inhabitants has its huge neo-Gothic church of Notre Dame, built at the turn of the century, and printing works employing about a quarter of the population. Beyond is Courgeon, also with its church of Notre Dame: this one dates from the early 17th century and is noted for its hexagonal belfry. One route back to Mortagne-au-Perche is via Loisail with its church of Saint Martin, presbytery and Norman house. Another is more direct, 7 km (4 miles) along the D9 from Courgeon to Mortagne-au-Perche.

A Countryside of Forest and River and the Duchy's Defences Against France

A mere snip of coastline provides Eure with just a whiff of the sea. Here they breathe the forest and river. Eure is Normandy's most wooded department and amongst the streams flowing through its countryside is the Seine. By way of the great river the outside world injected itself deep into Eure, but more frequent contact with the exterior was via Eure's eastern border, which in medieval times, was the Duchy of Normandy's frontline with the kingdom of France.

Evreux

An inner force in Evreux seems to have attracted ill fate like a powerful magnet. Vandals and Vikings came, in the 5th and 9th centuries respectively, plundered, and left the place in ruins; on occasions during the Middle Ages kings of England and of France, and a host of lesser nobles, held their final showdowns in Evreux, leaving the city in ashes or ruins and the population decimated or worse. In June 1940, the Germans bombed Evreux and the

Tiring work pitching the hay through the heat of an August day.

place burned for the best part of a week; four years later the Allies unleashed their devastating attack on the city.

With such a long history of destruction behind them, the people of Evreux are used to building upon rubble. The present city is predominantly modern, pleasant and thriving, with a population which has doubled to 50,000 since World War II. A few relics of the past have survived: monuments of the city's rich history and its resilience in the face of extermination.

The most notable survivor is the splendid **cathedral of Notre Dame**. Its origins are 12th century, the earlier cathedral was burnt down by King Henry I of England in 1119, but it has been restored frequently and built

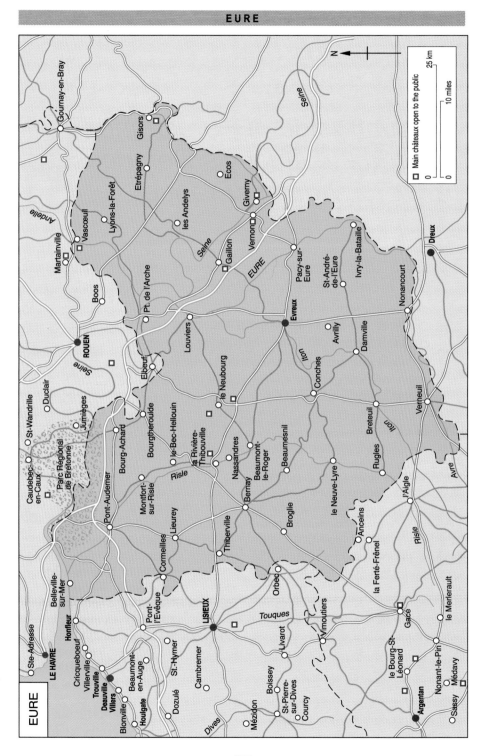

EURE

N

Main châteaux open to the public

25 km

10 miles

Gournay-en-Bray

Gisors

Etrépagny

Ecos

Lyons-la-Forêt

Giverny

Vascœuil

les Andelys

Vernon

Martainville

Gaillon

Pacy-sur-Eure

St-André-de-l'Eure

Ivry-la-Bataille

Nonancourt

Dreux

Boos

Pt. de l'Arche

EURE

Seine

Andelle

Seine

Seine

Évreux

Avrilly

Damville

ROUEN

Louviers

Duclair

Elbeuf

le Neubourg

Iton

Conches

Verneuil

St-Wandrille

Jumièges

Bourgtheroulde

le Bec-Hellouin

Nassandres

Beaumont-le-Roger

Beaumesnil

Breteuil

Rugles

Iton

Caudebec-en-Caux

Parc Régional de Brétonne

Bourg-Achard

la Rivière-Thibouville

Bernay

le Neuve-Lyre

l'Aigle

Risle

Pont-Audemer

Montfort-sur-Risle

Lieurey

Broglie

Anceins

la Ferté-Frênel

Belleville-sur-Mer

Cormeilles

Thiberville

Orbec

Vimoutiers

Gacé

le Merlerault

Ste-Adresse

Pont-l'Évêque

LISIEUX

Touques

Livarot

le Bourg-St-Léonard

Nonant-le-Pin

Médavy

LE HAVRE

Honfleur

Cricqueboeuf

Villerville

Trouville

Deauville

Villers

Beaumont-en-Auge

St-Hymer

St-Pierre-sur-Dives

Argentan

Sassy

Blonville

Houlgate

Dozulé

Cambremer

Boissey

Courcy

Mézidon

Dives

Risle

Ayre

Risle

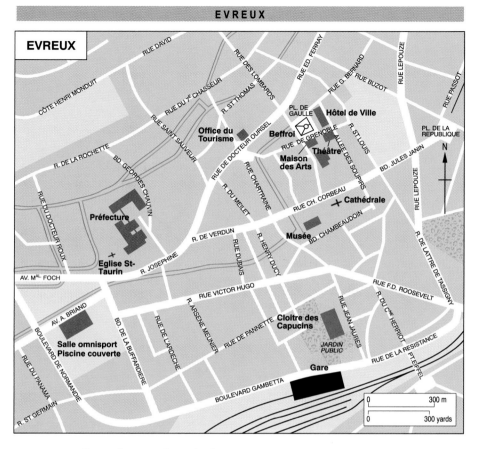

EVREUX

Town plan of Evreux.

upon over the subsequent centuries. Reconstruction after destruction appropriately reflects the tragic history of the city, but the overall spectacularity of the cathedral symbolizes the strength and spirit of Evreux.

In 1119 the cathedral was destroyed; it was rebuilt in 1137 only to be pulled down in 1194 by King Philippe-Auguste. Portions of the nave are all that remain from the 12th century. The chancel is 13th century, the transept, a gift from Louis XI, is 15th century. The south tower is also 15th century

Map of the Eure region.

and the north transept and doorway are 16th century; the great north tower is 17th century. Damage caused during the Revolution was repaired in the 19th century and some of the upper parts of the cathedral lost in the last World War have been restored. Notre Dame's 14th–15th-century stained glass which was removed for safe-keeping during the War has been replaced and is the cathedral's *pièce de résistance*. Of note are the carved wooden screens of the ambulatory chapels.

Just to the south of the cathedral is the fine late 15th-century Bishop's

Palace, built on a Gallo-Roman site, which now houses Evreux's particularly good **Municipal Museum**. The long, eventful history of the city and its surrounding country is well recounted with the aid of archaeological finds, displayed in the basement within the walls of the Gallo-Roman fortifications, along with medieval artefacts and more recent arts and crafts. *Opening times*: 10.00 a.m.–12.00 p.m.. and 2.00–5.00 p.m. daily except Mondays, open until 6.00 p.m. on Sundays; tel: 32-39-34-35.

A short walk to the south are the public gardens and the early 17th-century Capucin monastery which was restored in 1965 and is now a school, the College of Jean-Jaures. The cloisters, with the 30 panels promoting propaganda, can be visited; guided tours are on Wednesdays, Saturdays and Sundays in the afternoons and daily during July and August.

It is ½ km or so westwards down rue de Verdun from the cathedral to the church dedicated to Saint Taurin, who was the first Bishop of Evreux. Like the cathedral, this former abbey church of Saint Taurin suffered severe damage during the city's various destructions. The present church is predominantly 15th century, though the magnificent gold-plated silver shrine containing Saint Taurin's remains dates from the 13th century.

The rue Josephine leads to the centre of the city. Alternatively, there is a walk, promenade Robert de Flocques, which starts beside the cathedral and follows the course of the River Iton and the line of the old ramparts to the downtown. Here, the 44 m (144 ft) high, late 15th-century belfry still stands, on the site of the city's earlier gateway, and its 2,000 kg (4,400 lb) bell, cast in Mantes in 1406, continues to chime the hour. On the other side of the square is the late 19th-century Hôtel de Ville and the Municipal Theatre.

Roads Out of Evreux

There is a choice of roads to cover the 20 km (12 miles) from Evreux to Louviers to the north. The main one is the N154 which can be picked up just out of town. However, it is far more pleasant to veer off at Caer, a couple of kilometres after Gravigny, and take the D52 along the meandering course of the Iton; road and river rejoin the northbound thoroughfares just before Acquigny.

The N13 runs north-west from Evreux to Lisieux. However, its offshoots, the D39 and D31, cut their own paths across the flatlands to le Neubourg and Beaumont-le-Roger, 24 km (15 miles) and 30 km (19 miles) from Evreux respectively .

West of Evreux

Of the department of Eure, 20 per cent is covered by forest, a greater percentage than the other departments in Normandy.

The Forêt d'Evreux lies south-west of Evreux and here, on its northern edge by Bonneville-sur-Iton, are the remains of Notre-Dame-de-la-Noel, a Cistercian abbey founded in 1227 by Matilda, daughter of Henry I. Bonneville-sur-Iton is 12 km (7 1/2 miles) from Evreux by way of the pleasant forest route, the D55 and then right along the D74, and a little less via the main D830.

Conche-au-Ouche

The D830 continues 10 km (6 miles) westwards to Conche-au-Ouche, a medieval town strategically built on a high spur contained within a meander of the River Rouloir. From up here the views are over large tracts of forest. The "new" church of Sainte Foy with its sculpted bell tower and exceptionally fine stained-glass windows dates from the 15th–16th century. Originally, the church of Saint Cyprien stood here. Then, in the late 11th century, Raoul de Tosny, a prominent knight alongside William the Conqueror, made a pilgrimage to Conques-en-Rouergue in Aquitaine; he returned with the relics of Sainte Foy and placed them in the church, which he then renamed after the child saint. Indeed, a local legend claims that he went one step further and called his hilltop retreat "Conches" after "Conques". As the 15th century drew to a close, the old church was replaced by

The village baker-shop-keeper still survives despite the rise of the hypermarket in most towns.

the present one. The name of Sainte Foy, though, was retained. Number 12, rue Sainte Foy is La Maison des Seigneurs, the work of Jacques Martin, celebrated iron craftsman. The association "Richesse de l'Eure" holds, in its 18th-century house in place Astride Briand, exhibitions relating to local culture.

The town's 11th–12th-century fort is in the nearby public gardens, subterranean medieval passageways linked its dungeons to the cellars of La Maison des Seigneurs (these can be visited daily except Mondays), and was built on the site of Celtic and Roman settlements. Now in ruins, you can nevertheless appreciate its dramatic setting and the extensive panorama over the surrounding countryside. And indeed, there are impressive views of Conche itself from these lands below.

South-western Eure

Roads to the west cut through the pretty Forêt de Conche and deeper into the Pays d'Ouche. The D830 leads to the village of la Vieille-Lyre, 16 km (10 miles) from Conche, on the River Risle. From here roads lead north-west to Broglie and Bernay, 20 km (12½ miles) and 25 km (15½ miles) respectively. The D56 runs north by the Risle and through forest for the 8 km (5 miles) to Ferrière-sur-Risle, with its 13th-century church, 14th-century market building and nearby 20th-century amusement park. From here, the D23 heads to Beaumont-le-Roger, and the D140 to Beaumesnil, while southwards from la Vieille-Lyre the D830 follows the Risle upstream for 12 km (7½ miles) to Rugles.

Grison, red iron agglomerate, is rich in this region and Rugles, like l'Aigle 10 km (6 miles) to the south-west and other nearby towns, built its industry, as well as fame and prosperity, on forging iron. Rugles' noteworthy churches, the Notre Dame Outre-l'Eau and Saint Germain, have early medieval origins under their later additions. Following the line of the departmental border south-east, along the D54, you cross the River Iton at Bourth. A few kilometres downstream is Francheville with its iron-craft museum. Continuing eastwards it is a further 7 km (4 miles) via Mandres with its church of Saint Pierre, to Verneuil-sur-Avre, a total of 16 km (10 miles) from Rugles.

Alternatively, you can linger for a while in the countryside and dip into the relatively empty south-westernmost quarter of Eure. Bourth has a 12th–16th-century church dedicated to Saint Just and, to the south, there are other villages with churches of reasonable note. These include: Les Barils, which also has nearby the 19th-century Château des Bois Francs and Center Parcs residential park; Gournay-le-Guerin, with two châteaux and two churches; Saint Christophe-sur-Avre and Saint Victor-sur-Avre, both with churches originating from the 12th century and, *en route* to Verneuil, the village of Pullay and its church of Saint Gervais and Saint Protais.

Conches to Verneuil

A more direct route from Conches to Verneuil is south, along the D840, via Breteuil and is a total of 25 km (15½ miles). Touched by woodlands and embraced by an arm of the River Iton, the old market town of Breteuil has little to show of the medieval castle which stood in the present public gardens. However, the 11th–12th-century church of **Saint Sulpice**, with a notable organ gallery, does still stand and it was here that Adèle, daughter of William the Conqueror and mother of King Stephen of England, married Etienne, Count of Blois.

At 5 km (3 miles) to the east, just off the D833 to Damville, is the Louis XIII-style château of Chambray. To the west the D141 cuts through the pretty Forêt de Breteuil for the 15 km (9 miles) to Rugles.

Verneuil

Verneuil, on the River Avre, is a southern border town of Eure and Normandy. The department of Eure-et-Loire lies a few kilometres to the south. Indeed, during the 12th century, under Henry Beauclerk of England, Verneuil gained prominence as a front-line Normandy town facing France, and it constituted, with Tillières and Nonancourt just to the east, the "Avre defence". One of the bloodiest episodes of Verneuil's history was in 1424, during the Hundred Years War, when Charles VII of France, supported by some 7,000 tough Scots mercenaries, unsuccessfully attacked the town. It was not until 1449 that the French conclusively won Verneuil and that was only after Jean Bertin, a local miller, opened the city gates for the enemy.

The Tour Grise, on the southern side of town on the road bearing its name, was once the keep of Henry Beauclerk's castle and is today a sturdy medieval relic of those more beligerent times. On the other side of the road the 16th-century church of Saint Laurent has been converted into a museum of traditional crafts. There are many fine, aged half-timbered and stone houses of note on rue du Canon, running north of the church, and in the side roads of this quarter, such as in rue des Tanneries and along the "high street" of rue de la Madeleine at the top end.

The chequered-walled Maison à Tourelle Bibliotheque is at the junction of rue du Canon and rue de la Madeleine. Opposite is the church of La Madeleine, which is famed for its

---

The Hundred Years War: 1337–1453

This protracted struggle between England and France began after Edward III claimed the throne of France. The English won the all-important victories at Crécy in 1346 and Poitiers in 1356 before gaining peace at Bretigny in 1360. War resumed nine years later, continuing until 1395 when the English relinquished some of the French territories. On coming to the throne, Henry V set his sights on France, his "birthright" and with victory at Agincourt in 1415 and the subsequent submission of Normandy he was recognized by the French king as his regent at the Treaty of Troyes in 1420. However, not all France accepted the prospect of Henry as their monarch and a movement, spearheaded by Joan of Arc, regained lost soil until, in 1453, England's once vast French territory was reduced to the port of Calais alone.

---

three-tiered flamboyant 15th–16th-century tower adorned with statues and capped by a beautiful belfry. Inside, there is a further array of statues of saints and others.

Place de la Madeleine, car park-cum-market square, spreads before the church. Beyond the far end is the ruined church of Saint Jean and, just further on, is Jean Bertin's mill. Remains of the old ramparts and the moat still partly encircle the town and, from this point by the mill, they can be followed in either direction. Going left, southwest, you will eventually reach Tour Gelée. On the other side of rue Notre Dame is the 12th–15th-century church of Notre Dame, constructed of *grison*, the local red agglomerate building material. Though overshadowed by La Madeleine, Notre Dame does have its own fine collection of ecclesiastical statues, thanks partly to the resident school of statuary which flourished here in the 1500s. To the south of Notre Dame is the 17th-century Benedictine abbey of Saint Nicolas.

East Along the Avre

Barely 10 km (6 miles) east of Verneuil, on the N12, is Tillières-sur-Avre. A slightly longer, prettier route is through Bâlines and Courteilles and along the Avre, mostly on the D316 and D102 on the other side of the departmental border, via Montigny and its 17th-century château.

Tillières was, in 1013, the first of the Avre defences to be fortified; one of the rampart towers still stands. Unfortunately, its splendid church, part Romanesque, part Renaissance, was severely damaged by fire in 1969. Subsequently it has undergone restoration.

Nonancourt, split by the departmental border, is a further 11 km (9 miles) along the N12. As one of the three main medieval Avre defences, Nonancourt was made strong by Henry Beauclerk in the early 12th century. Today, the flamboyant churches of Saint Martin—with its early 13th-century belfry—and Saint Lubin are the town's most noteworthy features.

The Avre continues its eastward course from Nonancourt, all the time serving as frontier between the departments, until its confluence with the River Eure which constitutes the south-eastern corner of Eure department. North of Nonancourt the N154 runs a straight path across flatlands for the 29 km (18 miles) to Evreux.

Eure Valley

Here in the south-eastern corner of Eure, the River Eure forms the departmental boundary. On the eastern bank is the Forêt de Dreux of the Eure-et-Loire department; on the west bank the D143 follows the course of the Eure. At Marcilly the D52 bears left 23 km (14 miles) to Saint André and a further 18 km (10 miles) to Evreux. However, on the D143, the first riverside town of reasonable size is Ezy-sur-Eure, once the local horn comb capital, with the Musée du Peigne (the Comb Museum). Opening times: 10.00 a.m.–12.00 p.m.. and 2.00–6.00 p.m. on Saturdays and Sundays and Wednesday afternoons; tel: 37-64-64-69. On the far bank is the 16th-century château of Anet, reputed to have been one of the grandest Renaissance châteaux in France before it was partly dismantled after the Revolution. And 5 km (3 miles) north of Ezy is La Couture Boussey with its **Museum of Wind Instruments**. Opening times: 2.00–5.00 p.m. daily except Tuesdays; tel: 32-36-28-80. Obélisque d'Ivry is further along the D163. It was erected by Napoleon to commemorate Henry IV's victory against the Leaguers of Mayenne in 1590.

Downstream of Ezy-sur-Eure 4 km (2½ miles) is Ivry-la-Bataille, with ruined 11th-century fort and house of Henry IV. After this the river and border bifurcate. The Eure valley is now wholly in Eure department and it remains so until its conclusion. Continue on the west bank and 9 km (5½ miles) further on is Neuilly and the 16th-century château of Folletière. Either cut

A red dawn in central Normandy promises another sunny day. Dry, hot summers have been a feature of recent years.

"inland" to the 17th-century château and the 19th-century manor house at Boisset-les-Prevanches on the far side of Forêt de Merey, or cross the river and take the D836 downstream to Pacy-sur-Eure.

Pacy is a junction on the Eure. Traffic rocketing along the N13 between the Autoroute de Normandie 10 km (6 miles) to the east and Evreux 13 km (8 miles) to the west bypasses the southern fringes of the town. The D181 bears north-westwards to Bizy and Vernon, 13 km (8 miles) away on the banks of the Seine (see below). The D836 continues its more pleasant riverside route 7 km (4 miles) to Cocheral,

where the statesman Astride Briand lived earlier this century. However, Pacy itself is worthy of a pause, not least because of the 16th-century restored Gothic church of Saint Aubin.

Continuing along the river and beyond Cocheral is Chambray and then Autheuil-Authouillet; from here the D316 cuts northwards towards Gaillon 9 km (5½ miles) away near the banks of the Seine. But, keeping to the course of the Eure, cross back to the left bank and follow the pretty downstream route along the D71 from Saint Vigor through Crevecoeur and Cailly-sur-Eure and, as the north–south road begins to merge and tangle, travel to Acquigny for its 16th-century château and on to Louviers.

Louviers stretches along the streams of the Eure and was built on cloth, an industry which held the town in good stead from the 13th century until well into this century. Now the cloth has been replaced by hi-tech manufacture and unobtrusive trading roads have been superseded by the autoroute and routes nationales. Still, the old quarter of Louviers, in the southern part of the town, retains some of its character. The 13th-century church of Notre Dame, restored with a flourish in flamboyant style in the 15th century, is the town centre. The famous, finely crafted south portal reveals a dash of flair in the renovation. As for the interior, the 13th-century nave is lined with double aisles on both sides and the whole is enriched by the collection of religious art and stained glass found therein. East of the church, rue de la Poste spans streams of the Eure, and, past the post office, stands a portion of the former Penitents' Convent, a Franciscan convent which was founded in the mid-17th century and has, according to locals, "the only cloister in Europe built on water".

Traditional half-timbered Normandy houses survive in the quarter to the north of Notre Dame in rue du Quai, rue Tatin, rue Pierre Mendes-France and rue Ternaux. The House of the King's Fool, so-called because it belonged to Guillame Marchand, jester to King Henry IV, is in rue Maréchal Foch and is now used as a tourist office.

Marchand was Louviers' tenuous link with drama. That was until Georges Wakhevitch, illustrious designer of some 500 play and opera sets and 150 film sets, moved to nearby Tosny and left, on his death in 1984, an assorted collection of items from theatre and cinema. These, including 150 models of his sets, can be seen in the **Museum of Theatre, Opera and Film Scenery**, north of Notre Dame by the junction of the rue de l'Hôtel-de-Ville and place E Thorel. *Opening times*: 10.00 a.m.–12.00 p.m.. and 2.00–6.00 p.m. daily except Tuesdays; tel: 32-40-22-80.

East of Louviers 5 km (3 miles) away there is a viewpoint over the Seine from the church of Vironvay, on the other side of the N15. For Rouen, take the N15 northwards, through the pleasant Forêt de Bord, crossing the Seine at Pont de l'Arche. Here there is the rich flamboyant church of Notre-Dame-des-Arts and the claim to fame that Pont de l'Arche is the first bridging point over the lower Seine.

Epte: From Giverny to Gisors

The Epte, rising near Forges-les-Eaux in Seine-Maritime's Bray region, flows south-east to Gournay from where it forms the eastern frontier of Normandy, formerly the medieval border with France. It continues southwards through Gisors and the Vexin region to its confluence with the Seine just upstream of Giverny.

Travelling upstream from the Seine, the pretty valley route, the west bank's D5, leads 12 km (7½ miles) from Giverny through Gasny to Fourges and on to Bray-et-Lû, straddling the Epte and two departments. A turning to the left, just before Bray-et-Lû, runs to the ruins of the 11th-century Baudemont château. On the other side of the valley, in Val d'Oise department, is the 16th–17th-century château d'Ambleville 3 km (2 miles) from Bray-et-Lû along the D86 (tel: 34-67-71-76 for visiting hours).

Continue on the west bank, on the D146, through Aveny with its 15th-century bridge and Château-sur-Epte where William Rufus's once-important defence now lies in ruins, to Bordeaux-Saint-Clair. Across the bridge is the sister village of Saint-Clair-sur-Epte, one of the most historically significant spots in the western world. Here, in 911, Rollo the Viking, plunderer of the Seine valley, met with Charles the Simple, King of France. The result of their encounter was a pact which gave Rollo much of present day Normandy. Thus, the historical roots of Normandy, and hence England, can be traced back to this modest place.

Back on the west bank the D146 proceeds through Guerny to Dangu, with an 18th–19th-century château and Gothic church. A few kilometres away, on the other side of the river, is the 17th-century Château de Boury (tel: 32-55-15-10 for visiting hours). It is a further 9 km (5½ miles) from Dangu to Gisors; *en route* is Neaufles-Saint-Martin with ruins of yet another frontier fort, this one built by Henry II of England in the late 12th century.

Gisors

Life in medieval Gisors can not have been too comical. As an important border defence, the town was always overshadowed by the prospect of war, if not war itself. The inhabitants were living on the front line. The early dukes of Normandy fortified Gisors against attacks from across the Epte; these were strengthened by William Rufus in the 11th century and were further developed by Henry I and

---

> **Funny Times in Eastern Normandy**
> "Gournay is to Gisors what Lucullus was to Cicero. Here they are all out for glory, and people talk about the braggarts of Gisors. At Gournay their god is their belly and they are known as the gluttons of Gournay. Gisors looks down on Gournay, but Gournay laughs at Gisors. It is a very comical corner of the world."
>
> So related Monsieur Marabout to his friend Raoul Aubertin in Guy de Maupassant's *Madame Hussan's Rose King*.

Henry II during their reigns before they fell to Philippe-Auguste, who himself had the surrounding wall constructed in the late 12th century. Like the rest of Normandy, the people of Gisors suffered as the fortunes fluctuated between the French and English armies in the Hundred Years War and again, 500 years later, as the Allies battled with the Germans.

The **château fort**, built upon a hillock and with a suitably commanding view over the Epte valley, still has its 11th-century keep and a watchtower within Philippe-Auguste's walls. The French king was also responsible for the Maison du Governeur and the Tour du Prisonnier, with dungeons and walls defaced by the graffiti of 15th- and 16th-century inmates. The castle moat has been filled in and is now a public garden. *Opening times*: 10.00 a.m.–12.00 p.m. and 2.00–6.00 p.m. daily except Tuesdays from April to October and weekends only during the rest of the year; tel: 32-27-30-14.

Gisors' church of Saint Gervase and Saint Protase dates from the 12th century, though, as can be seen from the various styles of architecture, work

*S*olid healthy examples *of God's most beautiful creatures out grazing in the early morning.*

continued sporadically over the next 400 years.

Modern Gisors is a busy market town, as it seems to have been in the 19th century during the time of Guy de Maupassant. The light-hearted rivalry with Gournay also continues, though the "braggarts of Gisors" are from past folklore—at least that is what the present citizens of Gisors say!

The D915, the main road covering the 26 km (16 miles) north to Gournay in Seine-Maritime, runs along the east bank of the Epte. Near the departmental border a turning to the left leads to a First World War memorial, dedicated to those who thwarted a German raid. An alternative river route from Gisors is by the course of the Levrière: either cut through the Bois de Gisors north-west of the town or take the D14 Ecouis road and turn right after 5 km (3 miles) to follow the D17. Up the valley is Mainneville, which has 14th-century statues in the church.

Seine Valley

Vernon

Rollo, first duke of Normandy, conceived Vernon on the west bank of the Seine in the 10th century. Originally a town of Viking–Norman character, it gained English heritage some 200 years later, after Rollo's descendants, by now firmly secure as kings of England, returned to claim the land of their forefathers. Then, in the 13th century, the great Philippe-Auguste, King of France, came and conquered, and

something of the French breeding rubbed off in Vernon. These must have been interesting times, for, in the space of about 300 years, Vernon, like many other places in this part of the country, was exposed to and had absorbed a variety of cultures. Today, this pleasant Normandy border town continues to be "invaded" by the French or, more particularly, the Parisian day-tripper and weekender.

Henry I of England built a fort, now ruined, which extended on to the far bank so as to help protect Vernon's bridge.

The castle and remains of the wooden piles of the 12th-century span and the islands and Forêt de Vernon are visible from the present bridge. In town, the 12th-century collegiate church of Notre Dame is the focal point, though its 15th-century features, such as the nave and west front, are its highlights. Here too is the mausoleum of Marie Maignard. Nearby there are

A Norman's home is his château and pride in the garden is a further trait he shares with his brothers across the Channel.

half-timbered houses from the same period.

Along the extension of rue Carnot to the north is the **Museum of Alphonse Georges Poulain**, housed in a mansion once owned by the Le Moine de Belle Isle family. The museum was opened in 1983 and features the local history and fine art. The latter exhibition includes works by local artists, such as Monet, as well as others from further afield, such as impressionists from America. Animals in art is one of the museum's specialities. Opening times: 2.00–5.30 p.m. daily except Mondays and holidays; open also on Wednesday mornings in summer; tel: 32-21-28-09. Nearby, on rue Potard, is the restored Henry I–Philippe-Auguste keep, known as the Archives Tower. Number 6 on this road is another half-timbered house.

The D181 leads through the eastern outskirts of Vernon to the colonnaded **château of Bizy**, a little over 2 km (1 mile) from the town centre. Originally the home of Marshal Duc de Belle Isle, who had the château built in the early–mid-1700s, later occupants included Louis XV, Duc de Penthièvre, King Louis-Philippe, Baron de Schickler. Each of them, and particularly de Schickler, modified the château to their own taste and much of the original design has been lost.

The stables, which were created for de Belle Isle along the lines of Versailles, were left relatively untampered, though they now house vintage cars, fine examples of the early successors to the horse. Within the château, which is still the property of aristocrats who enjoy titles like their predecessors but not the power, the decor and furnishing are ornate and predominately 18th century; the carved woodwork, including the oak staircase, the tapestries and the mementoes of the Bonaparte family, are amongst the main features.

Outside, the original designer park was relaid by Louis-Philippe in the late 18th century and amongst its urns and fountains can be found sculptures including some curious sea horses. *Opening times*: 10.00 a.m.–12.00 p.m. and 2.00–6.00 p.m. every day except Fridays from April to November; no lunch break on Sundays in July and August; tel: 32-51-00-82).

Giverny

Upstream of Vernon, 2 km (1 mile) away, is Giverny. This is where **Claude Monet** lived. He moved to his house in the village in 1883 and it remained his home until his death in 1926. His son bequeathed the residence to the Acadamie des Beaux Arts in 1966. It opened as a museum 14 years later. The place itself was sometimes his inspiration—his garden appears in *The Garden, Nymphaes* and other works—and was the base from where he travelled, recording his impressions of Normandy with such luminosity on to canvas.

The house, studio and luxuriant garden with its famous pond and Japanese bridge are accessible to visitors; reproductions of his paintings and his collection of Japanese prints are displayed and rooms are restored to the same style as during Monet's time. Coming here, you are brought to the source of the man, his "bare canvas", whose art is now known universally through a million postcards and posters. Opening times: 10.00 a.m..–12.00 p.m. and 2.00–6.00 p.m. daily except Mondays (the garden is open through the day) from April to November; tel: 16-32-51-28-21.Monet is buried at the 12th-century church of Saint Radegone

The D313, along the Seine's east bank, running alongside the Forêt de Vernon, is the most attractive downstream route. Just beyond Port Mort, 12 km (7½ miles) from Vernon, is the Gravier de Gargantua, a dolmen, and the remains of an old château on the other side of the road from where there is a good view over the river.

On a headland on the far bank is Gaillon, birthplace of the Renaissance in Normandy thanks to Georges

---

Monet's Japanese Touch

At the age of five, Monet moved to Sainte Adresse—the Le Havre suburb—where his father set up business as a merchant-grocer. As a young teenager, Monet displayed his artistic talent by producing faithful caricatures which he was able to sell locally. However, it was a meeting with Boudin, and others from the Honfleur group, which exposed him to a new interpretation of his subjects. It opened his eyes to "impressionism", the style of painting he pursued during his long life as an artist.

Monet rejected the opportunity to go to the established Ecole des Beaux Arts in Paris, choosing to spend time with the modern artists of the day such as Boudin, Jongkind, Pissaro, Rodin, Sisley. He travelled to North Africa, Britain and the Netherlands—experiencing and capturing the different lights—and he became intrigued with art from afar, notably the decorative Japanese prints with their flat perspective.

In 1883, Monet settled in Giverny and seven years later he bought a stretch of marshland across the road from his house. A tributary of the Epte flowed through the plot, and he diverted this to create a pond with water lillies overhung by weeping willows and bamboo, and crossed at one end by a Japanese bridge. His exotic garden in the midst of Normandy—a work of environmental art in itself—was to be a major inspiration during his later life and was the subject for his vast murals at the Orangerie of the Tuileries which was later dubbed the "Sistine Chapel of Impressionism".

---

d'Amboise, cardinal minister during the reign of Louis XII. He went to Italy in the late 1400s and was so impressed by what he saw that, when he returned to Gaillon, he started work on a château, or rather modified the existing 12th-century one, in the latest Italian fashion. The fanciful style of the place caused controversy and after the Revolution, when châteaux throughout the land began to tumble, the d'Amboise pile was dismantled. The gatehouse, however, remains and the owners, the Ecole des Beaux Arts, have commissioned a restoration programme under the auspices of the *Conservation Régionale des Monuments Historiques.*

Château Gaillard

Beyond Port-Mort and Gaillon the Seine twists to form a tight meander. Both banks offer scenic views over the river. From Gaillon, the D65, merging into the D176, hugs this lovely curve of the Seine. It passes through Tosny before reaching the junction with the D135 which crosses the river straight in front of Château Gaillard perched up on its pedestal. From Port-Mort, the D313 cuts through the Forêt des Andelys, via Bouafles with its 17th-century dovecote, for the 10 km (6 miles) to Château Gaillard.

Chalk cliffs form part of the east bank; their white faces peer through the wooded hillsides. The evocative ruins of Château Gaillard crown a high chalk spur with a commanding, magnificent, panorama over the Seine. The great warrior crusader Richard the Lionheart, King of England, Duke of

Hligh above the Seine the ruined Château Gaillard, Richard the Lionheart's frontier defence against the French, is a powerful echo from the days of medieval warfare.

Normandy and Count of Anjou, had the castle built in 1196 on this eastern frontier of Normandy as a defence for Rouen, and the duchy as a whole, against possible attacks by Philippe-Auguste, King of France.

Built in a year, the château, high above the surrounds, must have been seen by the enemy as a symbol of strength, Gaillard means strong in French, and by the fact that it was a creation of a man of the Lionheart's repute made the imagery all the more awesome.

Indeed, Philippe-Auguste waited until Richard had been succeeded by his less capable brother King John before launching his assault on the fort in 1203. The French isolated the castle after occupying land to the south-east, thus cutting the supply line, and laying siege to it. After some months, those within were beleagured and those outside had made their preparations, filling in the moat with debris and mining the walls. While spirits were high, Philippe-Auguste pronounced the attack. It was a great success, and the French king subsequently pushed on to win Rouen.

Château Gaillard was a formidable asset to those who won these lands, including the English during the Hundred Years War, until Henry IV had it pulled down in 1603. What remains is a fraction of the original structure, but is still impressive. Access is gained either by means of the footpath up from

The Good Fortune of the Seine

The tantalizing river mouth tempts entry. The Vikings were enticed by the Seine into the unknown and as they pushed deeper upstream they discovered a rich world ripe for ravage. The beauty of the great river, its banks bejewelled by Paris, Rouen and the early monasteries of Christendom, brought cursed fortune to France as the Vikings raped the country of its wealth. However, the Vikings eventually settled here and their descendants soon enhanced these lands, bringing them prosperity and power. The allure of the Seine, once perceived as a damnation, finally proved to be a blessing in disguise.

The Seine, France's second largest river after the Loire, rises in the Langres Plateau, 29 kms (18 miles) north west of Dijon, and cuts a 780 kms (485 miles) north-westerly course through central and northern France before emitting its waters into the English Channel. It is a slow flow by the time it enters Normandy: the Seine's source in Mont Tasselot is at a height of 471 m (1545 ft); within 48 kms (30 miles) the river is less than 240 m (800 ft) above sea level and at Paris, 363 km (227 miles) from the coast, it is only 24 m (80 ft) above sea level. In the olden days it took 3 to 4 horses 36 hours to pull a barge from Paris to Rouen.

The river's twisting course—Seine is possibly derived from the Celtic word *squan* meaning curve—cuts its serpentile stream through chalk countryside and carves sheer white cliffs out of the landscape. Forts, such as Château Gaillard, the Normans' most powerful defence against the French in the medieval times, were built on these strategic hilltop vantages to guard against attacks along the valley below.

Besides a pathway to discovery, plunder and invasion, the river is, of course, an avenue of commerce and the slow moving Seine has a fast moving trade. There used to be a harbour by the deep waters on the outer bend of every meander and, in the 16th century, Rouen was France's premier seaport. However, increasingly, silting became

Pont de Tancarville, bridge over historic waters, is an essential link between Normans. Completed in 1959, it at long last provided a road across the Seine below Rouen.

a hazard and in the last century many a captain ran aground, especially between Quillebeuf and Villequier.

Dredging and the construction of canals and locks now allow modern vessels to sail upstream and, today, ships drawing up to 3.2 m (10 ft) can travel to the Paris port of Gennevilliers. Rouen, 126 km (78 miles) inland, is still a significant seaport, though now its importance is overshadowed by le Havre at the river mouth, which is currently France's second port after Marseilles with petrochemical products accounting for half its exports.

Some 200 years ago Napoleon summed up the value of the Seine when he said, "Le Havre, Rouen and Paris are but single towns of which the Seine is the main street". Without the "street" there would have been no "town".

A pathway to discovery, plunder, invasion and colonization, a high street for commerce, Seine the vein is also a spiritual lifeline, forever feeding those drawn to its banks with its flow of inspiration and nurturing the growth of greatness in many fields. A visitor to Normandy should make contact with the powerful river and travel a reach of its course so as to get a feel of its significant role.

Travelling downstream and on the right, near the confluence of the Seine and the Epte, is Giverny, home of Claude Monet. Beyond is Vernon and its Château of Bizy and then Pressagny l'Orgueilleux, home of writer Casimir Delavigne; further down, on the left bank, is Castle Gaillon before the bend in the river and Château de Gaillard high on the hill with les Andelys down in its shadows. The river twists two

A Scandinavian vessel travels up the Seine 1,000 years after the arrival of the Vikings.

Typically attractive rural scenery along the banks of the Seine.

tight meanders, topped by the Rocher de la Roque and the Côte des Deux Amants, before it turns towards Rouen. A creation of the Seine,.Normandy's capital is now the river's star attraction after Paris. They say that the waters are that much wiser after flowing through Rouen. Writers Gustave Flaubert and Pierre Corneille lived around the bend at Croisset and Petit Couronne respectively and Robert the Diabolical built his castle above the village of la Bouille.

Increasingly wide, slow and majestic, the Seine now enters a quieter land with a forest and monastery on every curve: Forêt de Roumare and the abbey of Saint Georges at St Martin-de-Boscherville; Forêt de Jumièges and the abbey of Jumièges; Forêt de Brotonne on the left bank and Forêt le Trait-Maulévrier on the right with the abbey of St Wandrille. Here, too, is Pont de Brotonne, the first span across the river since Rouen.

Downstream of Caudebec-en-Caux, where there is the Musée de la Marine de Seine (a museum about the history and activities of the Seine), is Villequier where Victor Hugo, France's "national writer" would spend his holidays. Beyond, on the right bank, are Château d'Etelan and the Roman town of Lillebonne and, on the left, the medieval port of Quillebeuf before Pont de Tancarville and the long entry to le Havre.

Layers of silt brought down by the Seine since its birth have built these lands on what was once the estuary and former ports are now far from the river. No such fate faces le Havre. Its vast petrochemical industry can be seen from afar, its fires burning above the plant as a healthy sign of wealth and progress as we enter the 21st century. Much has happened along the Seine since the Vikings turned their drakkars up river over 1,000 years ago.

A bottle of chilled cider, a farmer's Neufchâtel cheese and a fresh bagette. A simple satisfying lunch.

Le Petit Andely or from the car park at the end of rue Richard Coeur-de-Lion. First there is the redoubt, only one of its five towers stands; beyond is the moat and the main fort with vestiges of the keep—its 5 m (16½ ft) thick walls once stood three floors high—which served both as the final defence and as a grim prison for those who had fallen from royal favour.

One of those cast here, never to see the light of freedom again, was Marguerite, wife of Louis X, who, having been accused of adultery, was strangled with her own hair in her dark cell. History haunts these ruins.

Les Andelys

Les Andelys, below Château Gaillard, comprises the Petit Andelys, by the river, and the Grand Andelys. Its setting on this spot of the Seine is worthy of a stop in itself and can be appreciated all the more by taking a stroll down the waterfront, from where further relics of Richard's defences can be seen. As for the town, the humble 12th–13th-century church of Saint Sauveur, with its 17th-century organ, and its square with half-timbered houses are the main sights in the Petit Andelys.

The long avenue de la République leads from place Saint Saveur to Great Andelys and to its large predominantly flamboyant–Renaissance church of Notre Dame, also with a 17th-century organ of note, which has 16th-century stained glass in its south side. On the other side of avenue de la République is the wishing-well, of Saint Clotilde; its waters, it has been believed for over 1,000 years, have the astonishing curative power to heal ailing bodies. Nearby, on rue Saint Clotilde, is the Nicolas Poussin Museum. Poussin (1593–1665), court painter to Louis XIII, was born outside Les Andelys, and the museum houses works by the artist with his *Coriolan* as its centrepiece; other exhibits include furniture and silver from the Duc de Penthievre collection, as well as engravings, medieval religious art and 19th–20th-century paintings. *Opening times*: 2.00–6.00 p.m. daily except Tuesdays; tel: 32-54-10-50.

Beyond Les Andelys

The border town of Gisors is about 30 km (19 miles) by road to the east of Les Andelys, while Lyons-la-Forêt, in the heart of rich beech forest, is 20 km (12 ½ miles) on the D2 to the north. The twin-towered collegiate church of Notre Dame was built in the early 14th century at Ecouis, 8 km (5 miles) along the Lyons-la-Forêt road from Les Andelys. The enlightened Enguerrand de Marigny, Philip the Fair's minister of finances, founded the church for student clergy. Also a patron of the arts, he encouraged the sculpting of religious statues. However, de Marigny fell foul of Philip's fickle successor and he was put to death in 1315. His apparent failure in finance had led to this fate. However, he will be better remembered for his religious associations. The college flourished, and so did the output of sculptures. Today the church is a museum of religious art with splendid statues of saints and prominent prelates most of which were crafted in the 14th century.

Dovecotes, colombiers, are rich in this area, and can form the basis for an excursion into the countryside to the east of Les Andelys. A minor road leads south-east of the town to La Bucaille with its manor and 17th-century dovecote. Nearby, Guiseniers and la Grange de Bourgoult, D10 to Forêt la Folie and left along the D9, also have half-timbered dovecotes from this period; continue, and after crossing the Gambon, bear left along the D125 for Les Andelys and the 18th-century stone dovecote of Feuquerolles is off to the right.

However, the D313 continues its pretty course alongside the river bend between Seine and cliff. Splendid views are to be had from high vantages at Thuit and La Roquette (panorama de Notre Dame de Bellegarde). After Muids, the road "clips the corner" and cuts to Andé, a bridging point. But remain on this side, the more attractive of the two banks along this reach of the river, and pick up the D19 at Herqueville and follow it via Senneville with its manor and dovecote the 8 km (5 miles) to Amfreville-sous-les-Monts.

"Les Monts" which rise above Amfreville are the Côte des Deux Amants, a spur at the confluence of the Seine and the Andelle. The "Deux Amants", the Two Lovers, were, according to local legend, a young couple who had to prove their love to their parents. As a test, the boy had to carry his girl to the summit of the hill. This he did, but exhausted, he expired; heartbroken, his sweetheart slumped next to him and died. The grieving families, ashamed of their folly, buried the lovers here and named the hill in their honour. It is 5 km (3 miles) by road, from Amfreville to the hill top from where there is a splendid view over the two rivers and the surrounding countryside. Also visible are the Amfreville Locks, 220 m (240 yd) long, by 17 m (18½ yd) wide, and beyond is the Poses Dam, both of which regulate the flow of the Seine. The locks and the dam can be crossed on foot.

Downstream of its confluence with the Andelle, 8 km (5 miles) away, the Seine crosses the border into Seine-Maritime. Industry and urban developments feature on the river's banks with increasing dominance as the Seine turns its final sharp curve on its approach to Rouen.

Andelle Valley

The Andelle rises deep in the countryside of eastern Seine-Maritime and flows fast along its short course to the Seine. Its valley is more densely populated towards its end. Here, the roads running along either bank are linked by cross-river roads.

Travelling upstream from the confluence it is 4 km (2½ miles) by way of the D19, beneath the Côte des Deux Amants, to Pont Saint Pierre, a town straddling the Andelle.

The neighbouring village of Douville has a 14th-century dovecote. Further along and to the right is the Renaissance château of Bonnemare with its 17th-century chapel. *Opening times*: mid-May to mid-July; tel: 32-49-03-73.

Alternatively, turn into Pont Saint Pierre and there is the local château surrounded by park on the right and

then, down the street, the large 12th-century church. Continue along the river on the far bank and after 3 km (2 miles) there are, in their beautiful Elysian field by the Andelle, the ruins of Fontaine-Guérard, a 13th-century abbey, once the favoured nunnery amongst Normandy's aristocratic girls.

The abbey's chapel of Saint Michael is 15th century, though its church, chapter house and nuns' quarter are from the early years of construction. Some of the abbey's religious art can now be seen in the church at Pont Saint Paul.

The ruins at Radepont, just beyond Fontaine-Guérard, are of medieval defences, while the village château is 100 years old; there is a dovecote here as well.

The road continues to Fleur-sur-Andelle and Charleval by the confluence of the Andelle and the Lieure, strengthened by its tributary the Fouillebroc, approaching from the east. The lovely Forêt de Lyons lies between the arms of these rivers.

The D1 takes a pretty northward course along the Andelle valley the 10 km (6 miles) to the château of Vascoeuil on the Seine-Maritime border at the confluence of the Craven.

The 14th–16th-century red-brick château has now become a cultural centre hosting a variety of exhibitions and events. Appropriately so, for this is where Jules Michelet (1798–1874) wrote his 24-volume *Histoire de France* and the relatively modest 7-volume *Histoire de la Revolution*. Michelet mementoes are displayed. So is traditional Normandy as well, including a fine 17th-century dovecote, and, more incongruously, works by artists such as Salvador Dali and Braque. *Opening times*: Easter to November in the afternoons; tel: 35-23-62-35.

Forêt de Lyons

East of the Andelle stretches Forêt de Lyons, 10,700 hectares (26,429 acres) of lovely beech forest. Here the Romans built settlements, the Dukes of Normandy hunted stag and, through the centuries, many, from fugitives to freedom-fighters, found safe refuge amidst the dense foliage. And, in the heart of the forest, is the canton centre of Lyons-la-Forêt, a small town seemingly protected and preserved in all its picturesque Normandy tradition by the army of surrounding beeches.

Artists and monks also found their tranquillity in the forest. Maurice Ravel composed *Le Tombeau de Couperin* in 1917 at his house in rue de

Literary Champion of the Revolution
Born the son of a poor printer, Michelet—a largely self-educated man—became keeper of the national archives. He was, though, radically chic being anti-crown, anti-church, anti-bourgeois and highly sympathetic to the ideals of the masses and the revolution of 1789. His works on the history of France were suppressed and, with his refusal to swear allegiance to the Second Empire, he lost his position as professor at the College de France.

la République in Lyons-la-Forêt. The D2 and D6 run south out of town, and minor roads branch off and lead to the **Abbey de Mortemer**. However, the reclusive world of the Cistercian

*T*he rich foliage of the tall majestic beeches forms a panoply over the forest floor.

abbey, beautifully set just below the source of the Fouillebroc, was invaded by the most celebrated figures of the medieval period. Amongst the early visitors was Henry Beauclerk, who indulged excessively on a dinner of lampreys at the abbey and then died. Later guests, such as Beauclerk's son and heir, Richard the Lionheart, were not deterred and received the monks' hospitality without misfortune.

The abbey was founded in 1134 and building continued into the following century. However, what remains from this era is in ruins. The main conventual block is from the 17th century and has been extensively restored. A museum recounts monastic life. The abbey park is also open to visitors; the 15th-century dovecote was once used as a jail. *Opening times*: 2.00–6.00 p.m. Mondays to Fridays from April to mid-November and from 11.00 a.m.–6.00 p.m. on weekends and holidays; tel: 32-49-54-36.

Continue downstream along the D715 to Lisors, with its 14th-century Virgin in the church, and on, following the flow, to Menesqueville, with its 12th-century church. Beyond is Charleval. Alternatively, the D321 leads up the Lieure valley through Rosay, with its pretty church, back to Lyons-la-Forêt.

West out of Lyons-la-Forêt along the D14 is Beauficel-en-Lyons, again with a medieval Virgin in the church, and, beyond, the 17th-century château of Fleury-le-Forêt. The gardens and interior, furnished with the original pieces can be visited. *Opening times*: afternoons daily from Easter to mid-

September and Sunday afternoons through the year; tel: 32-49-54-36. The road continues into the department of Seine-Maritime

Northwards, there are attractive routes through the forest to Seine-Maritime, the main one, the D321, leads to la Feuille on the N31, the Gournay–Rouen road. To the west minor roads cut narrow paths towards the Andelle valley. Just out of Lyons-la-Forêt, off the D169 to Charleval, is the Chêne Saint Jean, an impressive oak in the beech-dominated Lyons-la-Forêt (70 per cent of the trees are beech, the remainder are mainly oak and lime).

West and North of Eure

Broglie

Broglie, on a pretty wooded stretch of the River Charentonne, is famed for its aristocratic Broglie family who lived here in the château, and gave the town its present name. Over the centuries this distinguished line included prominent soldiers, statesmen and scientists, most celebrated amongst the latter was Louis de Broglie who was Nobel Laureate for physics in 1929. The church of Saint Martin, of 11th-century origins, is partly built with Pays d'Ouche *grison*.

The N138 is 11 km (7 miles) between Broglie and Bernay; the minor D33 has a parallel though more pleasant path, interweaving its route between river and railway.

Bernay

Bernay's most famous citizen, Alexander de Bernay, was more literary than the sons of Broglie. It was he who, in the 12th century, devised the 12-syllable iambic line in poetry now known as the *alexandrine*. The town itself earned its fame from the abbey which was built here in the 11th century by Judith, wife of Duke Richard II of Normandy. The abbey church, modified in the 15th century, stands in the centre of Bernay; annexed to it was the old abbey complex, developed in Maurist style in the 17th century, only to fall into disrepair after the Revolution. Now restored, it serves as the Hôtel de Ville.

Just beyond is the **Municipal Museum** housed in what was once the abbot's chequered stone and brick residence. Ceramics, notably those of Rouen, are the main exhibits, but there are also collections of 16th–19th-century French, Flemish, Dutch and Italian paintings, early 20th-century paintings, 17th–18th-century furniture, local religious art and archaeological

T here is a crucifix in every village and every villager has someone he wishes to remember.

Alexander's Alexandrine

For the Prosodist, the alexandrine is a line of six iambic feet—the iambic hexameter—the standard heroic line in French verse, rather like the iambic pentameter is in English verse. It is probably derived from the *Li Romans d'Alexandrine,* a 12th-century French romance about the heroism of Alexander the Great, which was written in this style. The alexandrine never caught on in England except as the final line of the Spenserian stanza to contrast with the preceding iambic pentameter.

finds. *Opening times*: 10.00 a.m.–12.00 p.m.. and 2.30–6.00 p.m. daily except Tuesdays; tel: 32-43-49-11. Just north of this cluster of abbey buildings is rue Thiers, Bernay's long central high street. The church of Sainte Croix dominates this end of the street; it dates back to the 14th century and, within it, are the tombs of abbots, and the statues of saints. Alexander de Bernay was born in the street which bears his name at the eastern end of the church; at the western end, on the other side of rue Thiers, is the old covered market.

If you wander back, southwards, along rue Thiers you reach rue Gaston Folloppe on the right where there is the cart and local folklore museum, **Musée de la Charette**. *Opening times*: 10.00 a.m.–12.00 p.m.. and 3.00–7.00 p.m. daily except Mondays; tel: 32-43-05-47. Some old traditional Normandy half-timbered houses still stand in this quarter of town. Finally, at the southern end of town, down rue Kléber Mercier, there is the basilica of Notre Dame de la Couture where the 16th-century statue of the Virgin is greatly venerated and draws a large number of pilgrims.

The three main northbound roads from Bernay are: the D138, 13 km (8 miles) to Thiberville on the border with Calvados; the D834, 18 km (11 miles) to Lieurey and the N138, 16 km (10 miles) to Brionne. Eastwards, the D133 follows the courses of the Charentonne, via Serquigny and its church, and the Risle 17 km (10½ miles) to Beaumont-le-Roger; the D24 running along the other bank of the Charentonne leads through the attractive village of Fontaine l'Abbé.

Beaumont-le-Roger

Beaumont-le-Roger's best known figure is Regulus, the wooden Roman soldier who strikes the hourly chime from his perch in the tower of Saint Nicholas, the town's 14th–16th-century church. Saint Nicholas was damaged during the last War, however, Regulus remained unscathed and has maintained his hourly show with clockwork precision during war and peace for nearly 175 years. Here, on the banks of Risle, in the 13th century the monks of Bec Hellouin had a priory built; its ruins remain.

Roads run alongside the Risle: southwards via Grosley-sur-Risle, with its boating lake, and the farmhouses of le Val Gallerand to la Ferrière-sur-Risle; northwards via Nassandres and la Rivière Thibouville 15 km (9 miles) to Brionne. Northeastwards is le Neubourg 13 km (8 miles) along the D133; the D25 which is to the south cuts 11 km (7 miles) through the Forêt de Beaumont to Beaumesnil.

Beaumesnil

Beaumesnil is its **château**, and its celebrities are the array of aristocrats who owned this fantastic red-brick and stone Louis XIII "wedding cake" pile. It was created early in the 17th century, though a previous château once stood here. Earliest incumbent of the seat of Beaumesnil was Robert de Meulan, son of the man who looked after Normandy while William was away conquering England; some 350 years later Henry V of England was victorious on French soil and he gave Beaumesnil to Lord Willoughby, one of his commanders; it was the Marquis de Nonant who had the present château built in 1633, and he was succeeded by a variety of colourfully titled nobles, including Grand Duke Dimitri of Russia after World War I. Now the château is owned by the Foundation Furstenberg and houses a **Museum of**

316

Bookbinding, tracing the craft from the 16th century, and a splendid library. *Opening times* for château/museum: 2.30–6.00 p.m. from May to October, Fridays to Mondays; the park is open daily, except Tuesdays, from 9.00 a.m.–12.00 p.m.. and 2.30–6.00 p.m. from mid-May to October; tel: 32-44-40-09. At Thevray to the south there is an exhibition of steam-and fire-powered machines in **La Musée Tout Feu, Tout Flamme**. *Opening times*: Wednesdays, Sundays and holidays from mid-March to November and daily in June; tel: 32-40-78-25. The route west from Beaumesnil to Broglie is on cross-country lanes via Landepereuse.

Brionne

Brionne, built on islands and the banks of the Risle, has been a strategic stronghold, crossroads and market in the valley for centuries. The donjon of the 11th–12th-century castle, built by the Counts of Montfort, stands high above the town on the east bank and from here the views over the river and surrounding countryside are extensive. By the Risle is the 14th–15th-century church of Saint Martin with its 17th-century altar brought from Bec-Hellouin. The Jardin de Shaftesbury, Brionne on the far bank is "twinned" with the English town of Shaftesbury. In the south of the town, down Boulevard de la République, is Maison de Normandie, a traditional Normandy house exhibiting and selling local crafts and produce.

Much of the attention enjoyed by Brionne in the past, and in the present, has been due to its proximity to the le Bec-Hellouin abbey complex. Here in Brionne Duke William met Lanfranc and was introduced to the abbey; today, Bec Hellouin's numerous visitors often stay or pass through Brionne. For Bec-Hellouin take the N138 Rouen road and bear left after 4 km (2½ miles) for the final 3 km (2 miles) to the abbey.

Brionne to Le Neubourg

The D137 leads 15 km (9 miles) east across flat farmlands from Brionne to le Neubourg. Along the way: 7 km (4 miles) away is Harcourt, a medieval village, with a 13th-century church and old timbered market, which owes its fame and name to the great Harcourt knights. Indeed, it was Rollo the Viking, the first Duke of Normandy, who in the early 10th century gave Bernard le Danois, ancestor of the illustrious line of Harcourts, these lands. A castle was built just to the north of the village, though the one we see today was founded in the 12th century by Robert II of Harcourt and extended by his descendants over the following centuries. And then, in the 17th century, it was modified from a purpose-built defensive fort into a residential château by Françoise de Brancas, the Countess of Harcourt. Now, and since the aftermath of the Revolution, the château has been in the hands of the French Agricultural Academy. This worthy body created an arboretum in the grounds, where over 150 species of trees and bushes can be seen, and nurtured the surrounding forests which itself now comprises flourishing flora foreign to these parts. *Opening times*: 2.00–7.00 p.m. daily except Tuesdays from mid-March to mid-November; tel: 32-45-07-11.

A minor road leads from Harcourt to Sainte Opportune-du-Bosc and on to Champ de Bataille, another **"Harcourt" château**, gained through marriage though lost temporarily after the Revolution, which stands amidst wood and parklands. While the family no longer has the property which bears their name, they have managed to reclaim this estate. The large, unusual pink-brick and stone château is 17th century and comprises two long wings flanking a large grass court. The interior includes period decor and furniture as well as interesting mementoes belonging to the historic Harcourts. Further exhibits, flora and fauna (stuffed), are elsewhere in the grounds. *Opening times*: 10.30 a.m.–12.00 p.m.. and 2.00–6.30 p.m. Thursdays–Mondays from July to early September; Sundays, Mondays and Thursdays from mid-March to July; 2.00–5.00 p.m. Thursdays and holidays from mid-September to mid-March; tel: 32-35-03-72. The D39 leads the final 5 km (3 miles) from Champ de Bataille to le Neubourg.

Le Neubourg

Le Neubourg has long been a prosperous market centre on these rich arable flatlands, the Neubourg Plain, which covers this region of Normandy. The medieval fortifications were demolished in the 18th century, though some relics of the ramparts remain in place Aristide Briand. The town's

other notable sight from the past, besides several traditional Normandy houses, is the 16th-century church of Saint Pierre et Paul. Beyond the town, a few kilometres to the south, to the left off the D840, is le Tremblay-Omonville and the mid-18th-century Château d'Omonville and its gardens (visits on request; tel: 32-35-41-28).

Bec-Hellouin

In 1034 Hellouin, a warrior knight of some celebration, saw the light, turned his back on battle and, laying aside his sword, became an anchorite monk and immersed himself in a life of solitude and prayer in this lovely corner of Normandy. It proved to be a *volte face* of great significance. Over the subsequent years others followed Hellouin's example and, in 1042, Lanfranc, the distinguished Italian scholar and prelate, quit his post in Avranches to join the band of humble recluses here. He emerged from the shadows of society three years later and moved right into the limelight when he met Duke William while the latter was laying siege on nearby Brionne between 1047 and 1050.

A powerful relationship was established between duke and priest and each benefited from the other's influence. On marrying Matilda, his cousin, William received an interdict from Rome; however, Lanfranc went to discuss the matter with the pope and the result was the sanctioning of the union. And, as William's authority increased, so too did Lanfranc's prominence. He was made prior of the Abbey of Saint Etienne in Caen and then, after

318

William's conquest of England, he became Archbishop of Canterbury, a position which gave him virtual rulership of the country in William's absence.

Le Bec-Hellouin Abbey continued to attract the intellectual cream of the monastic fraternity and the link with Canterbury strengthened. Abbot Anselm of Bec, a scholar from Aosta, succeeded Lanfranc as England's senior primate in 1093; Theobald, too, made the same move in 1139. In addition to these three archbishops, Hellouin's order provided medieval England with a host of bishops and abbots.

The abbey complex was badly damaged in the 15th century during the Hundred Years War and, despite renovation, the order virtually disintegrated. There was a revival in the wake of the Maurist reform in the 17th century and Bec was enhanced by the workmanship of the great sculptor, Brother Guillame de la Tremblaye,

The stumps of pillars mark the site of Bec-Hellouin's old abbey church; behind stands the Saint Nicholas Tower on which there is a plaque listing the monks who went to serve in England.

who lived here at the turn of the 18th century. The abbey's nadir came 100 years later during the Revolution when the monks were purged and fled, and their church and other buildings were subsequently demolished. Monastic life in Bec was revived in 1948 when the estate was given to a Benedictine order. Since then, this once great and historic abbey has undergone restoration.

Enter the grounds and 50 m (55 yd) on the right is the 15th-century tower of Saint Nicholas, the best preserved part of the old abbey church; a plaque records Bec's early association with England. It is possible to climb the tower, and from the top there is a fine view.

Beyond the tower is the site of the old abbey church with a few stumps of pillars, scant and sad evidence that the great monument really did exist. And then there is the new abbey church, formerly the Maurist refectory; at the entrance there are several statues and Hellouin's 11th-century stairway which led the monks down from their dormitories to church for morning prayers.

The abbey shop sells crafts made by the monks and publications about Bec's history. The public can attend services in the abbey at 12.00 p.m. and 6.15 p.m.. *Opening times*: 9.30 a.m.–12.00 p.m.. and 2.30–6.00 p.m. daily except Tuesdays and during services on Sundays; guided tours: 10.00, 11.00 a.m., 3.00, 3.45, 4.30 p.m. (weekdays); 9.30 a.m., 12.00, 3.00, 3.30, 4.00, 6.00 p.m. (Sundays and holidays); tel: 32-44-86-09.

The village of Bec is pretty, and the parish church houses works of religious art salvaged from the abbey. A **Vintage Car Museum**, with 50 veteran cars all, apparently, in good working order, is down the lane to the right of the abbey's entrance, *Opening times*: 9.00 a.m.–12.00 p.m.. and 2.00–7.00 p.m. daily except Wednesdays and Thursdays during the winter; tel: 32-44-86-06.

Down the Risle to Pont Audemer

The road leads north from Bec to Pont Authou, a bridging point over the Risle. Across the river the D137 continues via Saint Georges-du-Vièvre the 15 km (9 miles) to Lieurey; beyond the D810 and its minor offshoots lead into the pretty borderland countryside around the canton centre of Cormeilles and villages such as Saint Pierre-de-Cormeilles, Saint Jean-d'Asnières and Bailleul-la-Vallée. However, at Saint Georges-du-Vièvre, 8 km (5 miles) from the Risle, the minor D33 to the south cuts a pleasant path back towards the Risle. A kilometre or so out of the village is the château of Launay on the left, with park and notable dovecote, and then the attractive hamlets of Saint Benoît-des-Ombres and Livet-sur-Authou, before the road rejoins the west bank of the Risle.

Continue downstream along the D39 with the river to the right. At Saint Philbert there is a bridge across to Montfort-sur-Risle, on the edge of the Forêt de Montfort, with the ruined remains of its 13th-century castle.

Roads east of Montfort lead in the direction of Rouen. The D91 runs through forest and then across country 13 km (8 miles) to Bourg-Achard, with finely crafted 15th–16th-century woodwork and stained glass in its church, and continues the other side of town into the Parc Régional Brotonne and the department of Seine-Maritime. Just before the border there is, on the left, the unique 13th-century stone mill of Hauville and, further west, the unusual bread oven and sabot museums at la Haye-de-Routot. Even more curious is the bonfire of Saint Clair, a 15 m (49 ft) high pyre burnt on the night of 16 July by the people of la Haye-de-Routot in honour of their village saint. Take the more south-eastward route from Montfort, the D130, and then bear left onto the D124, which bypasses the village of Ecaquelon to the left, with a 15th-century alabaster altar of local fame in its church, and the early 16th-century château at Tilly alongside relics of a medieval fort. Beyond, the road joins the busy N138 which, northwards, heads to Bourgtheroulde, with 16th-century stained glass in the church, before entering Seine-Maritime and its Forêt de la Londe.

Back at the Risle, the roads on either side of the river, the D130 on the east bank and the D39 on the west, follow a scenic path. The D130, the main avenue, continues through Appeville-Annebault, home for a while of Claude d'Annebault, a 16th-century governor of Normandy who helped to restore the 16th-century church and was duly honoured by local citizens who attached his name onto the name of their village. Cornville-sur-Risle, 6 km (4 miles) on, gave its name to the popular 19th-century operetta, *Les Cloches de Cornville*; the "Cloches" were a 12-bell carillon which now hang at the appropriately named Hôtel des Cloches. Pont-Audemer is 6 km (3½ miles) away.

Pont Audemer

It was at this point that Odemer, a local lord, built a bridge over the Risle. A town evolved and it bore the name Pont Audemer. Its development (it expanded along two parallel arms of the Risle and the connecting waterways), was largely due to its successful textile and leather industry. In the 11th century, work commenced on the church of Saint Ouen, and the monument reached its final grand proportions after a prolonged period of building in the 16th century. Construction, however, came to an abrupt halt after the coffers were scraped of their last and nobody was found to replenish them; thus the west front remains incomplete. None the less, Saint Ouen is a fine church and its 16th-century stained-glass windows, along with the modern ones by Max Ingrand, are one of its striking features.

Despite the damage caused during World War II, there still stand some of the ancient traditional half-timbered Normandy houses. Notably in the streets around Saint Ouen, in the main rue de la République, impasse Saint Ouen, impasse de l'Epée, cour Canal; and west of here, along rue Paul Clemencin to rue Notre-Dame-du-Pré, there is the 17th-century hotel Auberge du Vieux Puits. Alternatively, an impression of the old quarter of town can be had at a glance with the views from the bridge over the southern branch of the Risle, just a few metres from Saint Ouen.

Beyond Pont Audemer

Roads continue to flank the Risle over its final 15 km (9 miles) to its junction with the Seine. On the west bank, the N175 gives way to the D312 at Toutainville, which runs its pleasant course along the valley to Foulbec, a bridging point. It continues through

Conteville, Bervilles-sur-Mer and, turning parallel to the estuary, passes Mount Courel, with views over the Seine, and the château at la Pommeraye, then the ruined 11th-century abbey at Grestain, where Arlette, the Conqueror's mother was buried, before finally leading through Fiquefleur into Calvados.

On the east bank, the minor D39 passes through pretty patches. After some 10 km (6 miles) the choice is: either join the busy N178 which turns at Pointe de la Roque, with its panorama from the lighthouse over the estuary, and follows the Seine to Pont de Tancarville, the river's splendid crossing; or continue to Saint Samson-la-Roque and then find the way along the small roads to link with the D103 which traverses the 5,000 hectares (12,350 acre) Marais Vernier, once a bay in the estuary, now drained fenlands, to Quillebeuf.

Before the creation of the Marais Vernier, Quillebeuf had a significant position at what was the mouth of the Seine estuary. The Vikings moored their vessels here, as did others for centuries after. Now it has lost its purpose as a port, but the past still lingers. Not least is the story of the *Télémaque* which sank here in 1790 with, they say, its cargo of the French crown jewels. Henry IV stayed here, in the appropriately named Maison Henry IV, and it was during his reign in the late 16th century that Quillebeuf, enjoying royal attention, prospered. And so, during this period, the 12th-century Romanesque church of Notre Dame-de-Bon-Port, the town's main sight today, was modified. Across the waters Quillebeuf faces the realities of the late 20th century: the vast petrochemical plant of Port Jérôme. Today, the Quillebeuf–Port Jérôme ferry service links past with present.

From Quillebeuf, the D87, merging with the D89, follows the Seine upstream. At Trouville-le-Haule, a minor road bears left for the attractive run to the villages of Vieux Port and Aizier, with its chapel of Saint Thomas, and the border with Seine-Maritime. The **Maison des Métiers** at Bourneville, 5 km (3 miles) south of Aizier, is a collective where artisans continue a variety of Normandy crafts using traditional methods. *Opening times*: visitors are welcome from early April to late December, daily except for Tuesdays out of season; tel: 32-57-40-41. From Quillebeuf there is also the D810 turning off the D87 and passing through Sainte Opportune-la-Mare. Here traditional lifestyles have been revived for public display and include the old apple industry in the Maison de la Pomme and smithying in the forge. The road continues to Pont Audemer.

There is also a minor road south of Quillebeuf which follows the perimeter of the Marais Vernier. It skirts the waters of Grande Mare, part of the Mannevilles Nature Reserve, a protected area for local flora and fauna, and links to the D90, with its vantages over the fens, on its route to Saint Samson-de-la-Roque (*see* above).

In early summer foxgloves add a dash of colour to the depths of the forest.

The Right Place at the Right Price

Hotels

Whichever town you visit in Normandy there will be a good range of hotels from which to choose, with several dozen in each of the larger towns and cities. The Ministry of Tourism classifies hotels from one- to four-star on the basis of their facilities, but below an indication of price per room is given. French hotels normally charge per room which gives good value for couples. In the more expensive hotels most rooms will come with an adjoining bathroom.

The hotels listed below have been classified with regard to price as follows:

❚   up to 350F;
❚❚   350–600F;
❚❚❚   over 600F.

This is the cost per night for a room. Breakfast is usually charged as an extra. These price ranges should only be viewed as rough guides, as hotels may have some rooms available that fall into the price band above or below the one in which they have been placed, and prices vary from season to season.

L'Aigle

Hôtel Artus   ❚
7, rue Louis Pasteur
Tel: 33-24-52-01
16 rooms.

Hôtel du Dauphin   ❚❚
8, place de la Halle
Tel: 33-24-43-12
30 rooms. Restaurant. Best Western.

Hôtel de la Gare   ❚
61, rue Général de Gaulle
Tel: 33-24-10-31
9 rooms. Restaurant.

Alençon

Hôtel le Chapeau Rouge   ❚
1–3, boulevard Duchamp
Tel: 33-26-20-23
16 rooms.

Château de Saint Paterne   ❚❚
72610 Saint Paterne
Tel: 33-27-54-71
A few rooms and suites. On the south side of Alençon on the Pays de Loire-Normandy border. Restaurant.

La Faïencerie   ❚❚
61420 Saint Denis-sur-Sarthon
Tel: 33-27-30-16
17 rooms. 10 km (6 miles) west of Alençon. Restaurant.

Le Grand Cerf   ❚❚
21, rue Saint Blaise
Tel: 33-26-00-51
32 rooms. Best of the town hotels.

Hôtel le Grand St-Michel   ❚
7, rue de Temple
Tel: 33-26-04-77
13 rooms. Logis de France. Restaurant.

Hôtel de Paris   ❚
26, rue Denis Papin
Tel: 33-29-01-64
18 rooms.

Argentan

Hôtel de France   ❚
8, boulevard Carnot
Tel: 33-67-03-65
13 rooms. Logis de France. Restaurant.

Haras du Gazon "Neuvy au   ❚❚
Houlme"
61210 Putanges
Tel: 33-35-98-39
20 rooms. Some 20 km (12 miles) west of Argentan. 18th-century manor-farm-stud. Restaurant.

Hostellerie du Lion d'Or   ❚❚
1, rue Pigot
Tel: 33-35-16-92
Logis de France. Restaurant.

Hôtel la Renaissance   ❚
20, avenue de la 2e
Tel: 33-36-14-20
13 rooms. Logis de France. Restaurant.

Avranches

Hôtel de la Croix d'Or   ❚❚
83, rue de la Constitution
Tel: 33-58-04-88
29 rooms. Restaurant.

Normandie   ❚
2, boulevard Jozeau-Marigné
Tel: 33-58-01-33
15 rooms.

Bagnoles-de-l'Orne and Ferté Macé

Auberge d'Andaines   ❚
la Barbère, Ferté Macé
Tel: 33-37-20-28
15 rooms. Logis de France. Restaurant.

Hôtel Beaumont | I
26–28, boulevard Lemeunier-
  Rallière
Tel: 33-37-91-77
37 rooms. Logis de France.
Restaurant.

Hôtel Bois Joli   II
12, avenue Philippe du Rozier
Tel: 33-37-92-77
20 rooms. France-Accueil.

Hôtel Lutétia   II
boulevard Paul Chalvet
Tel: 33-37-94-77
33 rooms. Restaurant.

Hôtel Pavillon du Moulin   I
rue du Docteur Louvel
Tel: 33-37-83-43
22 rooms.

Barneville-Carteret
Hôtel les Isles   I
9, boulevard Maritime
Tel: 33-04-90-76
34 rooms. Sea views. Logis de
France. Restaurant.

Hôtel de la Marine   II
11, rue de Paris
Tel: 33-53-83-31
31 rooms. Sea views. Logis de
France. Restaurant.

Bavent
Hostellerie du Moulin du Pré   I
route de Gonneville-en-Auge
Tel: 31-78-83-68
10 rooms. Lake views. An old
mill, countryside alternative to
summertime's crowded coast.

Bayeux
Hôtel d'Argouge   I
21, rue Saint-Patrice
Tel: 31-92-88-86
25 rooms. In 18th-century
buildings.

Hôtel de Brunville   I
9, rue Genas-Duhomme
Tel: 31-21-18-00
38 rooms. France-Accueil.

Le Castel   II
7, rue de la Cambette
Tel: 31-92-05-86
4 rooms. Elegant 18th-century
town estate of Baronne de Ville
d'Avray.

Château d'Audrieu   IIII
14250 Audrieu
Tel: 31-80-21-52
21 rooms and 7 apartments. Pool
and parklands. .

Château du Molay   IIII
14330 Le Molay-Littry
Tel: 31-22-90-80
38 rooms. Set in estates with a
pool and tennis court..

Château de Sully   IIII
14490 Sully
Tel: 31-22-29-48
33 rooms. With restaurant.

Hôtel Churchill   II
14–16, rue Saint-Jean
Tel: 31-21-31-80
32 rooms.

Le Lion d'Or   II
71, rue Saint-Jean
Tel: 31-92-06-90
27 rooms. 18th-century inn. Logis
de France. Restaurant.

Manoir du Carel at Maisons   II
14400 Bayeaux
Tel: 31-22-37-00
4 rooms and a family apartment.

Notre Dame   I
44 rue des Cuisiners
Tel: 31-92-87-24
24 rooms. Logis de France.

Bernay
Acropole Hotel   II
La Grande Malouve
Tel: 32-46-06-06
51 rooms. A little out of town on
the N138. Restaurant.

Bezancourt
Château du Landel   II
76220 Bezancourt
Tel: 35-90-16-01
17 rooms. Still within the Forêt-
de-Lyons, this 17th-century
château, set in its own 60-hectare
(148-acre) park. Pool and tennis
court. Restaurant.

Bricquebec
Hôtel de Vieux Château   I
4, cours du Château
Tel: 33-52-24-49
28 rooms. Part of the original
medieval castle. A member of the
Châteaux-Hôtels Independants
group. Restaurant.

Cabourg
Auberge du Parc   I
31, avenue Général Leclerc
Tel: 31-91-00-82
10 rooms. Logis de France.
Restaurant.

Hôtel le Cabourg   II
5, avenue de la République
Tel: 31-24-42-55
7 rooms. Restaurant.

Hôtel le Cottage   I
24, avenue de Général Leclerc
Tel: 31-91-65-61
11 rooms. Restaurant.

Hôtel de l'Oie Qui Fume   I
avenue de la Brèche-Buhot
Tel: 31-91-27-79
20 rooms. Logis de France.
Restaurant.

Pullman Grand Hotel   IIII
promenade Marcel Proust
Tel: 31-91-01-79
70 rooms. Restaurant.

Caen
Hôtel Bristol   I
31, rue de 11 Novembre
Tel: 31-84-59-76
25 rooms. On the other side of the
racecourse, a little further away
from the hub of transport and
marginally closer to town.

Château des Riffets   II
14680 Bretteville-sur-Laize
Tel: 31-25-53-21
To the south of Caen en route to
Suisse Normande, set in parkland
with 4 rooms/suites and swimming
pool. A member of the Châteaux
Hôtels Independants group.

Hôtel au Départ   II
28, place de la Gare
Tel: 31-82-23-98
35 rooms.

Le Relais des Gourmets   IIII
15, rue de Geôle
Tel: 31-86-06-01
28 rooms including suites. In the
heart of town opposite the
château. Best Western.

Hôtel Malherbe   II
place Foch
Tel: 31-84-40-06
92 rooms. Centrally located.

Hôtel Mercure   II
1, place Courtonne
Tel: 31-93-07-62
130 rooms. Between the church
and bassin of Saint Pierre. Views
of the port.

Cherbourg
Hôtel France Symphonie   II
quartier Maupas
Tel: 32-20-18-00
Restaurant.

Grand Hôtel I
42, rue de la Marine
Tel: 33-43-04-02
32 rooms.

Hôtel Mercure II
Gare Maritime
Tel: 33-44-01-11
84 rooms. Views of port and sea.
Restaurant.

Clécy
Hostellerie du Moulin II
du Vey-Surosne
Vey
Tel: 31-69-71-08
19 rooms. An old mill down by the river just to the east of Clécy. Accommodation with character in this curious quarter of Normandy. A member of the Châteaux-Hôtels Independants group. Lake views.

Hôtel le Site Normand I
rue des Chatelets
Tel: 31-69-71-05
14 rooms. Logis de France.

Coutances-Coutainville
Hôtel Cositel II
route de Coutainville
Tel: 33-07-51-64
55 rooms. France-Accueil, Logis de France. Restaurant.

Hôtel le Relais du Viaduc I
24 avenue de Verdun
Tel: 33-45-02-68
10 rooms. Logis de France. Restaurant.

Deauville
Altéa Deauville III
boulevard Cornuché
Tel: 31-88-62-62
69 rooms. Sea views and views of port.

Hôtel l'Espérance I
32, rue Victor Hugo
Tel: 31-88-26-88
10 rooms.

Hôtel Ibis II
9, quai de la Marine
Tel: 31-88-09-71
95 rooms. Views of port. Large and reasonably priced.

Hôtel Royal III
boulevard Cornuché
Tel: 31-98-66-33
320 rooms. Sea views.

Dieppe
Hôtel Aguado II
30, boulevard de Verdun
Tel: 35-84-27-00
56 rooms. Sea views.

Hôtel de la Plage I
20, boulevard de Verdun
Tel: 35-84-18-28
40 rooms. Sea views.

Hôtel du Relais Gambetta I
95, avenue Gambetta
Tel: 35-84-12-91
17 rooms. Logis de France. Views of port.

Hôtel de l'Univers II
10, boulevard de Verdun
Tel: 35-84-12-55
30 rooms. France-Accueil. Sea views.

Etretat
Château de Diane I
76110 Ecrainville par Goderville
Tel: 35-27-76-02
20 rooms. 11 km (7 miles) from Etretat, off the D68 just south of Ecrainville near the town of Goderville..

Hôtel Dormy House II
40, route du Havre
Tel: 35-27-07-88
51 rooms. Sea views. Up on the cliff by the links; for golfers.

Hôtel l'Escale I
place Foch
Tel: 35-27-03-69
12 rooms.

Hôtel Normandie I
place Fochs
Tel: 35-27-06-99
17 rooms.

Hôtel Welcome II
10, avenue Verdun
Tel: 35-27-00-89
22 rooms.

Eu
Hôtel de la Gare I
20, avenue de la Gare
Tel: 35-86-16-64
22 rooms. Logis de France.

Pavillon de Joinville II
route du Tréport
Tel: 35-86-24-03
24 rooms. A member of the Châteaux-Hôtels Independants group. Pool and tennis court. Stylish restaurant.

Hôtel le Relais I
1, place Albery 1er
Tel: 35-86-14-88
14 rooms. Logis de France.

Evreux
Hôtel du Beffroi I
2, rue de l'Horloge
Tel: 32-39-08-49

Hôtel Climat de France I
boulevard Allende
Tel:32-23-07-07
42 rooms.

Hôtel de France I
12, rue St Thomas
Tel: 32-39-09-25
16 rooms. Logis de France.

Hôtel Normandy II
37, rue Edouard Feray
Tel: 32-33-14-40
25 rooms. Restaurant, serving traditional Normandy dishes.

Hôtel de l'Orme II
13, rue des Lombards
Tel: 32-39-34-12
65 rooms.

Fécamp
Château de Sassetot II
76540 Valmont
Tel: 35-28-00-11
30 rooms. Near Sassetot-le-Mauconduit, approximately 13 km (8 miles) north along the coast from Fécamp. Some 2 km (1 mile) from the sea and standing in a 10-hectare (24-acre) park.

Hôtel de la Plage I
87, rue de la Plage
Tel: 35-29-76-51
22 rooms. Sea views.

Manoir de Caniel II
50, route de Veulettes
76450 Cany-Barville
Tel: 35-97-88-43
6 rooms. A family manor house. A member of the Châteaux-Hôtels Independants group.

Flers
Auberge du Cèdre I
rue de la 11e DB
Tel: 33-64-06-00
8 rooms. Logis de France.

Hôtel le Normandie I
44 place Duhalde
Tel: 33-65-23-38
12 rooms. Restaurant.

Hôtel de l'Ouest   I
14, rue de la Boule
Tel: 33-64-32-43
12 rooms. Logis de France.

Forges-les-Eaux
Hotel Continental   I
avenue des Sources
Tel: 35-09-08-12
50 rooms.

Granville
Hôtel des Bains   III
19, rue Georges Clémenceau
Tel: 33-50-19-87
51 rooms. Central. Dates from Granville's heyday as an elegant resort. Sea views. Restaurant.

Hôtel Normandy Chaumière   I
20, rue Paul Poirier
Tel: 33-50-01-71
7 rooms. Logis de France. La Manche "Gastronomie de Terroir" restaurant.

Le Havre
Hôtel de Bordeaux   II
147, rue Louis Brindeau
Tel: 35-22-69-44
31 rooms. Lake views.

Hôtel Mercure   II
chaussée d'Angoulème
Tel: 35-21-23-45
96 rooms. Lake views.

Hôtel Parisien   I
1, cours de la République
Tel: 35-25-23-83
22 rooms. Petits Nids de France. Views of port.

Hôtel Voltaire   I
14, rue Voltaire
Tel: 35-41-30-91
24 rooms.

Honfleur
Hostellerie de Belvedere   I
36, rue Emile Renouf
Tel: 31-89-08-13

Hôtel du Cheval Blanc   II
2 quai des Passagers
Tel: 31-89-23-85
35 rooms. Views of port.

Hôtel Ferme de la Grande Court   I
Côte de Grâce Equemauville
Tel: 31-89-04-69
15 rooms. Logis de France.

Hôtel la Ferme Saint-Siméon   III
rue Adolphe Marais
Tel: 31-89-23-61
32 rooms. According to folklore, Impressionism evolved over the flow of flagons of cider. Sea views. Restaurant.

Hôtel Tilbury   II
30, place Hamelin
Tel: 31-98-83-33
7 rooms. Views of port.

Lisieux
Hôtel de la Coupe d'Or   I
49, rue Pont Mortain
Tel: 31-31-16-84
18 rooms. France-Accueil, Logis de France.

Hôtel le Latin   I
1, avenue Ste-Thérèse
Tel: 31-31-45-50
10 rooms.

Hôtel de la Place   II
67, rue Henri Chéron
Tel: 31-31-17-44
33 rooms. Usually referred to as the best hotel in town. A member of the Best Western group.

Hotel des Sports   I
29, rue Henry Chéron
Tel: 31-31-20-94
21 rooms.

Terrasse Hotel   I
25 avenue Ste-Thérèse
Tel: 31-62-17-65
17 rooms. Logis de France.

Louviers
Hôtel la Haye-le-Comte   I
4, route de la Haye-le-Comte, 27400 Louviers
Tel: 32-40-00-40
10 rooms. A 16th-century manor set in a 5-hectare (12-acre) park. Restaurant.

Hostellerie Saint Pierre   II
27430 Saint Pierre-du-Vauvray
Tel: 32-59-93-29
14 rooms. Convenient out-of-town halt on the way from Paris. Restaurants.

Lyons-La-Forêt
Château de Rosay   II
27790 Rosay-sur-Lieure
Tel: 32-49-66-51
27 rooms. Dates from the 17th century and is the most stylish of bases in the heart of this historic forest.

Hôtel Domaine Saint-Paul   II
D321, route de Forges-les-Eaux
Tel: 32-49-60-57
17 rooms. Logis de France. Restaurant.

Hôtel de la Licorne   II
place Benserade
Tel: 32-49-62-02
20 rooms. Logis de France. Restaurant.

Montpinchon
Château de la Salle   II
50210 Montpinchon
Tel: 33-46-95-19
10 rooms. In the heart of bocage countryside. A member of the Châteaux-Hôtels Independants group. Restaurant.

Mont-Saint-Michel
Hôtel de la Digue   II
Tel: 33-60-14-02
35 rooms. By the causeway. Logis de France

Hôtel les Terrasses Poulard   II
grande rue
Tel: 33-60-14-09
29 rooms. Sea views. Restaurant.

Hôtel Vieille Auberge   I
Tel: 33-60-13-34
13 rooms. Restaurant.

Mortagne-au-Perche
Hôtel Genty-Home   I
4, rue Notre Dame
Tel: 33-25-11-53
7 rooms. Restaurant.

Hôtel les Voyageurs   I
60, Faubourg St Eloi
Tel: 33-25-25-46
9 rooms. Restaurant.

Pont Audemer
Hôtel de l'Agriculture   I
84, avenue de la République
Tel: 32-41-01-23
10 rooms.

Hôtel Belle Isle-sur-Risle   III
112, route de Rouen
Tel: 32-56-96-22
14 rooms. On the route de Rouen, in its own gardens. Restaurant.

Auberge du Vieux Puits   II
6, rue Notre Dame du Pré
Tel: 32-41-01-48
Serves good local fare.

Pont l'Evêque

Hôtel Climat de France   I
base de Loisers
Tel: 31-64-64-00)
41 rooms. Lake views.

Hôtel le Lion d'Or   I
8, place du Calvaire
Tel: 31-65-01-55
*26 rooms. Mid-sized central hotel.
Restaurant.*

Rouen

Hôtel de la Cathédrale   I
12, rue St Romain
Tel: 35-71-57-95
*24 rooms. In its famous old
building.*

Hôtel Colin's   II
15, rue de la Pie
Tel: 35-71-00-88
*48 rooms. Well located just off
place du Vieux Marché.*

Hôtel de Normandie   I
19, rue du Bec
Tel:35-71-55-77
23 rooms.

Hôtel Normandya   I
32, rue du Cordier
Tel: 35-71-46-15
*13 rooms. Not far from the
Museum of Fine Arts.*

Hôtel du Petit Palais Royal   I
41, rue de la République
Tel: 35-71-28-04

Saint Hilaire-du-Harcouët

Hôtel le Cygne   I
rue Waldeck Rousseau
Tel: 33-49-11-18
*20 rooms. Logis de France.
France-Accueil. La Manche
"Gastronomie de Terroir"
restaurant.*

Hôtel le Relais de la Poste   I
11, rue de Mortain
Tel: 33-49-10-31
14 rooms. Restaurant.

Saint Lô

Hôtel le Marignan   I
place de la Gare
Tel: 33-05-15-15
18 rooms. Lake views. Restaurant.

Hôtel Régence   I
18, rue Saint Thomas
Tel: 33-05-50-80
20 rooms. Restaurant.

Hôtel le Terminus   I
3, avenue de Briovère
Tel: 33-05-08-60
*15 rooms. Lake views. Logis de
France.*

Saint-Vaast-la-Hougue

Hôtel de France
et des Fuchsias   I
18, rue Foch
Tel: 33-54-42-26
*32 rooms. Logis de France.
Restaurant.*

Hôtel la Granitière   II
rue Marechal Foch
Tel: 33-54-58-99
11 rooms.

Sées

Hôtel du Cheval Blanc   I
1, place St Pierre
Tel: 33-27-80-48
*9 rooms. Logis de France. One of
the best places to stay.
Restaurant.*

Hôtel le Dauphin   I
place des Halles
Tel: 33-27-80-07
*7 rooms. Logis de France. One of
the best places to stay.*

Le Tréport

Hôtel de Picardie   I
place de la Gare
Tel: 32-86-02-22
*32 rooms. Sea views and views
of port.*

Trouville

Beach Hotel   IIII
quai Albert 1ᵉʳ
Tel: 31-98-12-00
*110 rooms. Sea views and views
of port.*

Hôtel Florian-le-Cavendish   I
28–30, rue de la Plage
Tel: 31-88-17-40
29 rooms. Sea views.

Hôtel Mercure   II
place Foch
Tel: 31-87-38-38
80 rooms. Sea views.

Hôtel de la Paix   II
4, place Fernand Moureaux
Tel: 31-88-35-15
23 rooms. Views of port.

Restaurants

L'Aigle

Auberge la Jardinière
59, route de Paris-St Sulpice-sur-
Risle
Tel: 33-24-26-65

le Dauphin
8, place de la Halle
Tel: 33-24-43-12
The best restaurant in town.

Alençon

Au Petit Vatel
72, place Cdt Demeulles
Tel: 33-26-23-78
Celebrated local restaurant.

l'Escargot Dore
183 avenue du Général Leclerc
Tel: 33-26-05-40

les Trois Relais
44–46, rue de Quakenbruck
Tel: 33-29-03-72

*Most of the hotels have
restaurants. Notable are Grand
St-Michel and the de l'Industrie.*

Argentan

Hôtel la Renaissance
20, avenue de la 2e
Tel: 33-36-14-20
*Has the highest reputation of the
hotel restaurants.*

Avranches

Relais des Routiers
70, rue de la Constitution
Tel: 33-58-01-13

Le Littré
8, rue Dr Gilbert
Tel: 33-58-01-66
Bar-restaurant.

Bagnoles-de-l'Orne and Ferté Macé

Café de Paris
4, avenue Robert Cousin
Tel: 33-37-81-76
Serves good Italian dishes.

Hôtel de la Vallée de la Cour
Antoigny
Tel: 33-37-08-90
A popular restaurant.

Barneville-Carteret
l'Hermitage
promenade Abbé Lebouteiller
Tel: 33-54-96-29

la Port
Tel: 33-54-82-50
Down by the waterfront.

Bayeux
Bruneville
9, rue Genas-Duhomme
Tel: 31-21-18-00
Traditional Normandy cuisine.

Les Quatre Saisons
Grand Hôtel du Luxembourg
25, rue des Bouchers
Tel: 31-92-00-04
Traditional Normandy cuisine.

Taverne des Ducs
4, place St Patrice
Tel: 31-92-09-88
Less formal.

Cabourg
The pick of Cabourg's restaurants are in the hotels (prices are in keeping with their gradings).

Le Romantique
8, avenue Piat
Tel: 31-24-10-92

Caen
Alcide
1, place Courtonne
Tel: 31-44-18-06
Menu includes local tripe dishes.

le Buffet de la Gare Relais-Normandy
place de la Gare
Tel: 31-82-24-58
Traditional Normandy dishes.

l'Echevins
35, route Trouville
Tel: 31-84-10-17
Speciality, warmed oysters and winkles served with citrus fruits.
le Gastronome
43, rue St Saveur
Tel: 31-86-57-75
Less expensive restaurant.

Le Manior d'Hasting
18, avenue de la Côte de Nâcre
Tel: 31-44-62-43
At Bénouville, 10 km (6 miles) north of Caen. Famed in the region for its lobster and turbot "René Gilbert". A member of the prestigious l'Association des

Cuisiniers et Hôteliers de Métier. Talk "Tripe" in Caen and you win friends. A local delicacy. Chefs of tripes à la môde de Caen, tripe served in layers with onions, carrots and a variety of garnishes, may create a work of culinary art from this maligned cut of meat.

Cherbourg
Le Plouc
59 rue au Blé
Tel: 33-53-67-64
Selected as one of La Manche's "Gastronomie du Terroir" restaurants.

La Régence
42, quai de Caligny
Tel: 33-43-05-16

Clécy
Moulin du Vey
Vey
Tel: 31-69-71-08
Renowned restaurant.

le Site Normand
rue des Chatelets
Tel: 31-69-71-05
Renowned restaurant.

Coutances-Coutainville
Hôtel Cositel
route de Coutainville
Tel: 33-07-51-64
Regarded as the best of the hotel restaurants. La Manche "Gastronomie du Terroir" restaurant.

Crêperie Le Ratelier
3 rue Georges Clemençeau
Tel: 33-45-56-52
Popular restaurant.

le Relais du Viaduc
24 avenue de Verdun
Tel: 33-45-02-68
Member of the "Relais Routier" group of restaurants. La Manche "Gastronomie du Terroir" restaurant.

Deauville
Augusto
27, rue Désiré Le Hoc
Tel: 31-88-34-49

Chez Camillo
13, rue Désiré Le Hoc
Tel: 31-88-79-78
Less expensive.

Le Spinnaker
52, rue Mirabeau
Tel: 31-88-24-40

A rich Normandy cuisine offered at lavish prices is the norm at the better restaurants. The runaway costs of à la carte can be avoided in some restaurants by taking the reasonable "set menu" option.

Dieppe
l'Amorique
17, quai Henri IV
Tel: 35-84-28-14

Marmite Dieppoise
off quai Duquesne at
8, rue St Jean
Tel: 35-84-24-26
Takes its name from its speciality.

In Dieppe, home of the marmite Dieppoise, the excellent rich fish stew, and other less famed seafood dishes, there is the quai Henri IV alongside the ferry wharf: here there are many small informal restaurants.

Etretat
Le Bicorre
boulevard René Coty
Tel: 35-29-62-22

Eu
In Le Tréport it is a matter of wandering along quai Francois 1er and selecting from one of the many informal fish restaurants. In the back streets, away from the heaviest crowds, the restaurants tend to be less hectic.

Evreux
Le Royal Grillades
39, rue du Dr Oursel
Tel: 32-39-09-62

Fécamp
L'Escalier
101, quai Berigny
Tel: 35-28-26-79
Opposite the Bassin Berginy.

Viking
63, boulevard Albert I
Tel: 35-29-22-92
On the seafront.

As with all the coastal towns, it is the seafood which is the most interesting; meat dishes tend to be the predictable Normandy classics.

Flers

Auberge de Relais Fleuri
115, rue Schnetz
Tel: 33-65-23-89
*Famed locally for its traditional
Normandy cooking.*

le Normandie
44 place Duhalde
Tel: 33-65-23-38
Recommended.

Le Havre
la Huitrière
4, rue de Paris
Tel: 35-21-48-48
Features oysters.

Hôtel de Monaco
16 rue de Paris
Tel: 35-42-21-01
Recommended.

*Fish is a local speciality and is
served inexpensively at bistros and
cafés around the waterfront.*

Honfleur
l'Ancorage
12, rue Montpensier
Tel: 31-89-00-70

Lisieux
Parc
21, boulevard Herbert Fournet
Tel: 31-62-8-11

Mont-Saint-Michel
La Mère Poulard
grande rue
Tel: 33-60-14-09
*This is the place to eat "Annette
Poulard Omelette", Mont-Saint-
Michel's culinary speciality.
Expensive.*

Hôtel Vieille Auberge
Tel: 33-60-13-34

*Pré salé lamb, lamb grazed on the
nearby salty marshes, is an
alternative local delicacy to
Madame Poulard's omelettes.*

Mortagne-au-Perche
Croix d'Or
le Pin-la-Garenne
Tel: 33-83-80-33

Genty-Home
4, rue Notre Dame
Tel: 33-25-11-53
Good restaurant.

Pont l'Evêque
Auberge de la Touques
place de l'Eglise
Tel: 31-64-01-69
Recommended.

la Soupière
Climat de France
base de Loisers
Tel: 31-64-64-00
Recommended.

Rouen
Bertrand Warin
7–9, rue de la Pie
Tel: 35-89-26-69
*Just to the west off place Vieux
Marché; a pleasant alternative.*

la Cache Ribaud
10, rue Tambour
Tel: 35-71-04-82
*Less expensive and offers
traditional Normandy dishes.*

Chez Dufour
67, rue St Nicholas
Tel: 35-71-90-62
*One of Rouen's most highly rated
restaurants.*

la Couronne
31 place Vieux Marché
Tel: 35-71-40-90
*Its international popularity is
largely due to it being dubbed "the
oldest restaurant in France".*

La Marine
42, quai Cavalier-de-la-Salle
Tel: 35-73-10-01
*Reasonably priced fish restaurant
on the south bank and a little off
the tourist track.*

le Vieux Marché
2 place Vieux Marché
Tel: 35-75-59-09
*Less formal and expensive than
the nearby La Couronne, but
equally crowded.*

*While Caen boasts tripe, Rouen
presents duckling, the caneton
rouennais, as its culinary
showpiece. The local duckling is
specially bred around Duclair to
the west and is a hybrid of the
wild and domestic duck.*

Saint Hilaire-du-Harcouët
Hôtel le Relais de la Poste
11, rue de Mortain
Tel: 33-49-10-31
Good moderately priced menus.

Saint Lô
Hôtel le Marignan
place de la Gare
Tel: 33-05-15-15
*La Manche "Gastronomie de
Terroir" restaurant.*

Hôtel le Terminus
3, avenue de Briovère
Tel: 33-05-08-60
*One of the best of the hotel
restaurants.*

Saint-Vaast-la-Hougue
Café du Port
1, quai Vauban
Tel: 33-54-41-30

le Moyne de Saire
Reville
Tel: 33-54-46-06

*The celebrated St Va oysters are,
naturally, the local speciality.*

Sées
Au Normandy
20, place de Gaulle
Tel: 33-27-80-67
Informal. Also has a few rooms.

le Cheval Blanc
1, place St Pierre
Tel: 33-27-80-48
*The best known of the hotel
restaurants.*

Trouville
Le Charleston
place Fernand
Tel: 31-88-35-43

Roches Noires
16, boulevard Louis Breguet
Tel: 31-88-12-19

*Compared to Deauville, the style
and prices at restaurants are more
relaxed in Trouville.*

Index

Bold page numbers
refer to main entries.